INTERNATIONAL ECONOMIC LAW IN THE ERA OF DATAFICATION

This book addresses the challenges of datafication through the lens of international economic law. We are undergoing a wave of datafication practices. If such practices simply continue to evolve without being examined and repaired along the existing path of development, the same issues will continue to accumulate and will more than likely be amplified. The unprecedented economic and social influence of big tech has served as the catalyst for the concept of "digital sovereignty," which is rooted in the need to safeguard regulatory autonomy in a datafied world. The current wave of data-driven innovations has placed the policy debates on digital trade and data governance into an even more challenging context. The book's chapters are connected by the many facets of "data" and systematically explain how international economic law can reduce the perils of datafication instead of increasing them. This title is part of the Flip it Open Programme and may also be available Open Access. Check our website Cambridge Core for details.

SHIN-YI PENG is Distinguished Professor of Law at National Tsing Hua University. Professor Peng is a member of the Indicative List of Panelists for resolving WTO disputes. She has served as vice president of the Society of International Economic Law. In Taiwan, she is a former commissioner of the National Communications Commission, and the recipient of the Outstanding Research Awards from the National Science and Technology Council.

CAMBRIDGE INTERNATIONAL TRADE AND ECONOMIC LAW

Processes of economic regionalisation and globalisation have intensified
over the last decades, accompanied by increases in the regulation c
international trade and economics at the levels of international, regior
and national laws. At the same time, significant challenges have ari al
with respect to economic liberalization, rule-based systems of trade en
investment, and their political and social impacts. The subject mat and
this series is international economic law, in this contemporary con ter of
core is the regulation of international trade, investment, fin text. Its
cognate areas such as intellectual property and competition p nce and
series publishes books on related regulatory areas, in partic olicy. The
rights, labour, environment and culture, as well as sustain ular human
ment. These areas are horizontally interconnected and vert able develop-
the international, regional and national levels. The seri cally linked at
works on governance, dealing with the structure and o es also includes
national organisations related to the field of internati peration of inter-
and the way they interact with other subjects of inter onal economic law,
law. The series aims to include excellent legal doctr national and national
cutting-edge interdisciplinary works that engage nal treatises, as well as
ences and humanities. law and the social sci-

INTERNATIONAL ECONOMIC LAW IN THE ERA OF DATAFICATION

SHIN-YI PENG
National Tsing Hua University

CAMBRIDGE
UNIVERSITY PRESS

CAMBRIDGE
UNIVERSITY PRESS

Shaftesbury Road, Cambridge CB2 8EA, United Kingdom

One Liberty Plaza, 20th Floor, New York, NY 10006, USA

477 Williamstown Road, Port Melbourne, VIC 3207, Australia

314–321, 3rd Floor, Plot 3, Splendor Forum, Jasola District Centre, New Delhi – 110025, India

103 Penang Road, #05–06/07, Visioncrest Commercial, Singapore 238467

Cambridge University Press is part of Cambridge University Press & Assessment, a department of the University of Cambridge.

We share the University's mission to contribute to society through the pursuit of education, learning and research at the highest international levels of excellence.

www.cambridge.org
Information on this title: www.cambridge.org/9781009354981

DOI: 10.1017/9781009355025

First published 2024

A catalogue record for this publication is available from the British Library

Library of Congress Cataloging-in-Publication Data
Names: Peng, Shin-Yi, author.
Title: International economic law in the era of datafication / Shin-Yi Peng, National Tsing Hua University.
Description: Cambridge, United Kingdom ; New York, NY : Cambridge University Press, 2024. | Series: Cambridge international trade and economic law | Includes bibliographical references and index.
Identifiers: LCCN 2023045586 (print) | LCCN 2023045587 (ebook) | ISBN 9781009354981 (hardback) | ISBN 9781009355018 (paperback) | ISBN 9781009355025 (ebook)
Subjects: LCSH: Information technology–Law and legislation. | Foreign trade regulation. | Big data. | International trade–Technological innovations–Law and legislation. | Computer networks–Law and legislation. | Electronic commerce–Law and legislation. | Organizational change.
Classification: LCC K3820 .P46 2024 (print) | LCC K3820 (ebook) | DDC 343.09/99–dc23/eng/20231002
LC record available at https://lccn.loc.gov/2023045586
LC ebook record available at https://lccn.loc.gov/2023045587

ISBN 978-1-009-35498-1 Hardback

To my Parents

CONTENTS

ACKNOWLEDGMENTS

This book pursues the research question of how we should consider the trend of datafication – under which most dimensions of our lives are being transformed into data to create value – through the lens of international economic law. My initial intention was to provide a book-length treatment with a holistic assessment of the WTO Joint Initiative on E-commerce. But it soon became clear that what really interested me was the broader question of the interplay between datafication and international trade agreements. Having studied international trade law and digital technology governance for more than twenty years, I believe this is an optimal time to map out the dynamic questions posed by the data-driven economy and corresponding regulatory approaches with a fresh eye, and to capture the emerging shape of global trade governance in a datafied world. This book can therefore be seen as the accumulation and culmination of my enduring research interests in the interface between the digital revolution, national regulations, and international economic legal order. The framing of this book – the chapters of which are connected by the many facets of "data" – allows me to bring these various angles together in a more coherent context, which journal articles and book chapters cannot achieve.

National Tsing Hua University has been wonderfully supportive of my work. I am indebted to many colleagues here in Tsing Hua who, in one way or another, placed me in the position to complete this book. I owe so much to Yi-long Huang, who has served as an invaluable mentor throughout my academic journey. I am grateful to Shih-Chang Hung for his sage guidance and advice over the years. I thank my colleagues who worked with me at the Institute of Law for Science and Technology and the College of Technology Management, particularly Ching-Fu Lin, Han-Wei Liu, and Galit Shmueli, for their enjoyable collaboration on interdisciplinary projects. In Taiwan, special thanks go to Chang-fa Lo and Connie Guang-Hwa Yang, whom I have had the privilege of working with and learning from. I would also like to express my sincere appreciation to the National Science and Technology Council for its funding support of this book project.

This book has incorporated a number of different sources. My former governmental experience of serving as a telecommunications regulator in Taiwan helped to form my perspectives on complex regulatory issues. The ideas and arguments put forward in this book have been developed through many presentations and panel discussions at workshops and conferences, where I have benefited from productive conversations with scholars and practitioners. In particular, comments and questions from Lucian Cernat, Anupam Chander, Dan Ciuriak, Henry Gao, Aik Hoe Lim, Hamid Mamdouh, Bryan Mercurio, Neha Mishra, Andrew Mitchell, Pierre Sauvé, Gregory Shaffer, Thomas Streinz and Rolf Weber have insightfully informed my thinking on the issues explored in this book.

Parts of Chapters 1 and 5 were first published by Oxford University Press as "The Uneasy Interplay between Digital Inequality and International Economic Law" (2022) 33(1) *European Journal of International Law* 205–235. The valuable insights provided by Joseph Weiler and Chantal Thomas through the EJIL Symposium on Inequalities and International Law have guided me in carefully reflecting upon the topic. Parts of Chapter 2 were first published by Cambridge University Press as "Digital Economy and National Security: Contextualizing Cybersecurity-Related Exceptions" (2023) 117 *AJIL Unbound* 122. The feedback from the reviewers of the AJIL Unbound Symposium on Digital Trade – notably, Anne van Aaken and Mira Burri – was most thoughtful and helpful. Additionally, some parts of this book draw upon but substantially modify and extend materials in my previously published articles. These articles include "Private Cybersecurity Standards? Cyberspace Governance, Multistakeholderism, and the (Ir)relevance of the TBT Regime" and "Renegotiate the WTO Commitments? Technological Change and Treaty Interpretation," published in *Cornell International Law Journal*; "The Legality of Data Residency Requirements: How Can the Trans-Pacific Partnership Help?" and "GATS and the Over-the-Top Services: A Legal Outlook," published in the *Journal of World Trade*; and "Digital Trade," published in the *Oxford Handbook of International Trade Law*. I am grateful to the editors and reviewers of these articles for their comments, which have led me to reframe, refine, and more fully develop the arguments presented in this book.

My heartfelt thanks are for Charles Irish who awoke my interest in international trade law and policy during my studies at UW-Madison

Law School. The book has also been enriched through my engagement with many experts and friends in the community of international economic law over the years, especially Tomer Broude, Julien Chaisse, Wonmog Choi, Holger Hestermeyer, Meredith Kolsky Lewis, Gabrielle Marceau, Junji Nakagawa, Colin Picker, Lisa Toohey, Isabelle Van Damme, Peter Van den Bossche, Markus Wagner, Heng Wang, and Weihuan Zhou.

My sincere gratitude goes to Tom Randall, Sharon McCann, Gemma Smith, and the rest of the team at Cambridge University Press for their support and guidance throughout the process. Special thanks to Hsiang-lin Chiu and Yi-hsuan Chen for their research assistance, and to Nancy Dugan for proofreading the manuscript. I am also thankful to the anonymous readers of the book proposal for their constructive insights, and to Pierre Sauvé, Anne van Aaken, and Tania Voon for their generous comments on the back cover. Last, but most profoundly, I would like to thank my family for their love and support.

Introduction

The Trend of Datafication

We are rapidly moving toward a datafied world where our social activities are routinely transformed into machine-readable data.[1] Indeed, digital platforms today are capable of datafying more and more "subjects, objects, and practices"[2] – converting not only Facebook "likes" into social relationship profiles and shopping patterns into marketable records, but also other real-life events that were formerly unstorable into data. Increasingly, the term "datafication" is associated with platformization, which has been framed in the context of the penetration and influence of digital platforms.[3] Taken as a whole, nearly every aspect of our daily actions is being constantly and systematically harvested, turned into digital data, scaled and analyzed in real time, stored for the long term, aggregated, and sold. This is the phenomenon we are facing; it is growing, and we do not really know where it will lead us next.

Warnings about the perils of datafication are not new. The process of datafication has been critiqued by social scientists, who have underscored widespread issues surrounding the ways in which datafication causes problems, including, among others, digital inequality, information manipulation, data capitalism, algorithm discrimination, and privacy

1 Coined by Mayer-Schönberger and Cukier in 2013, the concept of datafication has been understood as datafying a phenomenon into "a quantified format so it can be tabulated and analyzed." See generally Viktor Mayer-Schonberger and Kenneth Cukier, *Big Data: A Revolution That Will Transform How We Live, Work, And Think* (Harper Business 2013), at 78.

2 Southerton defined datafication as "the process by which subjects, objects, and practices are transformed into digital data." Clare Southerton, "Datafication" in Laurie A. Schintler and Connie L. McNeely (eds), *Encyclopedia of Big Data* (Springer International 2022), at 358–360.

3 Marcus Burkhardt et al., "Introduction" in Marcus Burkhardt et al. (eds) *Interrogating Datafication: Towards a Praxeology of Data* (Transcript Publishing 2022), at 12–13.

intrusion.[4] Thought leaders like Cohen and Zuboff have reminded us how human experience is rapidly becoming raw material for datafication. Zuboff described datafication as "the application of software that allows computers and algorithms to process and analyze raw data" and claimed that the process of datafication "combined with (new and cheaper) storage technologies had translated 98 percent of the world's information into a digital format."[5] In her view, just as fat is rendered into oil, digital technologies are now designed to render our human actions into data: "Every time we encounter a digital interface we make our experience available to datafication."[6] Coined by Cohen as "information-era resources" and "information capitalism,"[7] human social interactions have now become "datafied inputs" for efficient exploitation and "profit extraction."[8] In Cohen's view, every day, we supply "raw material" to corporations, particularly big tech, and these firms then "translate" that raw data into a resource from which they can derive value.[9] Many critiques of datafication argue that from an economic perspective, it may unfairly benefit the rich and deepen the existing inequalities, and from a social perspective, it may violate personal dignity or autonomy.[10] As straightforward as it may be, some believe that "datafication is surveillance"[11] and caution that eventually, individuals are reduced to patterns of behavior and represented in algorithmically legible ways.[12]

To be sure, datafication today represents a paradigm shift as our society begins a new phase of the digital revolution. To date, however, scholarly literature on datafication has been dominated by discussions surrounding the risks and perils of such a trend. Assertions regarding "data colonialism" have reached an overwhelming level in the past few

[4] Southerton, supra note 2, at 358.

[5] Shoshana Zuboff, *The Age of Surveillance Capitalism: The Fight for a Human Future at the New Frontier of Power* (PublicAffairs 2019), at 187.

[6] *Ibid.*, at 233.

[7] Julie E. Cohen, *Between Truth and Power: The Legal Constructions of the Informational Capitalism* (Oxford University Press 2019), at 25, 37.

[8] *Ibid.*, at 16, 25.

[9] *Ibid.*, at 63–66.

[10] Salomé Viljoen, "A Relational Theory of Data Governance" (2021) 131 Yale Law Journal 573, at 581, 653.

[11] See, for example, Jasmine E. McNealy, "Sonic Privacy" (2022) 24 Yale Journal of Law and Technology 365, at 381.

[12] Viljoen, supra note 10, at 624.

years.[13] Humanities and social sciences scholars,[14] among other disciplines, have focused on how our preferences can be monetized by big tech, how our everyday relationships with data are becoming "colonial," and how data capitalism, combined with surveillance, is intensifying inequalities. Nevertheless, voices from the international economic law arena have remained relatively quiet.[15] This is where this book enters into the fray – to map the contours of this datafied economy, and to ensure balanced policy that fosters innovation while addressing challenges. Global governance of datafication entails multifaceted endeavors. While the dangers inherent in datafication should be fully addressed, the potential benefits and promises under such a trend are equally important and should also be carefully considered when formulating public policies. After all, how datafication is conceptualized shapes how domestic and international law respond to its implications – including how to promote the potential benefits as well as mitigate potential risks and harms arising from associated datafication practices.[16] Digital technologies simultaneously do both good and harm.[17] We would be wrong to treat them as disastrous, and we would be equally wrong to embrace them without

[13] Nick Couldry and Ulises A. Mejias, *The Costs of Connection: How Data Is Colonizing Human Life and Appropriating It for Capitalism* (Stanford University Press 2019), at 83–112.

[14] See, for example, Mikkel Flyverbom, *The Digital Prism – Transparency and Managed Visibilities in a Datafied World* (Cambridge University Press 2019), at 32–33 (explaining the "extensive stream of digital traces" produced by datafication); Arne Hintz et al., *Digital Citizenship in a Datafied Society* (Polity Press 2019), at 1–19 (identifying the ways in which actors involve in the datafication process).

[15] Weber's pioneering contribution is devoted to questions entwined in the very fabric of international economic law, which serves as the greatest source of inspiration for this book. Rolf H. Weber, "Global Law in the Face of Datafication and Artificial Intelligence" in Shin-yi Peng et al. (eds), *Artificial Intelligence and International Economic Law: Disruption, Regulation, and Reconfiguration* (Cambridge University Press 2021), at 54.

[16] See generally Viljoen, supra note 10.

[17] For example, the concepts associated with the datafication process have long been actively used in industries such as insurance, banking, and human resources. See Douglas W. Arner et al., "The Future of Data-Driven Finance and Regtech: Lessons from EU Big Bang II" (2020) 25 Stanford Journal of Law, Business & Finance 245, at 255 (explaining how the financial industry has been datafied). See also Margarita Shilova, "The Concept of Datafication: Definition & Examples" (*Data Science Central,* June 2, 2018) <www.datasciencecentral.com/the-concept-of-datafication-definition-amp-examples>.

reflection.[18] Depending upon the context, the term datafication can carry negative or positive connotations. We cannot talk about datafication without looking at both angles.

Challenges to Trade Governance

That said, the fundamental and foremost objective of this book is to explore datafication in the context of international economic law, with the assumption that international trade scholars and lawyers are more sympathetic toward datafication practices, whether digital trade liberalization or data capitalism. At its heart, this monograph is an attempt to systematically explain how international economic law may have contributed to the datafication ecosystem's architecture and may also help to change it. The tale I wish to tell in this book can best be summarized by the following two questions: Do trade rules perpetuate datafication practices and data capitalism in any manner? If so, what can be done to mitigate the damage?[19]

On these grounds, the setting of this book is regime-specific, focusing on international economic law and, more specifically, international trade law (noting that Chapters 1, 2, and 4 nevertheless address issues related to foreign investment). Over the past two decades, the (in)adequacy and even (ir)relevance of the conventional rules under the World Trade Organization (WTO), free trade agreements (FTAs), and bilateral investment treaties (BITs) in the governance of the digital economy have been at the center of discussions. Research on digital trade has mushroomed in recent years. The need to modernize relevant trade and investment rules to reflect technological developments is long overdue. Nonetheless, the current wave of data-driven innovations has placed the policy debates on digital trade and data governance into an even more challenging context. Datafication provides a new context that urgently demands further investigation in this research field. Core issues range from digital inclusion, critical infrastructure resilience, digital sovereignty, digital content moderation, and algorithmic transparency to privacy standards and

[18] Undeniably, datafying a wide range of phenomena into digital data for analysis has the potential to offer useful insights into digitally embedded lives and promote well-being. See Southerton, supra note 2, at 360.

[19] The author appreciates the insightful comments from the anonymous readers on this point.

cybersecurity norms. These emerging challenges lead this book to reflect upon and critically assess the following set of analytical questions:

First, what is datafication? How does datafication extend beyond digitalization? What role has the world trade system played in the story of data capitalism's emergence and evolution? Should trade and investment regimes be reconceptualized and reconstructed to more effectively respond to a platform-based, data-driven economy shaped by various disruptive technologies? If so, how can we confront the trend of datafication as a whole, and what is the role of international trade agreements? Bearing in mind the "inherently imperfect compass" and "political limits" of international economic law,[20] what optimal cross-border arrangements will yield a broadly effective policy environment that accommodates trade interests while balancing human rights, data autonomy, national security, freedom of speech, cultural diversity, fair competition, algorithmic transparency, privacy and cybersecurity protection, and other non-trade interests?

Second, can existing trade rules remain relevant, and, if so, to what extent? Why do trade rules fall short in addressing growing concerns related to datafication? In recent years, additional digital trade disciplines have been recognized in the FTAs, which to a large extent serve as indicators of future digital trade negotiations. At the time of the writing of this book, WTO members participating in the Joint Statement Initiative on E-commerce (JSI on E-commerce) are wrestling with questions about how digital trade should be addressed in the multilateral trading system. How can we assess existing and future e-commerce and digital trade rules under the international trade agreements – be they relatively broad agreements with high standards and deeper commitments or narrow agreements with limited scope – in governing datafication?

Finally, how can we most effectively engage in international regulatory cooperation in the formulation of data policies? Additionally, how can we foster public–private multistakeholder collaboration? Meanwhile, sectoral policymakers from many jurisdictions are formulating the shape of a new paradigm for data governance. What are the regional and national solutions to these issues? In what ways have (domestic) regulators intervened? How can regulatory convergence be successfully facilitated? To put it more concretely, to what extent will the future of data

[20] This statement benefited from the anonymous readers' thoughtful comments.

governance be influenced and even shaped by the key players, namely, the United States (US), Europe, and China? In this regard, will the private sector continue to assume an important role in the big data ecosystem? If so, why? In terms of Internet governance, inevitable clashes between multilateralism and multistakeholderism are imminent. How should (trade) governance arrangements respond to the trend of public–private convergence in the standardization process?

Structure of the Book

The structure of this book relies on network architecture, as illustrated by the International Organization for Standardization's Open Systems Interconnection (OSI) Reference Model,[21] which contains seven layers. Noting that the model is more than three decades old, it is still a relevant concept for creating a functional structure that can be used for regulatory purposes. By clustering and transposing the OSI technical model into the datafication context, this book is framed upon the three primary phases of the datafication process: infrastructure, application, and data flows. As shown in Figure 0.1, to better understand the relationship between datafication and international economic law, this book is divided into three main regulatory dimensions: first, the level of digital physical infrastructure that enables datafication (Part I); second, the level of digital applications and, in particular, the digital platform that drives datafication (Part II), and; third, the cross-border movement of data flows themselves (Part III). The three parts are technically bundled but, to a certain extent, legally separable, and they deserve independent analyses. Thus, the main premise of this book is the identification and investigation of the key issues associated with each conceptual phase, as each has its own challenges. Nonetheless, it goes without saying that full and complete comprehensiveness is impossible. Choices must be made, and some judgment calls are necessary.

With that caveat, we now turn to Figure 0.1 – a simplified datafication ecosystem. Vertically, the ecosystem has two layers from a regulatory point of view. The lower layer (Part I) is referred to as the network layer,

[21] Internet engineers typically adopt the International Standards Organization's Open Systems Interconnection (OSI) Reference Model to explain the network, which generally contains seven layers of function – 1. physical; 2. data link; 3. network; 4. transport; 5. sessions; 6. presentation; and 7. application. See, for example, IBM, "Networks" <www.ibm.com/docs/no/aix/7.1?topic=networks->.

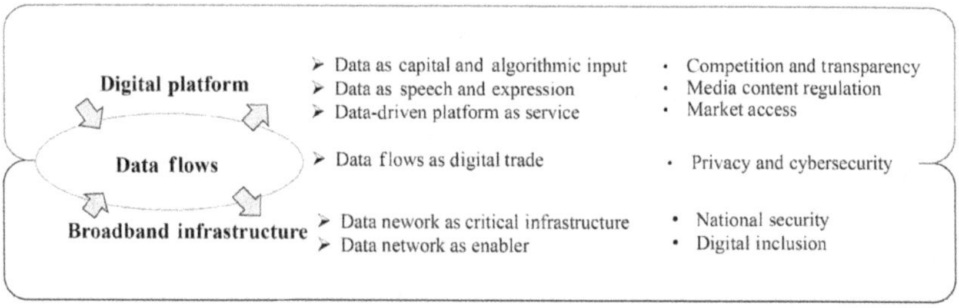

Figure 0.1 The interplay between datafication and international economic law

where the underlying telecommunications service function resides. The upper layer (Part II) is the application layer, where digital platforms such as social media reside. The data flow (Part III) takes place both vertically (between different layers) and horizontally (between different servers, applications, services, and facilities).[22] One interesting question regarding the structure is as follows: Given that digital application is contingent upon data flows, should not Part III come before Part II? Ideally, the issue of data flows should precede that of digital platforms. However, the flow of the book's arguments is easier to follow if the phenomenon of platformization can be explained before addressing the governance of "data flow" itself. At the end of the day, digital platforms are particularly potent data generators. When technically possible, they convert every bit of existence into data flows, which means that most aspects of our activities – whether at home or at work – become a part of the "flow." Because the framing of the book is rooted in the process of datafication, it is our hope that for those readers who are not familiar with this area, the foundation laid in the earlier parts of the book can provide a broader picture of how platforms control what becomes data (namely, what is being datafied),[23] how big tech drives profits using data, and how large-scale data reshapes the world.

The chapters in this book can be read separately. However, when read consecutively, they form a systematically conducted, holistic assessment of the interface between datafication and international economic law. Some chapters are meant to present the irony surrounding issues of

[22] Body of European Regulators for Electronic Communications (BEREC), "Draft BEREC Report on the Internet Ecosystem" BoR (22) 87 (June 9, 2022), at 10.

[23] See generally Angelina Fisher and Thomas Streinz, "Confronting Data Inequality" (2022) 60(3) Columbia Journal of Transnational Law 829.

datafication at each phase, which are so intertwined that their independent solutions might lead to contradictions. For example, the simple fact that the greater the "digital inclusion" (Chapter 1), the greater the "data extraction" (Chapter 5) proves the merits of an overall investigation. This book should therefore be seen as a methodical effort to jointly address major problems at different phases of datafication. The identified structural features of the book seek to provide the necessary context, furnish an integrated overview of the datafication process relevant to trade lawyers, and offer in-depth analyses of topical issues pertaining to related fields.

Overarching Themes

Part I consists of two chapters, which explore the underlying networks supporting a platform-driven, data-fueled world. Chapter 1 introduces the "enabling" character of broadband infrastructures. The main line of inquiry is how best to tackle the issue of "trade and development" in the digital economy. It concludes with an examination of the issue of digital inclusion from a broader policy perspective. Chapter 2 focuses on the role of broadband networks as critical infrastructures, stressing the tension between the security resilience across the information and communication technology (ICT) supply chain and the digital ecosystem. Core issues include how much risk in the broadband network would amount to a danger to "essential interests," as well as how to distinguish between "legitimate" security measures and those that solely represent protectionism. The chapter also discusses how the movement of datafication affects the application of the general exceptions and security exceptions under the WTO and FTAs.

The focus then shifts to digital applications that drive datafication, highlighting the phenomenon of platformization. Overall, Part II of the book is dedicated to exploring considerations pertaining to the regulation of digital platforms. Chapter 3 deals with the market access for data-driven platforms. It argues that the WTO commitments effectively leave the door open for big tech companies. Thus, this chapter calls for new domestic regulations to address the potential risks and harms brought about by trends in datafication. The next two chapters turn to the specific regulatory concerns of digital platforms. They explore how platforms can be regulated when data operates as "speech" or "capital," as well as what roles international trade agreements can play. Chapter 4 discusses the issues surrounding media platformization. Content regulations involve a broad set of issues that may be subject to trade negotiations or dispute settlement. After demonstrating the need to regulate content moderation on social media and, more fundamentally, to alter the power distribution in the Internet ecosystem, this chapter points out the potential contradictions of these necessary reforms with the international trade regime. Chapter 5 continues to explore competition rules for data-driven markets. There are growing concerns about the abuse of dominant market position by platform monopolies. The gap in competition policies and enforcement among jurisdictions, however, will likely leave any competition authority ill-equipped to effectively address anti-competitive practices among the big tech companies. At the same time, datafication and algorithm-based decision-making work hand in hand. What are the ramifications, and what roles should international economic law assume in its efforts to ensure the adequate transparency of algorithmic systems to supervise how digital platforms moderate, rank, and recommend content to their users? This chapter examines the fragmentation of platform regulation, embarks on both research and reflection regarding how international coordination of platform governance should proceed, and argues that a great deal of political support is needed to ensure cross-border policy coherence.

Part III is dedicated to the governance of "data flow" itself, encompassing concerns related to privacy and cybersecurity. Chapter 6 examines issues surrounding cross-border data flows in the context of public–private convergence, addressing whether the emergence of a multiplicity of new actors facilitates co-governance, and, if so, to what extent a soft law approach can help balance the interests between privacy, security, and digital trade. After establishing that international economic law alone is not adequate in terms of privacy and cybersecurity governance, the chapter calls for the reconfiguration of the roles of the public and private sectors and advocates for a (new) global architecture to govern cross-border data flows. Finally, while each angle of this book is valid on its own merits, merging the major arguments of various angles presents the complete picture. This leads the author to summarize this book's findings and make an aggregate assessment of international economic law in an increasingly datafied world.

Technological Dimensions

Methodologically, the book must decide how best to describe the entire datafication ecosystem, which involves multivarious technologies. Should we have addressed the problems of blockchain? Or should we have prioritized the debates over generative pre-trained transformers (GPT)? Should this book broaden its technological dimensions to more comprehensively address the Metaverse? These questions are intimately linked to the objectives of this book. As elaborated above, the goal of this book is to address major problems at different phases of datafication. Such a goal can be explored through many transformative technologies, including big data analytics, the Internet of Things (IoT), artificial intelligence (AI), and blockchain, to name just a few. Nonetheless, this book attempts to maintain a high degree of generality and capture the entire debate without focusing on any particular technology. Of course, technology-based arguments make sense when the legal claims are closely tied to that particular technology. As this book is presented, certain technological features are more thoroughly addressed in chapters and parts where relevant, such as 5G communications in Part I, AI and algorithms in Part II, and big data analytics and the IoT in Part III.

Another reason that it is preferable to maintain a more general tone rather than taking a technology-specific approach is to preserve the arguments presented in this book. Technology is organic and is rapidly changing, and new technological advances will be developed before the ink on the pages of this book is dry. The more this book strives to be specific in terms of technological features, the sooner it becomes obsolete. This book was written during a period spanning from the summer of 2021 to the spring of 2023, with the goal of remaining current as of May 2023. However, as the Greek philosopher Heraclitus so aptly put it, "There is nothing permanent except change." This is especially true in the field of technology governance, with global and geopolitics as well as technological innovations constantly evolving. Recognizing that the "faces" of datafication change daily, it is even more important to govern what is in existence. Otherwise, its effects will continue to accumulate and will more than likely be amplified.

PART I

Enabling Datafication
Broadband Infrastructure

1

Data Network as Enabler

Digital Inclusion and Trade Policy

1.1 Introduction

Efficient and affordable digital physical infrastructure is the prerequisite that enables people to meaningfully participate in the data-driven economy. In this broadband era, people who are connected are empowered in a manner that allows them to access information, online education, health and banking services, and much more. Broadband communications services, which include fixed-line and wireless communications networks, contribute not only to the integration of remote regions and disadvantaged groups, but also to key infrastructure in the economic development of virtually all sectors. In this context, broadband infrastructure is essential to improvements in the quality of life, for both developed and developing countries.[1]

The benefits of broadband development, however, are not evenly distributed. A long-debated concern expressed by developing economies is the inability to take advantage of evolving digital technology.[2] The reality is that digital transformation varies across countries and people.[3] Generally, this inability underscores the importance of greater "digital inclusion," which is defined as bridging the gap between individuals and groups, as well as economies.[4] In measuring digital development, it is

Parts of this chapter were first published by Oxford University Press as Shin-yi Peng, "The Uneasy Interplay between Digital Inequality and International Economic Law" (2022) 33(1) European Journal of International Law 205–235.

[1] See generally Tony Grubesic and Elizabeth Mack, *Broadband Telecommunications and Regional Development* (Routledge, 2016), at 1–7, 179–180.

[2] See, for example, UNCTAD, "The COVID-19 Crisis: Accentuating the Need to Bridge the Digital Divides" (2020) <https://unctad.org/publication/covid-19-crisis>.

[3] OECD, "Measuring the Digital Transformation: A Roadmap for the Future" (2019), at 1–3.

[4] *Ibid.*

important to note that, in 2019, only about 40 percent of people in developing countries were able to access and use the Internet.[5] According to International Telecommunications Union (ITU) statistics, although globally more than 1 billion new Internet users have been added from 2017 to 2022, outstanding digital divides persist between "connected countries, communities, and people."[6] By mid-2022, 5.3 billion people were Internet users, which means that almost 37 percent of the world's population does not use the Internet.[7] Most often, such divides stem from insufficient or slow connectivity, which is closely correlated to geography and socioeconomic status.[8] Substantial digital divides exist between countries,[9] with nearly 87 percent of people using the Internet in developed countries compared to approximately 44 percent in developing countries.[10] In least developed countries (LDCs), only 19 percent of individuals are online.[11] At the same time, intercontinentally, the trend of datafication continues to boost international Internet traffic and therefore requires more and more international bandwidth. It is evident that the demand for submarine cable infrastructure is quickly growing. Currently, transatlantic cable connections are the densest routes, with the highest traffic capacity, which continues to grow annually at the rate of 38 percent.[12] According to the American Chamber of Commerce, submarine communications cables that link the US and the European

[5] ITU, "Digital Inclusion of All" (2022) <https://www.itu.int/en/mediacentre/backgrounders/Pages/digital-inclusion-of-all.aspx>.

[6] *Ibid.* According to ITU statistics, digital divides are also evident within countries. Males, urban residents, and young people are more likely to access the Internet than women, rural residents, and the elderly. The ITU statistics also reveal that the digital gender gap is more substantial in developing and least developed countries.

[7] *Ibid.*

[8] *Ibid.*

[9] *Cf.*, under different framing and definitions of "digital divide," scholars refer to the "divide" between the digital trade strategies of the EU, the US, and China. See generally Susan Ariel Aaronson and Patrick Leblond, "Another Digital Divide: The Rise of Data Realms and Its Implications for the WTO" (2018) 21(2) Journal of International Economic Law 245; Henry Gao, "Digital or Trade? The Contrasting Approaches of China and US to Digital Trade" (2018) 21(2) Journal of International Economic Law 297; Mira Burri, "The Global Digital Divide as Impeded Access to Content" in Mira Burri and Thomas Cottier (eds), *Trade Governance in the Digital Age* (Cambridge University Press 2012), at 396 (discussing "the many divides" that contain not only infrastructure connectivity but also content access).

[10] ITU-D, "Digital Inclusion" (2023) <www.itu.int/itu-d/sites/digital-inclusion>.

[11] *Ibid.*

[12] Daniel S. Hamilton and Joseph P. Quinlan, "The Transatlantic Economy: Annual Survey of Jobs, Trade and Investment between the United States and Europe" (2021), at 56–57.

Union (EU), two of the most developed areas, carry 55 percent more data than transpacific routes and 40 percent more data than US–Latin American routes.[13]

Evidently, the "haves" – people who are connected to the Internet – are empowered. Digital infrastructure allows people to participate in a digital world, which in turn increases their overall well-being in these countries.[14] On the other hand, being "unconnected" means the "have-nots" cannot access online health services, make payments via mobile phone, or increase productivity through digital skills. The recent pandemic has convincingly demonstrated the need to bridge the digital divide. The COVID-19 crisis has stimulated a surge in the use of digital services. In the US, for example, home broadband traffic was up by roughly 20–40 percent from the onset of COVID-19.[15] The unprecedented demand during the pandemic for online delivery, including e-commerce, e-education, and e-health, has underscored the need for efficient and affordable digital services.[16] Even in developed countries, telecommunications regulators required Netflix and YouTube to reduce streaming loads in an attempt to prevent the Internet from collapsing under the strain of heavy usage due to the coronavirus pandemic. The need to address the challenges that hamper greater digital inclusion in developing countries, particularly in LDCs, is now more urgent than ever.[17]

Looking to the future, the core idea behind Industry 4.0,[18] as supported by the fifth generation (5G) network, is to connect machinery to the Internet, which encompasses technologies including 3D printing, the Internet of Things (IoT), artificial intelligence (AI), and big data analytics.[19] The connected devices associated with the IoT, for example, will dramatically increase demands on digital networks. Nearly every piece of technology we use will be part of an always-on, always-connected web of

[13] *Ibid.*, at 56. Note that content and cloud services suppliers are gradually displacing telecommunications operators as the major investors in (private) submarine cables.

[14] See UNCTAD, "Technology and Innovation Report" (2021), at 3, 78.

[15] Doug Brake, "Lessons from the Pandemic: Broadband Policy after COVID-19" Information Technology & Innovation Foundation (ITIF) (2020) <https://itif.org/publications/2020/07/13/lessons-pandemic-broadband-policy-after-covid-19>.

[16] WTO, "E-Commerce, Trade and the Covid-19 Pandemic Information Note" (2020).

[17] *Ibid.*

[18] Sudip Misra et al., *Introduction to Industrial Internet of Things and Industry 4.0* (Routledge 2020), at 51–71.

[19] *Ibid.*, at 3–9.

smart sensors and data feedback devices.[20] That in turn will unleash a torrent of data traffic across the Internet. However, the reality is that current networks are nowhere near ready to accommodate this level of Internet traffic.[21] Accommodating the technology evolution and meeting ensuing connectivity demands will require continued modernization of legacy telecommunications infrastructure, as well as the creation of additional broadband networks.[22] In light of the high levels of investment required to adopt 5G networks, developed countries' early deployment of 5G networks is expected to exacerbate the current digital divide.[23] According to industry estimations, the cost to deploy a 5G network may range from USD 6.8 million to USD 55.5 million, depending on the size of the city.[24] The ITU predicts that 5G penetration will be around 60 percent in developed economies by 2025, whereas the same network connectivity during this period will be below 10 percent in Latin America and below 5 percent in African countries.[25]

1.2 Opening the Services Market

1.2.1 Telecommunications Liberalization

In the context of international economic law, a few premise questions are in order. What role has the liberalization of telecommunications services played in the emergence of today's broadband "digital divide?" How might international trade agreements have contributed to such inequalities? How can the WTO help to narrow the digital divide, or even to promote digital inclusion? To answer these questions, a brief overview of the negotiating context of the relevant WTO treaty obligations is discussed below.

[20] The IoT refers to "a global, distributed network of physical objects that are capable of sensing or acting on their environment, and able to communicate with each other, other machines or computers." Rajkumar Buyya and Amir Dastjerdi (eds), *Internet of Things: Principles and Paradigms* (Elsevier 2016), at 3. The IoT should be seen as "the aggregation of many machine-to-machine (M2M) connections" which focus on the sharing of data and processing that takes place between these devices.

[21] ITU, "GSR Discussion Paper: Regulation and the Internet of Things" (2015) <www.itu.int/en/ITU-D/Conferences/GSR/Documents/GSR2015/Discussion_papers_and_Presentations/GSR_DiscussionPaper_IoT.pdf>.

[22] ITU, "Setting the Scene for 5G: Opportunities & Challenges" (2018) <www.itu.int/pub/D-PREF-BB.5G_01>, at 30.

[23] *Ibid.* See also UNCTAD, "Digital Economy Report" (2019) <https://unctad.org/webflyer/digital-economy-report-2019>, at 7.

[24] UNCTAD, supra note 22.

[25] *Ibid.*

Historically speaking, the pre-Uruguay Round General Agreement on Tariffs and Trade (GATT) system applied only to trade in goods. In light of the increased potential for international trade in services, the elimination of trade barriers to service sectors became a major priority of a number of developed countries in the Uruguay Round of trade negotiations in the early 1990s.[26] The conclusion of the General Agreement on Trade in Services (GATS) in 1994 forms an essential component of the legal framework for a global trading system.[27] The GATS is the first multilateral trade agreement to cover trade in services, through which WTO members commit to the liberalization of the services sectors. In scheduling their market access commitments, members indicate the limitations on market access for each services sector scheduled with regard to each of the "four modes of supply."[28]

Arguably, the GATS opened global telecommunications markets for multinational telecommunications companies in such a way that a critical mass of WTO members have included the telecommunications sector in their schedules of commitments. Overall, emerging economies have recorded a high incidence of commitments on Mode 3 (foreign investment). According to the WTO Secretariat, such unique patterns of commitment by emerging economies "illustrate the importance they have attached to foreign direct investment (FDI) as a means of improving and extending national telecommunications networks and universal access."[29] Over the years, the interplay between the liberalization of the telecommunications market and the possibility of attracting foreign investment in the sector has been repeatedly raised by WTO members – with divergent viewpoints. While some delegates from developing countries pointed out that the degree of liberalization in the telecommunications sector should be based on "the possibility for such liberalization to promote both growth and development,"[30] delegates from developed

[26] Andrew Lang, "GATS" in Daniel Bethlehem et al. (eds), *Oxford Handbook of International Trade Law* (Oxford University Press 2009).

[27] *Ibid.*

[28] At the most general level, the conceptual cornerstone of the GATS is its definition of trade in services. For the purposes of the GATS, trade in services is defined in Article I:2 by reference to four different ways in which such trade can occur: cross-border supply (Mode 1); consumption abroad (Mode 2); supply through commercial presence (Mode 3, *i.e.*, foreign investment); and supply through the presence of natural persons (Mode 4).

[29] WTO Secretariat, *Guide to the GATS: An Overview of Issues for Further Liberalization of Trade in Services* (Kluwer Law International 2001), at 540.

[30] "Multilateral Trade Negotiations the Uruguay Round Group of Negotiations on Services" MTN.GNS/23 (July 11, 1989), para. 12. (In the meeting, the delegate for Brazil "regretted

countries continued to stress that the liberalization of telecommunications could help modernize the economy, promote development, and bring "considerable growth effects" in the FDI host countries.[31]

For a long time, even before the broadband era, developing countries and LDCs have required injections of foreign capital into their telecommunications infrastructure. In the pre-GATS world, however, most states maintained state-monopoly control over telecommunications. Despite the enormous demand for capital to build large-scale networks, the telecommunications services sector was generally closed to FDI. When the GATS became effective, market forces were unleashed, and monopoly telecommunications incumbents began to face both domestic and foreign competition. In theory, competition driven by market forces should deliver services more effectively than monopoly-based schemes.[32] The economic assumption was that government-owned telecommunications companies were being privatized and confronted with the threat of entry from new competitors, thereby forcing these monopolies to become more efficient. At the same time, openness to foreign capital in the telecommunications industry could result in increased infrastructure investment and thus bridge the digital divide.[33]

1.2.2 From Monopoly to Competition

The promised economic benefit of market access commitments, however, has never been realized in many developing countries and LDCs. There is a missing link between telecommunications liberalization and broadband investment. Before the WTO opened the global telecommunications market, cross-subsidization within a monopolized market was the traditional means of pursuing "universal service" goals for most countries. Under such a monopoly scheme, losses incurred from less lucrative activities were financed by income earned from more profitable ones.[34]

the absence of development concerns" and stressed the gap between developed and developing countries regarding the capacities in supplying the telecommunications services.)

[31] "Note by the Secretariat, WTO Council for Trade in Services: Special Session" TN/S/M/2 (July 10, 2002), Report of the Meeting held on June 5 and 6, 2002, para. 48.

[32] See generally Gregory Sidak and Daniel Spulber, "Deregulation and Managed Competition in Network Industries" (1998) 15 Yale Journal on Regulation 117, at 120.

[33] *Ibid.*, at 122.

[34] Stuart Benjamin and James Speta, *Internet and Telecommunication Regulation* (Carolina Academic Press 2019), at 670.

The trend of telecommunications liberalization brought about by the GATS, however, has posed a significant threat to cross-subsidies.[35] As observed by Batura, in the pre-GATS age, monopolistic suppliers of telecommunications services financed universal service through cross-subsidization. Generally, one monopoly operator served the entire domestic telecommunications market and signed bilateral commercial agreements with the monopolists of other countries for international interconnection.[36] However, the operation had to be changed following the liberalization of the market. In competitive telecommunications markets, cross-subsidies have been squeezed out of the rate structure because prices in low-profit areas are not rebalanced to competitive levels. As a result, market forces may even broaden the digital divide.[37] Without governmental intervention, profit-motivated telecommunications network operators will prioritize serving densely populated, high-usage urban areas rather than rural areas or low-usage households – the "cream-skimming" or "cherry-picking" effect.[38]

The transitional stages from a monopolistic to a competitive telecommunications market, therefore, have been a bumpy road in terms of reshaping universal service policies, especially for developing countries and LDCs, where infrastructure development needs are urgent. According to the United Nations Conference on Trade and Development (UNCTAD), a dominant part of FDI has been concentrated in a select few countries, leaving the LDCs to receive less than 2 percent of global FDI.[39] Over the past decade, FDI flows to LDCs have increased only marginally.[40] Among all infrastructure sectors, FDI in renewable energy generation and distribution services has increased since 2021, while FDI in other infrastructure sectors, including telecommunications services, barely grew.[41]

35 *Ibid.*, at 672.

36 Olga Batura, *Universal Service in WTO and EU Law: Liberalization and Social Regulation in Telecommunications* (Springer 2016), at 87.

37 See Benjamin and Speta, supra note 34, at 672. See also Thomas Bonnett, *Telewars in the States: Telecommunications Issues in a New Era of Competition* (Council of Governors' Policy Advisors 1996), at 100.

38 Benjamin and Speta, *ibid.*, at 672. See also Stuart M. Benjamin, *Telecommunications Law and Policy* (Carolina Academic Press 2012), at 631–632 (explaining why, in competitive telecommunications markets, the cost of supplying telecommunications service per subscriber is lower in more densely populated areas).

39 United Nations, "World Investment Report 2016" (2016), at 37.

40 United Nations, "World Investment Report 2022" (2022), at 12–13.

41 *Ibid.*, at 13.

As Shaffer observed in a broader context, international trade liberalization results in the more efficient use of resources, but the gain from such economic efficiency may not be "inclusively shared."[42] Rather, international trade, together with "other primary culprits," can contribute to increased inequality.[43] Evidently, market liberalization alone failed to promote broadband equality. In order to promote affordable access to physical networks, the challenge for governments is how to utilize competition to maximize access while enforcing a digital inclusion policy to minimize geographic inequalities. After all, while competition delivers broadband services in "abundance," it distributes them unequally.[44] As discussed below, the domestic 'funding' mechanism therefore becomes the central issue in the alleviation of the digital divide.

1.3 Bridging the Digital Divide

1.3.1 Universal Broadband Service

The lack of "universal access" to telecommunications services has been addressed nationally – primarily via "universal service" mechanisms administered by national communications regulators to spur infrastructure development in high-cost areas.[45] From a historical perspective, the contemporary concept of "universal service" carries a somewhat different meaning today than when it was coined by Theodore Vail, the chief architect of the Bell system.[46] When Vail first advocated for "one policy, one system, universal service" in 1908, the term "universal service" was conceived as a single provider offering a single telephone network, to which all customers were connected.[47] In that context, the losses could easily be "cross-subsidized" by the profits within a monopoly scheme – just as the Bell system did in the US.[48]

[42] Gregory Shaffer, "Reconceiving Trade Agreements for Social Inclusion" in Manfred Elsig et al. (eds), *The Shifting Landscape of Global Trade Governance* (Cambridge University Press 2019), at 157, 159, 161.

[43] *Ibid.*, at 161.

[44] See Shin-yi Peng, "Universal Telecommunications Service in China: Trade Liberalization, Subsidy, and Technology in the Making of Information Equality in the Broadband Era" (2003) 4 Asian-Pacific Law & Policy Journal 21, at 36.

[45] Benjamin and Speta, supra note 34, at 665–685.

[46] *Ibid.*, at 665.

[47] *Ibid.*

[48] *Ibid.*, at 670.

Following the liberalization of telecommunications in the 1990s, it has been generally recognized by regulators around the world that increased competition, coupled with a domestic universal service fund,[49] may provide a nation with the best opportunity to achieve the goal of digital inclusion.[50] To bridge the digital divide, governments have typically turned to public policies that aim to both promote market efficiency and improve social welfare – namely, pro-competitive regulations complemented by "universal service" mechanisms that mitigate the digital divide between commercially viable and nonviable areas.[51] The modern concept of "universal service" therefore means the availability of telecommunications services for all customers at an affordable price, supported by subsidies.[52] One striking example is Section 254 of the US Telecommunications Act of 1996, which employs a funding mechanism to finance universal service through equitable contributions by all telecommunications operators.[53] The basic rationale is that while competition can foster affordability by reducing costs and prices in profitable areas, a "universal service fund" can help to ensure that "basic services" are provided to unprofitable rural areas.[54]

Neither "universal" nor "service," however, are self-defining terms. Considering the uncertainty surrounding technological developments, it is necessary for regulators to operate in a reactive manner, implementing universal service policies that can adjust to unique changes in digital technologies. Consequently, most jurisdictions use vague language in their regulations to offer a fair degree of interpretive flexibility.[55] For example, the scope of the universal service scheme in the US remains

[49] For best practices in universal service funds, see ITU, "Universal Service Funds and Digital Inclusion for All" (2013) <www.itu.int/en/ITU-D/Digital-Inclusion/Documents/USF_final-en.pdf>, at16–19.

[50] *Ibid.* It should also be noted that several innovative broadband infrastructure projects are emerging, including Loon (Internet-beaming balloons) and SpaceX (low Earth orbit satellite). These disruptive technologies have the potential to substantially change broadband policy in the coming years. Zoe Kleinman, "Satellites Beat Balloons in Race for Flying Internet" (*The BBC News*, January 25, 2021).

[51] *Ibid.*

[52] Benjamin and Speta, supra note 34, at 684.

[53] *Ibid. Cf.*, infra notes 80 & 81. Currently, a relevant debate is whether to ask big tech companies to contribute to universal service funds.

[54] OECD, "Universal Service Obligations in a Competitive Telecommunications Environment" (1995) <www.oecd.org/sti/broadband/2349175.pdf> (offering a comprehensive examination of the rationale of universal service policies).

[55] For comparative studies of universal service policy across countries, see ITU, supra note 49, at 30–32.

dynamic, which comprises "an evolving level of telecommunications services" that regulators must periodically revisit and reevaluate.[56]

1.3.2 Evolving Technologies

In practice, the definition of "universal service" is pragmatic in order to ensure that policies will keep pace with technological developments. As technology evolves, much of the debate focuses on what should be included under the definition of universal service. In this regard, "universal service" in many jurisdictions essentially refers to the provision of "minimum" telecommunications service to people at an affordable price.[57] Nevertheless, the core question is as follows: What level of telecommunications service represents the "minimum"? Should it include both fixed and mobile broadband Internet access? If yes, how "broad" is the broadband of the network? How should the definition of universal service evolve toward a higher standard of service as digital technologies improve and demands for advanced services increase?

There are variations in the definitions of universal service, and policy tools and financing approaches differ from country to country.[58] Broadband Internet access has been advocated as a "fundamental right."[59] Finland, as a Utopian example, is the first country in the world to enshrine broadband access as a right in law – legally guaranteeing the Finnish people a 1 MB speed by 2010 and a 100Mbps (megabit per

[56] Section 254 of the US Telecommunications Act requires the Federal-State Joint Board to consider the extent to which such services: first, are essential to education, public health, and safety; second, have been subscribed to by a substantial majority of residential consumers; third, are being deployed in public telecommunications networks by telecommunications carriers; and fourth, are consistent with public interest, convenience, and necessity.

[57] Charles Kennedy, *An Introduction to U.S. Telecommunications Law* (Artech House 2001), at 185–199. The U.S. Telecommunications Act of 1996 was drafted in recognition of the fact that cross-subsidization funding mechanisms could not survive under the new competitive regime. The Act employs funding mechanisms financed through equitable contributions by all service providers. Every telecom carrier that provides telecom services contributes, on an equitable basis, to the universal service support mechanisms. An eligible telecom carrier can receive support from these mechanisms for the provision of facilities and services within the scope of the universal service policy.

[58] ITU, supra note 49, at 30–32.

[59] For example, Satya Nadella, the CEO of Microsoft, is the advocator for "broadband fundamental rights." Clare Duffy, "Broadband Internet Access Is a Fundamental Right" (*CNN Business News*, July 15, 2020).

second) broadband connection by the end of 2015.[60] Similarly, the UK government has recognized that access to the Internet is "the passport to the information society"[61] and an "essential element to participate in the economy," which is "as vital as access to electricity a century ago." In practice, the UK government announced a new "legal right" to 25 Mbps broadband in 2015, which ensures that all residents and businesses in the UK have access to broadband through a "Universal Broadband Obligation."[62] The government has also used "coverage obligations" attached to the mobile operators' licenses and has required operators to reach 95 percent of the UK population by 2025.[63] In this context, Taiwan, which is classified as a developing country, was also set to ensure "broadband human rights" to "all disadvantaged people," enabling access to 25 Mbps broadband services.[64] At the other end of the spectrum, however, the United Nations' 2025 targets for 25 Mbps broadband-Internet user penetration are 65 percent in developing countries and 35 percent in LDCs.[65]

It should be noted, however, that the above fundamental right-oriented approach was to guarantee minimum broadband access to disadvantaged groups in rural areas. The reality is that a "broadband human right" is "not enough" in developed countries. Despite the relatively low floor set by developed countries in terms of standards,[66] the EU also has ambitious digital plans for 2025, including Gigabit (1000 Mbps) connectivity for all main socioeconomic drivers, such as schools,

[60] Finland became the first country in the world to make broadband a legal right for every citizen. Since July 1, 2010, every Finn has the right to access to a 1Mbps (megabit per second) broadband connection. "Finland Makes Broadband A 'Legal Right'" (*BBC News*, July 1, 2010).

[61] UK Parliament, "Universal Broadband Obligation" (2009) <https://edm.parliament.uk/early-day-motion/37476/universal-broadband-obligation>.

[62] "UK Government Makes 10Mbps Universal Broadband Obligation" (*Telecoms News*, November 9, 2015) <https://telecoms.com/451742/uk-government-makes-10mbps-universal-broadband-obligation/>.

[63] UK Government, "£1 billion Deal Set to Solve Poor Mobile Coverage" (October 25, 2015) <www.gov.uk/government/news/1-billion-deal-set-to-solve-poor-mobile-coverage>.

[64] Executive Yuan, "E-Competitiveness Annual Report" (December 2018), at 48.

[65] ITU, "The State of Broadband 2020: Tackling Digital Inequalities" (September 2020) <www.itu.int/dms_pub/itu-s/opb/pol/S-POL-BROADBAND.21-2020-PDF-E.pdf>, at 5.

[66] The EU has also announced its connectivity objectives that 100 Mbps networks will reach "all European households" by 2025. EU, "Connectivity for a European Gigabit Society" (February 26, 2021) <https://ec.europa.eu/digital-single-market/en/news/connectivity-european-gigabit-society-brochure>.

transport hubs, hospitals, and public administrations.[67] On the other side of the Atlantic, the US Federal Communications Commission (FCC) has allocated $9.2 billion from its Rural Digital Opportunity Fund for high-speed broadband services – with the vast majority of locations receiving Gigabit broadband.[68] Indeed, as Moyn pointed out, it is critical to note that "sufficiency" and "equality" are different.[69] The "basic needs," "human rights" oriented solutions to digital inclusion – providing the minimum broadband speed – "coexist with a crisis of material inequality."[70]

To conclude, at present, a universal service policy has been the most popular legal mechanism for countries in the promotion of digital inclusion.[71] Generally, a universal service policy provides a certain level of interpretive flexibility as technology evolves. Textually speaking, "universal" may mean that everyone is entitled to services that meet their needs, regardless of their ability to pay.[72] "Minimum" may also be defined as "something people actually want"[73] – as part of their "basic needs."[74] In today's digital age, how much broadband do we need? Based on the UN's 2025 targets, 25 Mbps seems to be the answer for developing countries and LDCs – a wide gap compared to the EU 2025 Gigabit connectivity goal. This reconfirms both the theory and the experience that human rights are rarely an effective tool to address socioeconomic inequalities.

1.4 Digital Inclusion under International Trade Agreements

1.4.1 The GATS Telecommunications Reference Paper: Universal Service

Universal service policies, which are now generally accomplished through national funding, are explicitly recognized by the GATS

[67] *Ibid.*

[68] FCC, "Successful Rural Digital Opportunity Fund Auction to Expand Broadband to Over 10 Million Rural Americans" (*FCC News*, December 7, 2020) <https://docs.fcc.gov/public/attachments/DOC-368588A1.pdf>.

[69] Samuel Moyn, *Not Enough: Human Rights in an Unequal World* (Harvard University Press 2018), at 3.

[70] Moyn, *ibid.*, at 218.

[71] Bonnett, supra note 37, at 100.

[72] See generally Ian Gough, "Universal Basic Services: A Theoretical and Moral Framework" (2019) 90(3) The Political Quarterly 2.

[73] *Ibid.*

[74] Kennedy, supra note 57, at 185–199.

Telecommunications Reference Paper (Telecom Reference Paper). More specifically, in stipulating that WTO members have the right to define the kind of universal service obligations they wish to adopt, Section 3 (Universal Service) of the Telecom Reference Paper implicitly permits members to establish a universal service support fund, stating the following:

> Any Member has the right to define the kind of universal service obligation it wishes to maintain. Such obligations will not be regarded as anti-competitive per se, provided they are administered in a *transparent, non-discriminatory and competitively neutral manner* and are not more burdensome than necessary for the kind of universal service defined by the Member.[75] (emphasis added)

Section 3 of the Telecom Reference Paper, however, is silent as to whether such a fund should be maintained through operator levies or the general tax system. As a whole, the Telecom Reference Paper does not impose a single method by which universal service providers should be chosen or a specific mechanism by which universal service should be funded.[76] Rather, it leaves WTO members free to define the scope and method of a universal service policy that suits them depending on unique national circumstances. Such flexibility allows members to pursue universal service objectives through a wide range of methods, as long as these social objectives are achieved in a transparent, non-discriminatory manner.[77] In addition, Section 3 requires that the collection and distribution of a subsidy fund should be performed in a competitively neutral manner, and that the funding levied should not be more than is necessary to meet the member's universal service policy requirements.[78] In practice, a member's universal service scheme should be administered in alignment with the general principles required by Section 3 of the Telecom Reference Paper. For example, when implementing a universal service fund, a member should specify that such a fund is to be financed by all physical network operators, regardless of whether they are domestic or foreign enterprises or joint ventures. Nevertheless, WTO members

[75] Telecom Reference Paper, Section 3 (Universal Service).

[76] Damien Geradin and Michel Kerf, "Levelling the Playing Field: Is the WTO Adequately Equipped to Prevent Anti-Competitive Practices in Telecommunications?" in Damien Geradin & David Luff (eds), *The WTO and Global Convergence in Telecommunications and Audio-Visual Services* (Cambridge University Press 2004), at 131, 146.

[77] *Ibid.*, at 154–155.

[78] *Ibid.*

have the discretion to impose self-defined universal service obligations on services suppliers. A member's telecommunications regulator has wide policy space in advancing universal broadband service.

In this datafied world, potential reform in this regard is moving toward a requirement that big tech companies contribute their fair share to support the universal service mechanism. In the "FCC Reports to Congress on Future of the Universal Service Fund," the FCC Commissioners, and in particular Brendan Carr, advocated for a new approach to funding the government's universal service system.[79] After pointing out that Netflix, YouTube, Amazon Prime, Disney+, and Microsoft have been "enjoying a free ride on . . . Internet infrastructure," Carr specifically asked the US Federal-State Joint Board on Universal Service to ensure that "the businesses that derived the greatest benefit from a communications network . . . are required to pay the lion's share of the costs."[80] Similarly, the EU has launched a public consultation surrounding how to fund infrastructure upgrades needed for transformative digital technologies, including AI and Metaverse/virtual reality (VR) applications.[81] By underscoring that all players benefiting from the digital economy should "fairly contribute to the required investments," and that the entire industry should make "proportionate contribution to the costs" of public infrastructure,[82] it is clear that EU policymakers recognize the need for big tech companies to bear greater responsibility for the universal service goal. Turning back to the Telecom Reference Paper, this book contends that the proposed reforms to the member's universal service system are aligned with Section 3, which provides sufficient policy leeway to accommodate the divergent policy needs of WTO members and structural changes to the broadband market, as long as they are administered in a transparent, non-discriminatory, and competitively neutral manner. Despite this, the *Mexico–Telecom* case below demonstrates how a WTO member's universal service policy can go too far.

[79] FCC, "Reports to Congress on Future of the Universal Service Fund" (August 15 2022) <www.fcc.gov/document/fcc-reports-congress-future-universal-service-fund>, at 63.

[80] FCC, "Carr Calls for Ending Big Tech's Free Ride on the Internet" (*FCC News*, May 24, 2021) <https://docs.fcc.gov/public/attachments/DOC-372688A1.pdf>.

[81] European Commission, "The Future of the Electronic Communications Sector and Its Infrastructure, Consultation Questionnaire" (February 23, 2023) <https://digital-strategy.ec.europa.eu/en/consultations/future-electronic-communications-sector-and-its-infrastructure>.

[82] *Ibid.*

1.4.2 *The* Mexico–Telecom *Case: Cost-Oriented Rates*

The *Mexico–Telecom* dispute[83] was the first WTO panel proceeding to solely address the GATS, and it is also the only dispute settlement case to address international trade of telecommunications services.[84] The US asserted that Mexico's rules governing connection rates for international telecommunications traffic violated its WTO commitments to provide interconnection at reasonable rates. It claimed that the interconnection rates negotiated by Telmex, the incumbent telecommunications supplier in Mexico, were not consistent with the "cost-oriented" requirement imposed by Section 2.2(b) of the Telecom Reference Paper.[85] Mexico argued that the US erroneously interpreted "cost-oriented" rates as simply equal to the "bare cost" of supplying the telecommunications services, and that instead, the term must be interpreted by taking into account the qualifying phrase "transparent, reasonable, and economically feasible" in Section 2.2(b) of the Telecom Reference Paper.[86] In the view of Mexico, relevant factors in assessing whether cost-oriented rates were "reasonable" include "the state of a WTO member's telecommunications industry; the coverage and quality of its telecommunications network; and the return on investment."[87] Mexico further argued that in assessing whether the cost-oriented rates were "economically feasible," key factors should include "the efficient use of income and wealth" and "the needs of the operator and the policy goals of the country."[88] In this respect, Mexico's policy objectives to promote universal service, which "depended to a large extent on interconnection revenues," should be taken into

[83] Panel Report, *Mexico – Measures Affecting Telecommunications Services (Mexico – Telecom)*, WT/DS204/R, April 2, 2004.

[84] See generally Shin-yi Peng, "Trade in Telecommunications Services: Doha and Beyond" (2007) 41(2) Journal of World Trade 293.

[85] Telecom Reference Paper, Section 2 (Interconnection), 2.2 (Interconnection to be ensured):

> Interconnection with a major supplier will be ensured at any technically feasible point in the network. Such interconnection is provided. . . . (b) in a timely fashion, on terms, conditions (including technical standards and specifications) and cost-oriented rates that are transparent, reasonable, having regard to economic feasibility, and sufficiently unbundled so that the supplier need not pay for network components or facilities that it does not require for the service to be provided; . . ..

[86] Panel Report, *Mexico – Telecom*, para. 7.164.

[87] *Ibid.*

[88] *Ibid.*, para. 4.180.

consideration.[89] Throughout the litigation, Mexico repeatedly stressed the need for "infrastructure development" and "universal service."[90] The main argument is clear: The term "economic feasibility" in Section 2.2(b) of the Telecom Reference Paper provides great latitude in allowing its major supplier, Telmex, to include charges for infrastructure development or universal service.[91]

In response to Mexico's arguments, the US clarified the relationship between Section 2.2 (cost-oriented rate) and Section 3 (universal service) of the Telecom Reference Paper. In the view of the US, "interconnection charges are limited to the specific network components and facilities required for the interconnection service provided."[92] Therefore, Telmex's interconnection charge, which includes a universal service component, violates the "cost-orientation" requirement in Section 2.2. At the same time, the recovery of universal service subsidies hidden in Mexico's interconnection charges also violates the "transparent administration" of universal service obligations in Section 3.[93] The US further pointed out that the Telecom Reference Paper separates the disciplines on cost-orientation rates in Section 2 from the disciplines on universal service in Section 3.[94] The US delegation argued that if Mexico wished to promote "investment" in its national telecommunications infrastructure, it should "fund" its rollout costs in a way that is consistent with Section 3 of the Telecom Reference Paper. The US contended that Mexico's recovery of universal service subsidies paid to Telmex through the levy of hidden, inflated interconnection rates from foreign suppliers would be inconsistent with the Section 3 requirement that universal service obligations be administered in a transparent, non-discriminatory and competitively neutral manner.[95] Interestingly enough, during the oral hearing in the litigation, the US delegation "lectured" that Mexico's above-cost interconnection rates had not and could not lead to infrastructure rollout and increase the country's teledensity. The statement went on as follows: "competition, along with … the imposition of a universal service

89 *Ibid.*, para.7.164.

90 Oral Statement of the United States at the Second Meeting of the Panel, *Mexico–Telecom*, WT/DS204/R, March 12, 2003, para. 3.

91 *Ibid.*, para. 59.

92 *Ibid.*, paras. 61–63.

93 *Ibid.*

94 *Ibid.*

95 Answers of the United States to the Panel's Questions to the Parties at the Second Meeting, *Mexico–Telecom*, WT/DS204/R, March 27, 2003, para. 53.

obligation that is consistent with the requirements of Section 3 of the Telecom Reference Paper, will help Mexico achieve infrastructure rollout and increased teledensity."[96]

While recognizing that the high degree of flexibility embedded in the term "cost-oriented" implies that more than one pricing methodology can be employed when calculating "cost-oriented" rates, the panel nevertheless noted that the widespread use of long-term incremental cost methodologies among WTO members should serve as a reference in determining the costs incurred in supplying the service.[97] On that basis, the panel concluded that Mexico was in violation of its "cost-orientation rate" commitments under Section 2.2(b) of the Telecom Reference Paper, because the interconnection rates charged by Telmex were substantially higher than the costs actually incurred in supplying the interconnection services.[98] The panel's interpretation of the cost-orientation principle, which did not consider domestic regulatory objectives and practices, has been criticized by Howse as "laissez-faire ideology" and a "hyperliberal teleological view" toward the liberalization and deregulation of the telecommunications sector.[99] Twenty years after the *Mexico–Telecom* case, the issue of universal service, although framed in different legal contexts, once again came to the fore in the *Brazil – Taxation* case.

1.4.3 The Brazil Taxation *Case: Public Morals Exception*

Digital inclusion measures that extend beyond the context of the Telecom Reference Paper might also violate other WTO obligations and therefore raise the question of whether such measures can be justified by the WTO's general exceptions. At the core of the issue is to what extent digital inclusion falls within the scope of the "public morals" exceptions. In this regard, the *Brazil – Taxation* dispute represents a remarkable case surrounding the challenges faced by international economic law in striking a balance between trade efficiency and digital

96 Comments of the United States on Mexico's Answers to the Panel's Questions at the Second Meeting, *Mexico – Telecom*, WT/DS204/R, April 30, 2003, para. 43.

97 Panel Report, *Mexico – Telecom*, para. 7.177.

98 *Ibid.*, 7.216.

99 Robert Howse, "Importing Regulatory Standards and Principles into WTO Dispute Settlement: The Challenge of Interpreting the GATS Arrangements on Telecommunications" in Ioannis Lianos and Okeoghene Odudu (eds), *Regulating Trade in Services in the EU and the WTO: Trust, Distrust and Economic Integration* (Cambridge University Press, 2012), at 445, 464–467.

inclusion.[100] The measures at issue concerned four Brazilian tax incentive programs.[101] Among others, under the Brazilian Digital Inclusion Program, only goods eligible for tax benefits are Brazilian domestic products,[102] representing a straightforward situation of incentives that are provided in respect of a preference for domestic over imported goods. The complaining parties – the EU and Japan – claimed that the Digital Inclusion Program is inconsistent with Article III:4 National Treatment principle of the GATT.[103]

One key issue in the dispute was whether the discriminatory aspects of the measures could be justified under Article XX(a) of the GATT 1994[104] – the public morals exception.[105] In the litigation, Brazil argued that "there is a gap between demographics and regions that have access to modern information and telecommunications technology and those that do not have access or have restricted access."[106] According to Brazil, the measures in dispute represented an important means to "bridge this digital divide and promote social inclusion," which would in turn "improve literacy, democracy, social mobility, economic quality, and growth."[107] To support its overarching policy goals, Brazil submitted as evidence the United Nations' Millennium Development Goals Report, which stressed that "ICT access and use are unequally distributed within and between countries," and that "it will be essential to address the

[100] Request for Consultations by the European Union, *Brazil – Certain Measures Concerning Taxation and Charges (Brazil – Taxation)*, WT/DS472/1, January 8, 2014. Panel Report, *Brazil – Taxation*, WT/DS472/R, January 11, 2019, para. 7.622.

[101] Panel Report, *Brazil – Taxation*, paras. 8.5, 8.16. The measures at issue include the Informatics Program, the Program of Incentives for the Semiconductor Sector (PADIS), the Program of Support for the Technological Development of the Digital TV Equipment Industry (PATVD), and the Digital Inclusion Program (acronyms represent Brazilian-language versions of these programs).

[102] *Ibid.*, paras. 7.315–7.317. The retailers in turn only obtain the tax benefits to the extent that they have purchased these domestic goods (for resale), instead of like foreign goods.

[103] *Ibid.*, para. 7.3.2.

[104] *Ibid.*, paras. 7.3.6.3.

[105] GATT, Article XX (General Exceptions):

> Subject to the requirement that such measures are not applied in a manner which would constitute a means of arbitrary or unjustifiable discrimination between countries where the same conditions prevail, or a disguised restriction on international trade, nothing in this Agreement shall be construed to prevent the adoption or enforcement by any contracting party of measures: (a) necessary to protect public morals; . . ..

[106] Panel Report, *Brazil – Taxation*, para. 7.544.

[107] *Ibid.*, para. 7.545.

widening digital divide."[108] It further stated: "Only then will the transformative power of ICTs and the data revolution be harnessed to deliver sustainable development for all."[109] In this regard, the EU argued that the social and economic development objectives claimed by Brazil may "characterize any governmental action."[110] According to the EU, if objectives such as access to information were protected under Article XX, "then any governmental action taken in the public interest could be justifiable under Article XX."[111]

The panel found that a concern existed in Brazilian society with respect to the need to bridge the digital divide, and that such concern was within the meaning of Article XX(a) of the GATT 1994.[112] The panel therefore proceeded to examine whether the measures at issue satisfied the "necessity test" – the principle of proportionality in the context of international economic law. Under this "necessity test" practice, a central question is whether the discriminatory aspects of the measure are necessary to achieve the claimed objective: closing the digital divide.[113] More specifically, the central question in *Brazil – Taxation* concerned whether the alternative measures proposed by the complaining parties were WTO-consistent measures that were reasonably available to Brazil, that were less trade restrictive than the measures at issue, and that could achieve an equal or higher level of contribution to the objective of bridging the digital divide.[114] The panel found that the alternatives proposed by the complaining parties would not only be WTO-consistent and less trade restrictive than the Brazilian tax incentive programs,[115] but that they would also make a more substantial contribution to the claimed objective than the measures at issue.[116] The panel therefore concluded that Brazil had not demonstrated that the measures at issue were "necessary" to achieve digital inclusion within the meaning of Article XX(a) of

108 *Ibid.*, para. 7.563.
109 *Ibid.*
110 *Ibid.*
111 *Ibid.*, para. 7.548.
112 *Ibid.*, paras. 7.568–7.569.
113 *Ibid.*, para 7.596.
114 *Ibid.*, para. 7.549. See also European Union's opening statement at the first meeting of the Panel, *Brazil –Taxation*, WT/DS472/R, para. 165.
115 Panel Report, para. 7.609. Both complaining parties have proposed certain WTO-consistent, less trade-restrictive alternative measures that they consider are reasonably available to Brazil, including nondiscriminatory tax exemptions on digital TV transmitters, or the overall elimination of import tariffs on digital TV transmitters.
116 *Ibid.* para.7.618.

the GATT 1994.[117] In other words, Brazil's developmental concerns could not justify the imposition of national-origin measures.

In a broader sense, it is an awkward task for a WTO panel to address the "digital divide" within the context of Article XX of the GATT. Limited to its mandate, the panel's primary task is to safeguard trade interests and address problems that arise when digital policies have an impact on trade. Nonetheless, the development of network infrastructure is the foundation upon which individuals are empowered to benefit from digital opportunities. Infrastructural dimensions, including enhancements to teledensity and Internet density by wireline, as well as wireless connections, often involve WTO-inconsistent subsidization measures that grant tax exemptions or subsidize ICT-related sectors in any possible way. The mere fact that a responding party must have attempted to stretch the scope of the "public morals" exception to justify its digital inclusion policy within the WTO indicates that the interplay between international economic law and digital inequality invites further reflection.

The WTO's general exceptions provide a hierarchical framework by which to balance international trade commitments against national social preferences, ranging from the protection of public morals to the maintenance of public health.[118] WTO members can, for example, justify violations of their obligations assumed under the GATS through recourse based upon one of the grounds delineated in GATS Article XIV.[119] The opening sentence of Article XIV (the Chapeau) indicates that the negotiators' intent was that all grounds listed in this provision "trump" trade obligations delineated in the rest of the GATS.[120] In other words, trade liberalization is not the supreme goal that all WTO members must strive to achieve at the expense of other public objectives. Domestic measures aimed at bridging the digital divide, if successfully invoked under GATS

[117] *Ibid.*, paras. 7.544–7.568. The finding of the panel in this case raised a critical question as to what constitutes public morals and how to distinguish between public policies that fall under public morals and those that do not. Unfortunately, in the appeal, while the EU and Japan each appealed certain issues of law and legal interpretations developed in the Panel Reports, both parties did not appeal the issue of Article XX(a). The key questions remain unanswered.

[118] See, for example, GATS, Article XIV.

[119] *Ibid.*

[120] Petros C. Mavroidis, *Trade in Goods* (Oxford University Press 2012), at Ch. 5 (Deviating from WTO Obligations).

Article XIV, may provide WTO members with a lawful escape route from their GATS obligations.

Although the term "public morals" is not further defined in the WTO's general exceptions, WTO jurisprudence offers examples of public policies that have been found by panels or the Appellate Body to pertain to public morals,[121] which include preventing underage gambling,[122] combatting money laundering,[123] protecting national culture and traditional values,[124] safeguarding animal welfare,[125] and, as demonstrated in the *Brazil – Taxation* case, bridging the digital divide and promoting social inclusion.[126] Nevertheless, only measures that are necessary to protect public morals will be deemed consistent with the GATS. In this context, the criteria for the "necessity test" have been consistently reproduced and emphasized in WTO jurisprudence, under which WTO members "have the right to decide which level of protection of the objectives it pursues."[127] In this particular respect, it is up to WTO members to determine the level of protection of digital inclusion they consider appropriate, and other WTO members cannot challenge the level of digital inclusion pursued.[128] However, the "necessity test" requires the consideration of alternatives to the measure taken in order to determine whether existing options are "less trade restrictive" while "providing an equivalent contribution to the achievement of the objective pursued."[129]

[121] See also Christian Delev, "A Moral Stretch? US–Tariff Measures and the Public Morals Exception in WTO Law" (2021) World Trade Review 1–12. Panel Report, *United States – Tariff Measures on Certain Goods from China (US Tariff Measures)*, WT/DS543/R, not yet adopted, para. 7.113.

[122] See Appellate Body Report, *United States – Measures Affecting the Cross-Border Supply of Gambling and Betting Services (US-Gambling)*, WT/DS285/AB/R, April 20, 2005, para. 278.

[123] *Ibid.*

[124] Appellate Body Report, *China – Measures Affecting Trading Rights and Distribution Services for Certain Publications and Audiovisual Entertainment Products (China – Publications and Audiovisual Products)*, WT/DS363/AB/R, January 19, 2010, paras. 141–143.

[125] See, for example, Appellate Body Report, *European Communities – Measures Prohibiting the Importation and Marketing of Seal Products (EC – Seal Products)*, WT/DS400/AB/R, WT/DS401/AB/R, June 18, 2014, paras. 5.199–5.203.

[126] *Brazil – Taxation*, paras, *7.552–7.568*.

[127] See, for example, Panel Report, *Argentina – Measures Relating to Trade in Goods and Services (Argentina – Financial Services)*, WT/DS453/AB/R9, April 14, 2016, para. 7.684.

[128] See, for example, Appellate Body Report, *EC – Seal Products*, para. 5.214.

[129] Panel Report, *EC – Seal*, paras. 5.260–5.264. Appellate Body Report, *Brazil – Measures Affecting Imports of Retreaded Tyres (Brazil – Tyres)*, WT/DS332/AB/R, December 17, 2007, paras. 141, 143, 156, 178.

As evidenced in *Brazil – Taxation*, the overall structure of the necessity test developed by the dispute settlement organs of the WTO serves as a critical tool by which to balance the public interests of the regulating member and the trade interests of other WTO members. Consistent with overall Article XX jurisprudence, while the panel in *Brazil – Taxation* reaffirmed the validity of "digital divide" concerns for purposes of the public morals exception, it also reinforced the necessity test as a limit in terms of how such measures can be applied. To conclude, when trade policy collides with digital inclusion policy, it leads to a dilemma between trade and non-trade values. Faced with such a dilemma, the WTO remains the most effective forum for balancing competing interests. Normatively speaking, however, there is little room for the panels to further expand the reach of the exceptions, and this is attributable to the prominence of the "necessity test" in applying the GATT/GATS general exception language.

1.4.4 DEPA: Digital Inclusion Module

Further disciplines of digital trade have been realized in FTAs and other preferential trade agreements (PTAs) in recent years.[130] In particular, significant achievements have been advanced by the Comprehensive and Progressive Agreement for Trans-Pacific Partnership (CPTPP)[131] and the United States–Mexico–Canada Agreement (USMCA).[132] Moreover, the Digital Economy Partnership Agreement (DEPA) between Singapore, Chile, and New Zealand represents an innovative and collaborative approach to digital trade issues.[133] Other recently concluded FTAs, such

[130] The concept of "digital trade," which in this book is understood in a broad sense, encompasses international trade enabled by digital technologies. There is no single definition of digital trade. OECD defines it as "Digitally enabled transactions of trade in goods and services that can either be digitally or physically delivered." OECD, "The Impact of Digitalization on Trade" (2021) < https://search.oecd.org/trade/topics/digital-trade/>.

[131] The Comprehensive and Progressive Agreement for Trans-Pacific Partnership (CPTPP) Agreement, available at, for example, the website of the MFAT, <www.mfat.govt.nz/en/trade/free-trade-agreements/free-trade-agreements-in-force/comprehensive-and-progressive-agreement-for-trans-pacific-partnership-cptpp>.

[132] United States–Mexico–Canada Agreement (USMCA), available at, for example, the website of the USTR, <https://ustr.gov/usmca>.

[133] Digital Economy Partnership (DEPA) between Singapore, Chile, and New Zealand, available at <www.mti.gov.sg/Trade/Digital-Economy-Agreements/The-Digital-Economy-Partnership-Agreement >.

as the EU–UK Trade and Cooperation Agreement (EU–UK TCA),[134] the Regional Comprehensive Economic Partnership (RCEP) and the EU-New Zealand Free Trade Agreement (EU–NZ FTA), also serve as indicators of future digital trade negotiations.[135]

One important feature of these FTAs, although it may not immediately affect digital inclusion policies, is worth emphasizing: There has been increasing recognition of a state's "right to regulate." Moving beyond the GATS preamble, participating parties have increasingly reserved a more concrete "right to regulate" in the FTAs. The Preamble of the CPTPP, for example, includes language stipulating that CPTPP members recognize their inherent right to regulate and resolve issues, preserving the flexibility of the parties to "set legislative and regulatory priorities, safeguard public welfare, and protect legitimate public welfare objectives," including "public morals."[136] As another example, in the Digital Trade Chapter, the parties of the EU–UK TCA reaffirm the right to regulate for the purpose of achieving legitimate policy objectives, such as "public morals."[137] Over the long run, this trend may help to strike a balance between trade efficiency and digital inclusion, especially in trade dispute litigation where the preamble of a treaty is a source of interpretative guidance.

Nonetheless, the DEPA represents a new form of digital trade agreement that directly addresses the issue of digital inclusion.[138] The Digital Inclusion module in the DEPA – the first of its kind – establishes new collaborations pertaining to digital trade issues, including reduced disparities between developed and developing countries, and among haves and have-nots within a given country.[139] Article 11 stipulates that the parties acknowledge "the importance of digital inclusion to ensure that all people and businesses have what they need to participate in,

[134] The EU-UK Trade and Cooperation Agreement (EU-UK TCA), available at <https://commission.europa.eu/strategy-and-policy/relations-non-eu-countries/relations-united-kingdom/eu-uk-trade-and-cooperation-agreement_en>.

[135] The Regional Comprehensive Economic Partnership (RCEP), available at <https://rcepsec.org/>; The EU-New Zealand Free Trade Agreement (EU–NZ FTA), available at <https://policy.trade.ec.europa.eu/eu-trade-relationships-country-and-region/countries-and-regions/new-zealand/eu-new-zealand-agreement/text-agreement_en>.

[136] CPTPP, supra note 131, the Preamble.

[137] EU-UK TCA, supra note 134, Article 198.

[138] Other FTAs, whether in the Telecommunication Chapters or the E-Commerce/Digital Trade Chapters, did not substantively go beyond the WTO Agreement in this regard.

[139] Module 11 Digital Inclusion of the DEPA.

contribute to, and benefit from the digital economy."[140] The parties also recognize "the importance of improving access for women, rural populations and low socio-economic groups."[141] Toward that end, the parties have agreed to cooperate on matters relating to digital inclusion, which may comprise, in part, the promotion of "inclusive and sustainable economic growth," to ensure that the benefits and opportunities of the digital economy are more widely shared.[142]

Surely, the language in Article 11 is relatively "soft" in terms of enforceability. The parties simply "acknowledge" or "recognize" the importance of digital inclusion, a scenario that does not provide countries involved with adequate legal tools by which to enhance their broadband infrastructure. It should be noted, however, that Article 14 renders Article 11 subject to dispute settlement.[143] A party may request the appointment of an arbitral tribunal to settle disputes among the parties concerning their rights and obligations with regard to digital inclusion. Overall, there is still a long way to go in transforming "digital inclusion" from a "shield" (*i.e.*, a defense) to a "sword" (*i.e.*, an affirmative obligation) under international trade agreements. However, a relatively softer cross-border regime like DEPA provides an early signal of the direction that stronger international commitments to digital inclusion may eventually take in the future. To conclude, a DEPA-type digital inclusion provision that requires cooperation in bridging the digital divide is a feasible starting point.[144] DEPA has apparently resulted in minor but highly symbolic progress in global digital inclusion efforts.

1.4.5 WTO JSI on E-Commerce: Digital Trade and Development

At the multilateral level, the dynamics in the interplay between trade liberalization and digital (in)equality likely will continue. Recent negotiating proposals in the WTO JSI on E-commerce reveal the uneasy relationship between digital trade and development.[145] Central debates

[140] DEPA, Article 11.1.1.
[141] DEPA, Article 11.1.2.
[142] DEPA, Article 11.1.3.
[143] DEPA. Article 14.
[144] Andrew Mitchell and Neha Mishra, "Digital Trade Integration in Preferential Trade Agreements" (2020) 191 Asia-Pacific Research and Training Network on Trade Working Paper Series.
[145] WTO, "Joint Statement on Electronic Commerce" WT/L/1056 (January 25, 2019). G20 trade negotiators in June 2019 issued a joint statement on digital economic policies that

include how to promote digital capacity and take into account the special constraints that developing countries face in the digital economy.[146] Communication from Côte d'Ivoire, among other interventions, called for the WTO Secretariat to be responsible for establishing a multilateral cooperation forum to "ensure universal benefits from the digital economy."[147] Reiterating the fact that they "lack the infrastructure to fully exploit the potential of e-commerce,"[148] developing countries' position is that they "have not felt the effects of trade digitalization on their economic development," and that the ongoing e-commerce negotiations may "ignore the development interests of low-income countries."[149] Similar communications from developing country members also requested that the WTO Secretariat establish a fund to support the integration of developing countries and LDCs into the digital economy. In their view, the WTO "should be responsible" for identifying and cataloguing the various programs, which are aimed at "providing technical assistance and implementing pilot projects for the development of e-commerce."[150] In summary, developing countries have been pressing for "development-focused digital industrialization,"[151] stressing that needs more pressing than digital liberalization include the promotion of digital capacity and the safeguarding of universal benefits of the data-driven economy.[152] They have clearly positioned themselves in support of the argument that the WTO JSI on E-commerce should specifically

has paved the way for the WTO's plurilateral e-commerce talks. A consolidated text had been distributed to WTO members in December 2020, which is now the basis for negotiations. As of May 2023, participating countries have not yet agreed on divisive issues such as cross-border data flows. See generally WTO, "Electronic Commerce" <www.wto.org/english/tratop_e/ecom_e/ecom_e.htm>.

146 Communication from Argentina, Colombia, and Costa Rica, "WTO Negotiations on Trade-Related Aspects of E-Commerce" INF/ECOM/1 (March 25, 2019). Non-Paper from Brazil, "Exploratory Work on Electronic Commerce" INF/ECOM/3 (March 25, 2019).

147 Communication from Côte d'Ivoire, INF/ECOM/46 (November 14, 2019). Communication from Côte d'Ivoire, INF/ECOM/49 (December 16, 2019).

148 *Ibid.*

149 *Ibid.*

150 *Ibid.*

151 Communication from the African Group, "Report of Panel Discussion on Digital Industrial Policy and Development" JOB/GC/133 (July 21, 2017). See Non-Paper from Brazil, JOB/GC/98 (July 20, 2016). Communication from China, "Joint Statement on Electronic Commerce" INF/ECOM/19 (April 24, 2019).

152 Inside US Trade, "WTO E-Commerce Talks Co-Convener: No Conclusions on Legal Path" (March 16, 2021).

address the urgent needs of digital connectivity, namely, the enabling infrastructure of e-commerce activities.[153]

Drawing upon the experiences of the FTA negotiations, the issue of how to tackle digital trade and development will continue to be one of the primary battles in the WTO JSI on E-commerce.[154] Among others, one key issue is how to extend special and differential (S&D) treatment in the area of digital trade, which typically offers trade preferences, flexibility, transition periods, and technical assistance to developing countries.[155] The concept of S&D has been incorporated into the E-Commerce/Digital Trade Chapters of the FTA. In the CPTPP, Vietnam has been given a transition period, during which its existing data localization measures cannot be challenged by other parties. Similarly, a grace period has also been extended to both Vietnam and Malaysia for existing measures concerning the cross-border transfer of information by electronic means.[156] By the same token, obligations concerning interactive computer services will not apply to Mexico until three years after the USMCA becomes effective.[157] It remains to be seen how S&D provisions will be incorporated into the WTO e-commerce trade rules.[158]

Amid the JSI negotiations, it is important to save the WTO e-commerce trade deal from being a digital "haves" trade agreement. In the digital world, developed countries might just as well be from Mars, while developing countries might just as well be from Venus. In the meantime, the latter are still at the stage where they are struggling to provide Internet access in rural areas and among disadvantaged groups, whereas the former are already focusing on cutting edge issues

153 Shin-yi Peng, "Digital Trade" in Daniel Bethlehem et al. (eds), *The Oxford Handbook of International Trade Law* (Oxford University Press 2022), chapter 29.

154 See, for example, Rolf Weber, "Global Law in the Face of Datafication and Artificial Intelligence" in Peng et al. (eds), *Artificial Intelligence and International Economic Law: Disruption, Regulation, and Reconfiguration* (Cambridge University Press, 2021) (discussing the further transformation of the global trade regime).

155 The WTO Agreements contain over 150 special and differential treatment provisions (S&D). For more general discussion on S & D, see WTO, "Proposals to Enhance Special Treatment for Developing Countries" (2020) <www.wto.org/english/news_e/news20_e/devel_21sep20_e.htm>. See generally Seung Wha Chang, "WTO for Trade and Development Post-Doha" (2007) 10(3) Journal of International Economic Law 553.

156 CPTPP, supra note 131, Article 14.18.

157 USMCA, supra note 132, Chapter 19, ANNEX 19-A. See Mark Wu, "Digital Trade-Related Provisions in Regional Trade Agreements: Existing Models and Lessons for the Multilateral Trade System" RTA Exchange, ICTSD and IDB (November 2017).

158 Peng, supra note 153.

such as open government data, e-invoicing facilitation, etc.[159] Such gaps have posed challenges to the promotion of the more widespread adoption of multilateral e-commerce trade rules. The WTO must be very careful not to give emerging economies a reason to think they are being excluded from the multilateral process. Priority in the negotiating agenda should be given to addressing the issues surrounding infrastructure development, including both goods (*e.g.*, tax measures on ICT products)[160] and services (*e.g.*, broadband FDI).[161] It remains to be seen how WTO members can find the common ground needed to balance digital trade liberalization and development needs. Unless infrastructure concerns from developing countries and LDCs are addressed, the ongoing e-commerce trade deal may end up being labeled a digital "haves" trade agreement.

1.5 Broadband Investment in a Broader Policy Context

1.5.1 Network Neutrality

From a broader policy perspective, a long and painful debate that has been repeatedly asserted as central to broadband investment centers on the regulations regarding network neutrality.[162] Briefly, the erosion of broadband telecommunications revenues has had a disruptive effect on the sector over the past decade. Digital applications such as WhatsApp have become practical alternatives to "traditional" telecommunications services.[163] Voice and messaging services provided by Internet applications have dramatically drawn voice and short messaging service (SMS) traffic away from mobile operators, causing a significant impact on "traditional" network volumes and revenues.[164] In addition to these revenue-eroding trends, streaming content delivered by suppliers such

159 See for example, Communication from New Zealand, INF/ECOM/36 (July 5, 2019).

160 As discussed above in Section 1.4.3 (the *Brazil – Taxation* case).

161 As discussed above in Section 1.2.1 (the lack of foreign capital in broadband investment).

162 Tim Wu, "A Proposal for Network Neutrality" (2003) < www.timwu.org/OriginalNNProposal.pdf>. See also Tim Wu, "Network Neutrality, Broadband Discrimination" (2002) 2 Journal of Telecommunications & High Technology Law, at 141. For discussions on both sides of the debate regarding network neutrality, Tim Wu & Christopher S. Yoo, "Keeping the Internet Neutral? Tim Wu and Christopher Yoo Debate" (2007) 59 Federal Communications Law Journal, at 575.

163 See, for example, Mansoor Iqbal, "WhatsApp Revenue and Usage Statistics" (*Business of Apps*, 2023).

164 *Ibid.*

as Netflix has resulted in the growing demand for broadband infrastructure to seamlessly connect data. Taken together, broadband infrastructure itself is becoming the so-called dumb pipe.[165] Internet content and applications "piggyback" on physical network infrastructure for delivery,[166] while at the same time directly competing with services offered by infrastructure operators. Because of these perceived vulnerabilities, some broadband operators have resorted to blocking or degrading Internet traffic.[167]

Against this backdrop, network neutrality is a term that encompasses various levels of equal treatment of online traffic. The primary concept behind network neutrality is that "all data traffic on a network should be treated indiscriminately."[168] This means that in practice, Internet service providers (ISPs) would be restricted from blocking, degrading, or prioritizing the delivery of online content and applications at their discretion.[169] Whether network neutrality should be imposed as a regulatory requirement has become a controversial issue in many jurisdictions, with politically powerful advocates both in favor of and against its imposition.[170] Especially in the US, since network neutrality's emergence as an academic idea in the early 2000s, the controversy surrounding it has never ceased.[171] Network neutrality opponents have claimed,[172] among other issues, that incentives for physical network operators to continually

165 See, for example, Daniel L. Brenner, "Creating Effective Broadband Network Regulation" (2010) 62 Federal Communications Law Journal 13 (discussing the "near-religious war" between network neutrality advocates who envision a dumb pipe provided by broadband operators).

166 Shin-yi Peng, "GATS and the Over-the-Top Services: A Legal Outlook" (2016) 50(1) Journal of World Trade 21 (explaining the vertical competition between broadband operators and OTT services suppliers).

167 FCC, "In the Matter of Protecting and Promoting the Open Internet" GN Docket No. 14-28 (March 12, 2015), para. 7.

168 Boston Human Rights Commission, "Broadband Access in Boston Project Report" (2021) <www.boston.gov/sites/default/files/file/2022/07/Broadband-Access%20Spring%202021.pdf>, at 22.

169 Wu, supra note 162. See also EU, "Open Internet – Sharing Europe's Digital Future" (2022) <https://ec.europa.eu/digital-single-market/en/open-internet>.

170 Relevant issues, among others, include the impact of network neutrality policy on consumer choices, see Christopher S. Yoo, "Beyond Network Neutrality" (2005) 19 Harvard Journal of Law & Technology 1, at 50; and the consideration of mobile broadband, see Christopher S. Yoo, "Wireless Network Neutrality: Technological Challenges and Policy Implications" (2016) 31 Berkeley Technology Law Journal 1409.

171 In 2018, the FCC under the Trump administration decided to "remedy the marketplace intrusions" of the 2015 Open Internet Order that "have harmed competition, broadband infrastructure investment, and innovation." The current FCC of the Biden administration is now in the process of "restoring" the Obama-era network neutrality rules.

172 See generally Yoo, supra note 162.

invest in broadband infrastructure may be reduced if operators cannot realize revenues from the additional traffic generated by online content and application suppliers such as Netflix and YouTube.[173] In their view, increasing Internet traffic has resulted in a congestion problem, and without new sources of revenue, necessary infrastructure investments in the transmission network layer will be at risk.[174] Based on some empirical data, network neutrality opponents have argued that "the digital divide would have widened" if network neutrality rules were restored.[175] On the other hand, based on an analysis of broadband economics, supporters of network neutrality have advanced arguments suggesting that the neutrality policy would not overly interfere with broadband operators' ability to "earn a return on their infrastructure investment."[176]

In the arena of international economic law, a looming version of network neutrality – "Open Networks, Network Access and Use" – has emerged since the early 2010s in both bilateral and plurilateral trade negotiations.[177] More recently, a quasi-network neutrality provision, "Principles on Access to and Use of the Internet for Electronic Commerce/Digital Trade" (Access Principles), has been incorporated into the FTAs such as CPTPP's E-Commerce Chapter and the USMCA's Digital Trade Chapter.[178] In other words, although the provision did not come closer to a comprehensive approach to network

[173] See for example, Comcast, "Notice of Ex Parte Communication, Protecting and Promoting the Open Internet" GN Docket No. 14-28; "Framework for Broadband Internet Service" GN Docket No. 10-127 (December 24, 2014).

[174] *Ibid.* Such a viewpoint seems to be shared by the telecom regulator – the Ofcom of the UK – where there is currently maintained a network neutrality framework. Ofcom, "Net Neutrality Review" (October 21, 2022) <www.ofcom.org.uk/__data/assets/pdf_file/0028/245926/net-neutrality-review.pdf>.

[175] American Consumer Institute, "Bridging the Digital Divide: Net Neutrality and Rural Connectivity" (November 9, 2020).

[176] Wu, supra note 162, at 9.

[177] "Open Networks, Network Access and Use" was incorporated into the TISA negotiating texts of the Annex on e-commerce. Jane Kelsey and Burcu Kilic, "Briefing on US TISA Proposal on E-Commerce, Technology Transfer, Cross-border Data Flows and Net Neutrality" (2014) <www.world-psi.org/en/briefing-us-tisa-proposal-e-commerce-technology-transfer-cross-border-data-flows-and-net-neutrality>. A similar provision can be found in Article 2 of the US-EU Trade Principles on Information, Communication Technology Services; Article 3 of the Japan-US Trade Principles for ICT Services states that: "[g]overnments recognize that Internet access providers should strive to avoid unreasonable discrimination in transmitting lawful network traffic."

[178] USMCA, supra note 132, Article 19.10 (Principles on Access to and Use of the Internet for Digital Trade): "The Parties recognize that it is beneficial for consumers in their territories to be able to: (a) access and use services and applications of a consumer's choice available on the Internet, subject to reasonable network management..."

neutrality, a miniature concept of this has been injected into FTAs, with one outstanding caveat: reasonableness.

To illustrate, under both trade agreements, broadband operators within the territories of the parties are still allowed to maintain "reasonable network management." In this regard, it is permissible for broadband operators within the CPTPP parties to offer their subscribers certain content on an exclusive basis.[179] It should be noted that the concept of "reasonable network management" has been highly controversial within the domestic context, and there is no guidance surrounding its meaning in most jurisdictions. Some broadband operators have claimed that "reasonable network management" may require practices "to reduce or mitigate congestion on the network, ensure quality-of-service, or address traffic that is unwanted or harmful to users, among other things."[180] If so, this caveat creates a space for broadband operators to throttle Internet traffic or downgrade bandwidth for certain data flows.[181]

After all, if we borrow from the WTO's jurisprudence on the "reasonableness" standard, the term "reasonable" is defined by several WTO panels as "in accordance with reason," "not irrational or absurd," "sensible," "within the limits of reason,"[182] and "not greatly less or more than might be thought likely or appropriate."[183] Compared with other, more "advanced" standards, such as necessity and proportionality, reasonableness represents a basic standard, which merely requires that the acts are not "irrational or absurd."[184] It can be argued, however, that under the "reasonableness test," the question of whether a broadband operator's

[179] CPTPP, supra note 131, Article 14.10, footnote 6: "The Parties recognize that an Internet access service supplier that offers its subscribers certain content on an exclusive basis would not be acting contrary to this principle."

[180] AT&T, "AT&T Open Internet Policy Statement" <www.att.com/legal/terms.openinternetpolicy.html>.

[181] However, arguably, the Access Principles in the international trade agreements merely address the most basic standard: no blocking. See Rodrigo Polanco Lazo and Sebastián Gómez Fiedler, "A Requiem for The Trans-Pacific Partnership: Something New, Something Old and Something Borrowed? A Requiem for the TPP" (2018) 18(2) Melbourne Journal of International Law 298.

[182] Panel Reports, *China – Measures Related to the Exportation of Various Raw Materials (China – Raw Materials)*, WT/DS394/R/WT/DS395/R/WT/DS398/R, February 22, 2012, paras. 7.696, 7.741.

[183] Panel Reports, *United States – Certain Country of Origin Labelling Requirements (US-COOL)*, WT/DS384/R / WT/DS386/R, July 23, 2012, paras 7.850–7.851.

[184] *Ibid.* See Shin-yi Peng, "The Rule of Law in Times of Technological Uncertainty: Is International Economic Law Ready for Emerging Supervisory Trends?" (2019) 22(1) Journal of International Economic Law 1, at 19.

network management practices violate the Access Principles should be examined under specific country conditions. Namely, the state of broadband development of a party, especially in the developing world, should be taken into account. When viewed in this light, "reasonableness" is to be determined in context, accommodating local development needs.[185] For example, broadband operators' practices in Vietnam might be more likely to be considered "reasonable" Internet traffic management if the degraded service was due to traffic congestion concerns. On the other hand, an ISP's degrading of Internet traffic in Singapore, a leading country in the world in terms of broadband speeds,[186] might be found "unreasonable" as a whole.

In any event, these quasi-network neutrality "rules" under the FTAs are of a soft law nature. The parties merely "recognize" the benefits of the Access Principles, which are subject to a party's domestic "policies, laws and regulations." To a large extent, these provisions do not impose mandatory or legally binding obligations. Such obligations carry little institutionalized enforcement for noncompliant behavior. The softness of these provisions reflects the political sensitivity surrounding this issue.

1.5.2 Digital Silk Road

From a foreign policy angle, there has been unconventional but potentially overwhelming progress regarding digital connectivity: the Digital Silk Road (DSR) component of China's Belt and Road Initiative (BRI).[187] The BRI, as China's most significant strategic agenda following its accession to the WTO, has centered its initiatives on infrastructure development. Despite mounting concerns regarding debt sustainability and the commercial as well as the political rationale behind the initiative, China's actions to bridge the global infrastructure gap – whether roads, railways,

[185] See Arturo J. Carrilloa, "Having Your Cake and Eating It Too? Zero-Rating, Net Neutrality, and International Law" (2016) 19 Stanford Technology Law Review 364.

[186] Singapore ranked top on the Internet Quality Index 2020. Katharina Buchholz "The Best & Worst Places for Internet Quality" (*Statista*, February 23, 2021) <www.statista.com/chart/24261/internet-quality-ranking/>.

[187] See Heng Wang, "The Belt and Road Initiative Agreements: Characteristics, Rationale, and Challenges" (2021) 20 World Trade Review 282, at 287; Gregory Shaffer and Henry Gao, "A New Chinese Economic Order?" (2020) 23(3) Journal of International Economic Law 607, at 614–620; Julien Chaisse & Mitsuo Matsushita, "China's 'Belt and Road' Initiative: Mapping the World Trade Normative and Strategic Implications" (2018) 52 Journal of World Trade 163, at 167.

ports, electricity, or telecommunications infrastructure – are nevertheless welcome in many developing countries and LDCs.[188] Under the umbrella of the BRI, the DSR has gained its own momentum since its emergence in 2015 and is becoming more and more central to the BRI.[189]

The DSR's primary undertaking is straightforward: rolling out broadband in dozens of countries in BRI regions where digital infrastructure is underdeveloped or even nonexistent, and upgrading existing Internet connections to a higher broadband across BRI regions.[190] Under the DSR, dozens of projects have been implemented with the help of Chinese government investments, which generally involve financial aid and technical support for digital infrastructure and related industries. For example, China has been deeply involved in the Infrastructure Consortium for Africa, including the establishment of national broadband networks. Several African countries have substantially benefited from the DSR, primarily in the areas of 5G networks and fiber-optic cables.[191] Overall, the DSR has been concentrating on the urgent needs of broadband connectivity in the Global South.[192]

From a "legal" perspective,[193] China has signed memoranda of understanding (MoU) along the path of the DSR, with at least sixteen countries agreeing to closer cooperation in the development of digital infrastructure.[194] In the Belt and Road Digital Economy Cooperation Initiative, for example, the parties to the MoU declare their intentions to "expand broadband access and improve quality, improve the construction of regional communication, Internet, satellite navigation, as well as other important information infrastructure and facilitate interconnection."[195]

188 See generally Jeremy Garlick, *The Impact of China's Belt and Roald Initiative* (Routledge 2019), at 170–203.

189 Deloitte, "BRI Update 2019" (2019).

190 *Ibid.*

191 This includes, at the least, Angola, Ethiopia, Nigeria, Zambia, and Zimbabwe. Steven Feldstein, "Testimony before the U.S.-China Economic and Security Review Commission Hearing on China's Strategic Aims in Africa" (May 8, 2020) <www.uscc.gov/sites/default/files/Feldstein_Testimony.pdf>. It should be noted that the 5G networks being developed around the DSR will increase transmission capacity, which is essential to IoT and AI applications.

192 *Ibid.* China has signed DSR cooperation agreements with at least sixteen countries.

193 BRI agreements are often of a "soft law" nature – taking advantage of the elements of soft law instruments to address sensitive issues such as cooperation in the digital sphere. Wang, supra note 187, at 297.

194 Council on Foreign Relations, "Assessing China's Digital Road Initiative" <www.cfr.org/china-digital-silk-road/>.

195 *Ibid.*

The parties also stress the priority to "explore ways to expand high-speed Internet access and connectivity at [an] affordable price," as well as to "promote broadband network coverage and improve service capacity and quality."[196]

In practice, the DSR is driven by China's private companies. Supported by the DSR, telecommunications services suppliers such as China Telecom Corporation, China Mobile, and China Unicom, together with telecommunications equipment vendors such as Huawei and ZTE, take advantage of the "DSR label" to expand their 5G markets overseas.[197] These Chinese companies work together, supply integrated solutions, and – at the same time – "transplant" Chinese standards to the DSR regions.[198] In the long run, the more the DSR's beneficiary countries depend on Chinese systems in their digital infrastructure, the more progress China realizes in leading the way in global standards for 5G and beyond. In addition to its technical standard-setting efforts, China's involvement in digital infrastructure through the DSR is increasingly leading to geopolitical and security implications.[199] Concerns have been raised that China can leverage the DSR to "export" its model of technology-enabled authoritarianism to recipient regions,[200] which would compromise personal data protection and human rights in those countries.[201] More specifically, commentators argue that China, through the DSR, will further influence recipient countries to adopt surveillance measures that are detrimental to Internet freedoms.[202] In this context, the 2021 G7 summit in Cornwall highlighted such concerns.[203] During

196 *Ibid.*

197 Matthew S. Erie & Thomas Streinz, "The Beijing Effect: China's Digital Silk Road as Transnational Data Governance" (2021) 54(1) New York University Journal of International Law & Policy 1, at 22.

198 *Ibid.*, at 14, 75.

199 Francisco Jose Leandro, "The OBOR Global Geopolitical Drive: The Chinese Access Security Strategy" in Julien Chaisse and Jedrzej Gorski (eds), *The Belt and Road Initiative: Law Economics and Politics* (Brill Nijhoff 2018), at 88; Joshua Meltzer, "China's One Belt One Road Initiative: A View from the United States" (*Brookings Report*, June 19, 2017).

200 See for example, Human Rights Watch, "China's Techno-Authoritarianism Has Gone Global" (April 8, 2021) <www.hrw.org/news/2021/04/08/chinas-techno-authoritarianism-has-gone-global>.

201 *Ibid.*

202 Richard Fontaine and Daniel Kliman, "On China's New Silk Road, Democracy Pays a Toll" (*Foreign Policy*, May 16, 2018) <https://foreignpolicy.com/2018/05/16/on-chinas-new-silk-road-democracy-pays-a-toll/>.

203 G7 Rivals China with Grand Infrastructure Plan, Reuters (*Reuters*, June 13, 2021).

the 2021 summit, allied leaders announced a "global infrastructure plan" – the Build Back Better World program – to "provide an infrastructure alternative to China's BRI."[204] At the 2022 Summit, G7 leaders formally launched "the Partnership for Global Infrastructure and Investment," which aims to "close the infrastructure gap in developing countries,"[205] and to offer, if not rival, an alternative to China's BRI in developing countries and LDCs.

In summary, although primarily driven by a political agenda and strategic propaganda, the DSR represents an indispensable component in mapping the whole contours of the issues surrounding digital inclusion. The DSR has often been conceptualized as a strategic extension of China's digital technologies and authoritarian policies, and China's digital push for development cooperation has long been framed as a part of the Chinese effort to assert itself as the dominant technological power in the world.[206] In any event, China's support for major telecommunications infrastructure projects under the DSR has proven to be a rather strategic and thus effective approach to influencing the developing and the less developed worlds. Admittedly, the DSR can help to enhance digital connectivity in underserved regions, improve broadband access in developing countries, and, at the end of the day, narrow the infrastructure gap.[207] Of course, the most pressing challenge facing recipient countries undergoing digital development with the aid of China is how to bargain for their "digital sovereignty."[208]

1.6 Conclusion

The "enabling" character of digital physical infrastructure raises questions regarding how best to tackle the issue of "trade and development" in a datafied world. In this chapter, we have examined the issue of digital inclusion at the broadband infrastructure level. This chapter should be read in conjunction with Chapters 5 and 6 of this book. After all, the remedy for broadband access (Chapter 1) cannot be meaningfully

[204] *Ibid.* The program, if implemented, will help narrow a US $40 trillion need for infrastructure projects across the developing world.

[205] "President Biden and G7 Leaders Formally Launch the Partnership for Global Infrastructure and Investment" (*White House Press*, June 26, 2022).

[206] Feldstein, supra note 191; Erie and Streinz, supra note 197.

[207] To some extent, the G7's response to the BRI of creating its own B3W shows recognition of BRI's impact.

[208] See Section 3.5.1 of this book for additional discussion.

realized without ensuring it is in sync with digital application (Chapter 5) and data flow (Chapter 6). Put simply, this is attributable to the fact that the more people access the Internet, the more data digital platforms gain. The far-reaching datafication of human activities goes hand in hand with communications on the 5G broadband. Moreover, as Chapter 2 will continue to address, cybersecurity risks have been growing in parallel with the increasing penetration of broadband networks. Increasing Internet connectivity has led to a surge in cybersecurity threats. Although Huawei's campaign has emphasized how its exclusion from many countries' telecommunications markets would "exacerbate the digital divide,"[209] the digital economy relies not only on the availability, but also on the resilience, of broadband infrastructure.[210] Secure and trusted broadband services are equally, if not more, important to a universal broadband service in this datafied world. The security and availability of 5G networks in some way conflict.

[209] Huawei, "Corporate Fact Sheet: What Is the Impact of Huawei's Exclusion from the U.S. Market?" <www.huawei.com/en/facts/questionanswer/what_is_the_impact_of_huaweis_exclusion_from_the_us_market>.

[210] Since the telecommunications liberalization in the 1990s, the central dimension of the broadband policy has been the universal service and competition law. In the recent decades, however, the cybersecurity critical infrastructure dimension has been shifting to the center.

2

Data Network as Critical Infrastructure

National Security and the Digital Economy

2.1 Introduction

Digital technologies have significantly transformed the way we live our lives. The workings of both the public and private sectors have become reliant on digital infrastructure that enables data flows. The rapid development of "smart cities," in conjunction with progress in the IoT and AI, has converted more and more social and economic activities into digital data, which has in turn produced new forms of vulnerabilities: the multiplication of cybersecurity risks. Cybersecurity threats, for which digital technology suppliers can build back doors into hardware or software, have become major concerns for policymakers in this datafied era.[1] Along with digitalization, platformization, and datafication, the probability of cyberattacks against critical infrastructure increases as well. Therefore, supply chains of critical industries become intrinsically linked to broader digital and national security policies.

More specifically, the global data network has generated vulnerabilities for states in terms of protecting national security. Cyber risks in the supply chains of critical industries are specifically perceived as threats to the integrity of a state's critical infrastructure. A cyberattack to a critical national infrastructure is far beyond a mere criminal offence that the nation's judicial organs can meaningfully address.[2] Rather, it is a matter

Parts of this chapter are derived from the author's previous work: Shin-yi Peng, "Digital Economy and National Security: Contextualizing Cybersecurity-Related Exceptions" (2023) 117 AJIL Unbound 122.

[1] OECD, "Reviews of Risk Management Policies Good Governance for Critical Infrastructure Resilience" (2019) <www.oecd.org/gov/good-governance-for-critical-infrastructure-resilience-02f0e5a0-en.htm>, at 18–24.

[2] Cyberattacks had led to approximate global annual cybercrime costs of €5.5 trillion by 2021. See European Commission, "Proposal for a Regulation of the European Parliament

of national security that affects the foundation of a sovereign.[3] Due to the relatively low cost and wide availability of digital technologies, cyberattacks and cyber terrorists now represent key methods of warfare.[4] High-profile, hostile incidents over the years[5] and the recent war in Ukraine offer lessons to other countries about the importance of a cyber defense.[6] As the backbone infrastructural sector and an interactive central nervous system for the digital economy, 5G networks face acute challenges as a result of cyber espionage, surveillance, and other cybersecurity risks, creating an intertwined relationship between data networks, cybersecurity, and national security.

In terms of national regulations, the mobile telecommunications sector has long been subject to heavy regulations. Traditional command and control mechanisms have been in place, primarily because the sector involves spectrum allocation and other public interests. More recently, controversies surrounding vulnerabilities in 5G goods and services have become a common concern, which has in turn amplified the role of state oversight. National security is now the central theme in the global 5G crisis,[7] and it is becoming more and more acute given the increasing tensions between the US and China. Taking in the entire picture, the US–China trade war has been intensified due to, or partially under the pretext of, US national security concerns. It has become a general perception that China's leading role in the 5G standardization process and Huawei's potential dominance in the global 5G market increase security risks, which could be exploited for spying and industrial espionage.[8] Facing

and of the Council on Horizontal Cybersecurity Requirements for Products with Digital Elements and Amending Regulation" (2022).

3 Sean M. Condron, "Getting It Right: Protecting American Critical Infrastructure in Cyberspace" (2007) 20(2) Harvard Journal of Law & Technology 403, at 404–407.

4 *Ibid.*, at 407–408.

5 See, for example, "Cyberattack Disrupts UK's NHS 111 Emergency Line" (*Economic Times*, August 8, 2022).

6 For example, Taiwan's Ministry of Digital Development announced efforts to secure satellite Internet backup and diversify its satellite Internet services to mitigate the risks of cyberattacks. See "Taiwan Has to Secure Satellite Internet" (*Taipei Times*, October 30, 2022).

7 See generally Berna Akcali Gur, "Cybersecurity, European Digital Sovereignty and the 5G Rollout Crisis" (2022) 46 Computer Law & Security Review 1, at 1–8.

8 *Ibid.*, at 14. Note that Huawei, Nokia, and Ericsson are the major global suppliers of 5G telecommunications equipment, including base stations and cell towers that create the wireless broadband network through which our data pass. The dependence on Huawei products has become the key source of the claimed cybersecurity concerns.

the potential threat of a "Cyber Pearl Harbor,"[9] states have resorted to domestic regulation to protect their cybersecurity interests, leveraging their regulatory power to address such concerns, especially in critical industries in which the integrity of critical infrastructure would be in peril if not properly guarded.[10]

At the same time, the interdependencies and interconnectedness of cyberspace cannot be fully understood without considering their transnational dimension.[11] Cyber risks do not stop at national borders. Critical infrastructure resilience should therefore be examined in the cross-border context. Recent initiatives, such as the EU–US Trade and Technology Council (TTC) and the Pillar of Supply Chain of the Indo-Pacific Economic Framework (IPEF), further demonstrate policy directions to promote supply chain security and strengthen the resilience of ICT ecosystems. With regard to transatlantic allies, the impact of Russia's invasion of Ukraine on Europe's supply chains presents an urgent need to "identify and address supply chain vulnerabilities."[12] Thus, the main agenda for TTC is to cooperate on trust and security issues in the areas of ICT goods and services – namely, to prevent political and economic disruption caused by the over-concentration of resources in key supply chains. If the US is able to replicate the TTC level of cooperation and momentum under the IPEF, the transpacific allies may move forward to establish criteria, jointly identify goods and services critical to their national security, and "increase resiliency and investment in critical sectors."[13] Evidently, strengthening international cooperation toward critical infrastructure resilience is a compelling policy option among geopolitical allies.

2.2 Critical Infrastructure as the Backbone of the Digital Economy

2.2.1 Critical Infrastructure and Cyber Resilience

The concept of "critical infrastructure" is constantly evolving. In order to reflect and respond to new challenges in network security, both the

[9] See generally Lawrence J. Trautman, "Is Cyberattack the Next Pearl Harbor?" (2016) 18 North Carolina Journal of Law & Technology 233, at 233–235.

[10] Akcali Gur, supra note 7, at 14.

[11] OECD, supra note 1, at 38–39.

[12] European Commission, "EU-US Joint Statement of the Trade and Technology Council" (2022) <https://ec.europa.eu/commission/presscorner/detail/en/STATEMENT_22_7516>.

[13] USTR, "Ministerial Statement for Pillar II of The Indo-Pacific Economic Framework For Prosperity, Indo-Pacific Economic Framework for Prosperity (IPEF)-Pillar II – Supply Chains" (2022) <https://ustr.gov/trade-agreements/agreements-under-negotiation/indo-pacific-economic-framework-prosperity-ipef/trade-pillar>.

number and variety of critical infrastructure are rapidly increasing. Critical infrastructure is now a term commonly used to identify services of a sensitive nature that have the potential to "cause massive disruption to dependent systems/services if they are compromised or destroyed."[14] Public utilities and emergency services, among others,[15] are most frequently associated with the concept of critical infrastructure.[16] In this datafied age, however, critical infrastructure operates across both the physical and the digital world,[17] and as a result, cybersecurity threats may originate from both the hardware and software components. Indeed, critical infrastructure is "increasingly if not exclusively controlled by computers."[18] In other words, infrastructure systems have undergone a digital transformation, with consequences to cyber risks and vulnerabilities. Cyberattacks can damage critical infrastructure in various ways, including directly taking control of industrial processes to block the functioning of energy distribution or transport services.

The complex ecosystem of critical infrastructure therefore requires a holistic and convergent security approach that protects both physical security and cybersecurity. Taking the energy sector as an example, the development of a smart grid and other innovative services means that the sector is increasingly reliant on data flows. Thus, an aggregate level of safety is necessary to mitigate both physical and cyber risks to energy systems.[19] Ultimately, critical infrastructure resilience is multifaceted. The disruption of critical infrastructure – whether 5G networks, transportation systems, water or energy supplies, or emergency hospital services – can lead to significant harm to societies and cause cascading effects across sectors. The cross-sectoral, systematically interdependent

[14] The US Patriot Act defines critical infrastructure as: "systems and assets, whether physical or virtual, so vital to the United States that the incapacity or destruction of such systems and assets would have a debilitating impact on security, national economic security, national public health or safety, or any combination of those matters." Condron, supra note 3, at 404–407.

[15] For example, there are thirteen national infrastructure sectors in the UK, including "Chemicals, Civil Nuclear, Communications, Defence, Emergency Services, Energy, Finance, Food, Government, Health, Space, Transport and Water." Several sectors have defined subsectors; Emergency Services, for example, can be split into "Police, Ambulance, Fire Services and Coast Guard." See UK's National Protective Security Authority, "Critical National Infrastructure" (2023) <www.cpni.gov.uk/critical-national-infrastructure-0>.

[16] Condron, supra note 3, at 404–407.

[17] See Section 6.4.1 for more discussions in this regard.

[18] Nigel Wilson, "Australia's National Broadband Network: A Cybersecure Critical Infrastructure?" (2014) 30 Computer Law & Security 699, at 702.

[19] OECD, supra note 1, at 18–24.

nature of critical infrastructure therefore calls for a comprehensive resilience strategy through which security risks are assessed in their entirety.[20]

Notably, some infrastructure assets are the key components of a wider, complex system. In this regard, the 5G broadband infrastructure has been considered one of the most critical utilities, which "if destroyed, degraded or rendered unavailable for an extended period, would adversely impact the social or economic well-being of the nation or affect a state's ability to ensure national security."[21] Ensuring the cyber resilience of the 5G broadband infrastructure and preventing it from being either a direct target or an indirect vehicle for cyber threats has become a prominent mission of the national security efforts of most countries. That being said, such an infrastructure is generally owned and operated by the private sector. As discussed in Chapter 1, telecommunications services have undergone privatization over the last several decades, and currently, government control over telecommunications infrastructure assets has, to a large extent, decreased. The need for cyber resilience, however, has resulted in escalating governmental intervention.[22] To tackle cross-border security challenges, governments have reviewed and strengthened their national security strategies and have adopted more far-reaching regulations, with the aim of fostering a secure and resilient ICT environment against cyberattacks.

2.2.2 Trade-Restrictive Critical Infrastructure Security Measures

The cyber arms race and digital tit-for-tat have intensified geopolitical frictions. The major geopolitical players in the digital economy have adopted increasingly comprehensive security measures at the national level. By stressing that the backbone of the digital economy must be trusted and reliable, the Biden administration has accelerated the implementation of a set of trade measures to diversify supply chains and thereby secure the infrastructural resilience of 5G networks.[23] In fact, under both Trump and Biden, 5G supply chain security has been at the center of the national security strategy of the US. At the data network

[20] *Ibid.*, at 38–39.

[21] Wilson supra note 18, at 702.

[22] OECD, supra note 1, at 42.

[23] The US White House, "National Security Strategy" (2022) <www.whitehouse.gov/wp-content/uploads/2022/10/Biden-Harris-Administrations-National-Security-Strategy-10.2022.pdf>, at 33–35.

level, following Trump's "Clean Network" and "Clean Path" initiatives,[24] the current FCC of the Biden administration, citing the same national security grounds, has continued to order US telecommunications companies to remove Huawei equipment from their networks.[25] At the digital platform level, although the Biden administration has withdrawn Trump's executive orders that banned transactions with eight Chinese software applications,[26] the current FCC proceeded to request that US digital platforms remove TikTok from their app stores.[27] Overall, the government has been actively engaged and has closely scrutinized transactions in the ICT sector. Among other measures, the Committee on Foreign Investment in the United States (CFIUS)[28] ordered ByteDance, a Chinese startup, to divest in TikTok due to national security concerns. Although that order was not enforced by the Biden administration, the CFIUS has continued to monitor whether TikTok's partnership with Oracle can sufficiently resolve national security issues.[29]

Across the Atlantic, recognizing that digital technologies are now a vulnerable target, protecting resilience against cybersecurity threats has been placed at the center of the EU's cybersecurity policies. The adoption of the "5G Toolbox of Risk-Mitigating Measures" (the "5G Toolbox"),[30]

[24] The US Department of State, "The Clean Network" (2021) <https://2017–2021.state.gov/the-clean-network/index.html>.

[25] David Shepardson, "U.S. FCC Set to Ban Approvals of New Huawei, ZTE Equipment" (*Reuters*, October 13, 2022) <available at www.reuters.com/technology/us-fcc-set-ban-all-us-sales-huawei-zte-equipment-axios-2022-10-13/>.

[26] The US White House, "Executive Order on Protecting Americans' Sensitive Data from Foreign Adversaries" (June 9, 2021) <www.whitehouse.gov/briefing-room/presidential-actions/2021/06/09/executive-order-on-protecting-americans-sensitive-data-from-foreign-adversaries/>.

[27] Brian Fung, "FCC Commissioner Calls on Apple and Google to Remove TikTok from Their App Stores" (*CNN*, June 29, 2022).

[28] CFIUS is an interagency committee tasked to "block or suspend proposed or pending foreign mergers, acquisitions, or takeovers of persons engaged in interstate commerce in the U.S. that threaten to impair the national security." Defense Production Act of 1950, 50 USC §4565 (2018). See Lizzie Knight and Tania Voon, "The Evolution of National Security at the Interface Between Domestic and International Investment Law and Policy: The Role of China" (2020) 21 Journal of World Investment and Trade 104, at 139.

[29] The US Congress, "TikTok: How Congress Can Safeguard American Data Privacy and Protect Children from Online Harms" (March 23, 2023) <www.congress.gov/event/118th-congress/house-event/115519?s=1&r=18> (TikTok chief executive Shou Chew testified before the US Congressional Hearing explaining the platform's business practices and defending the company from charges that it poses national security threats).

[30] On January 29, 2020, the EU adopted Cybersecurity of 5G networks EU Toolbox of risk mitigating measures (the "5G Toolbox"). European Commission, "Cybersecurity of 5G

which delineates potential areas of risk and remedial measures connected with suppliers of 5G infrastructure, sought to achieve diversity among suppliers and reduce Chinese companies' (especially Huawei's) participation in the 5G rollout.[31] In practice, one important category in the 5G Toolbox is the risks connected with suppliers of 5G infrastructure. Among all possible strategic remedial measures, the 5G Toolbox underscores the importance of restricting or excluding "high risk suppliers" to ensure that dependencies on certain suppliers do not "negatively affect the security of networks and/or services."[32] Along this policy path, the proposed EU Cyber Resilience Act is expected to "bolster cybersecurity rules to ensure more secure hardware and software products."[33]

Other striking cases of trade-restrictive security measures surrounding 5G and its applications include the Australian government's ban on Huawei's participation in building the nation's broadband infrastructure and India's decision to block access to dozens of mobile applications originating in China, including WeChat.[34] It should also be noted that after joining the so-called Five Eyes intelligence-sharing network, which consists of the US, Canada, the UK, Australia, and New Zealand, Canada decided to ban Huawei/ZTE 5G equipment to protect its national security. Retroactively, Canadian telecommunications operators that already have this equipment installed are required to remove it by June 2024.[35]

At the same time, from "Great Firewall" to direct virtual private network (VPN) blocking,[36] VPN traffic is generally filtered in China to ensure compliance with its social stability and national security agendas.

Networks – EU Toolbox of Risk Mitigating Measures" (2020) <https://digital-strategy.ec.europa.eu/en/library/cybersecurity-5g-networks-eu-toolbox-risk-mitigating-measures>.

31 *Ibid.*

32 *Ibid.*

33 European Commission, "Cyber Resilience Act" (September 15, 2022) <https://digital-strategy.ec.europa.eu/en/library/cyber-resilience-act>.

34 WeChat is Tencent's flagship social media platform, providing messaging, online shopping, payments, and other digital services. The app's more than one billion users are based in China, and it is also used by millions of people, mainly Mandarin speakers, around the globe.

35 Andy Blatchford, "Canada Joins Five Eyes in Ban on Huawei and ZTE" (*Politico*, May 19, 2022).

36 The Great Firewall of China restricts users within the country from accessing certain websites. Virtual private networks (VPNs) are one of the most popular tools to bypass the firewall. For commentaries on the trade aspects of the Great Firewall, see Henry Gao, "E-commerce Joint Statement Initiative Negotiation and China" in Shin-yi Peng et al. (eds), *Artificial Intelligence and International Economic Law: Disruption, Regulation, and Reconfiguration* (Cambridge University Press, 2021), at 295, 316.

China's cybersecurity regime has become even more complex and strict since its Cybersecurity Law was implemented,[37] primarily due to its lack of tailored definitions and transparent guidance. The vague language and broad scope of China's Cybersecurity Law accord the government even wider latitude to facilitate its political and economic agendas.[38] The Chinese government has issued implementation measures for its cybersecurity law, including the "cybersecurity review," which imposes restrictions on foreign ICT goods and services based on "potential national security risks" related to the reliability of supply chains. Moreover, the Chinese Cryptography Law contains trade-restrictive requirements for encryption products that involve national security.[39] Under the Chinese regulatory framework, loosely defined "encryption products," which encompass a wide range of ICT goods and services, must mandatorily undergo a cybersecurity risk assessment.[40]

2.2.3 The Inherent Clash with International Trade Rules

Through a broader lens, security-related trade restrictions – regardless of whether or not they directly address critical infrastructure – have the potential to clash with international trade rules in many ways, at both the multilateral and regional levels. Country-specific bans on ICT goods and services may violate the most-favored-nation principle, given the fact that the competitors of other countries will be the beneficiaries of such restrictions.[41] Security measures may be inconsistent with national treatment obligations if the domestic ICT goods or services and the banned foreign goods or services are "like products" or "like services."[42] Moreover, non-discrimination provisions in the Electronic Commerce/Digital Trade Chapters of the FTAs also require the parties to ensure

[37] *Zhonghua Renmin Gongheguo Wanglao Anquan Fa* (China's Cybersecurity Law), effective June 1, 2017.

[38] USTR, "Report to Congress on China's WTO Compliance" (2021) <https://ustr.gov/sites/default/files/files/Press/Reports/2021USTR%20ReportCongressChinaWTO.pdf>, at 34.

[39] *Zhonghua Renmin Gongheguo Mima Fa* (China's Cryptography Law), effective January 1, 2020.

[40] USTR, supra note 38, at 35.

[41] Most-favored-nation (MFN), for example, GATT, Article I; GATS, Article II. Arguably, major competitors of Huawei from Europe (Nokia and Ericsson) and South Korea (Samsung) will be the beneficiaries of the Huawei ban in the US.

[42] The National Treatment (NT), for example, GATT, Article III; GATS, Article XVII.

non-discriminatory treatment of "like digital products."[43] In other words, a violation could be found by comparing domestic and foreign digital products. If they are "like" digital goods or services, the adverse treatment of foreign digital products may be considered discrimination. Furthermore, security measures can simultaneously constitute quantitative restrictions on international trade in goods and violate the obligations to eliminate such restrictions.[44] Similarly, when a state undertakes market access commitments in relevant services sectors, these measures may restrict ICT services and violate relevant market access obligations.[45] Additionally, security-related trade restrictions in the public procurement of network equipment may breach a state's market access schedules of commitment under the Government Procurement Agreement (GPA), which lists the procurement activities open to international competition.

In cases in which the security standards constitute "technical regulations" under the Technical Barriers to Trade Agreement (TBT Agreement), unique security standards that accord less favorable treatment to imported products than that accorded to like products of national origin may also breach non-discrimination obligations.[46] Given the technical characteristics of cybersecurity measures, the TBT Agreement has become the legal battleground for trade-restrictive security measures. To be more straightforward, China and the EU have been accusing each other of using mandatory cybersecurity standards to protect their own 5G equipment suppliers, namely, Huawei/ZTE and Ericsson/Nokia. On the one hand, China's paradigmatic approach to the use of technical standards in the ICT sector, which in many instances appears designed to favor China-specific approaches, has caused substantial worldwide concern within the industry. In particular, the EU has consistently claimed that the requirement of the Chinese ICT security certification regime "appears to extend well beyond what the EU would consider justified for national security protection, which was cited by China as the legitimate objective to be achieved."[47] The EU also

[43] Non-discrimination provisions in the Electronic Commerce/Digital Trade Chapters of the FTAs, see for example, CPTPP, Article 14.4; USMCA, Article 19.4.

[44] The obligations to eliminate quantitative restrictions, for example, GATT, Article XI.

[45] GATS, Article XVI. Note that China claimed that the US violated its market access commitments under the GATS when the Trump administration imposed restrictions on TikTok and WeChat. See Section 3.1 for more discussions.

[46] TBT Agreement, Article 2.1.

[47] Communication from the European Commission, "China's Transitional Review Mechanism" G/TBT/W/326 (October 29, 2009), para. 12.

repeatedly requested that China clarify the rationale for its cybersecurity measures and their relationship to national security. On the other hand, the EU 5G policy – notably, trade-related cybersecurity measures designed to decrease (over)dependence on non-EU goods and services – has been criticized by China for being inconsistent with the EU's dedication to open market principles. In particular, China has raised concerns about the measures adopted by Sweden, which aims to remove Huawei and ZTE from its 5G infrastructure by 2025 based on the EU 5G Toolbox.[48] The delegate for China in the WTO meetings also claimed that the Swedish decision violates the WTO rules of transparency and non-discrimination, that the assessment criteria in the 5G Toolbox have led to *de facto* discrimination, and that the favorable treatment of Ericsson is inconsistent with the TBT Agreement.[49] Similarly, at the same WTO meeting, China reiterated its "regret" that Chinese companies cannot participate in Australia's 5G network construction, and that their equipment in the existing 4G network has also been removed in Australia.[50] Interestingly, China asserted that "the issue of telecommunication network security should be addressed based on scientific verifiable facts and data, rather than the origin of suppliers."[51] China urged Australia to amend its 5G policy to bring its measures in line with WTO rules. In response to China's assertion, the Australian government stressed that its 5G policy is "country-agnostic, transparent, risk-based, non-discriminatory, and fully WTO-consistent."[52]

2.3 Contextualizing Security-Related Exceptions: Possible Reconciliation

Nonetheless, general and security exceptions provide a normative framework by which to balance free trade obligations against national policy interests. Thus, the key issues here relate to whether and how those

48 *Ibid.* The delegate for China pointed out that the Swedish government established its 5G licensing requirements in October 2020, under which the 5G spectrum auction must not be carried out with base station equipment from the Chinese companies. In addition, the existing equipment of Huawei and ZTE, no matter the 4G or 5G system within Sweden, should be removed in the coming years. See also European Commission, supra note 30.

49 WTO, "Minutes of the Meeting of the Council for Trade in Goods" G/C/M/139 (June 16, 2021), paras. 13.2–13.7.

50 *Ibid.*

51 *Ibid.*, paras. 40.3–40.5.

52 *Ibid.*, para. 40.5.

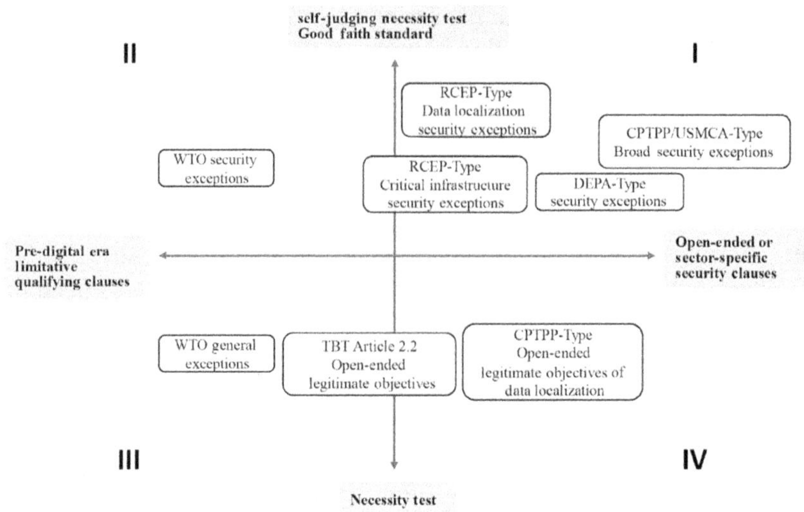

Figure 2.1 Contextualizing security-related exceptions

exceptions would protect a state's policy space through regulatory actions directed at national security matters. In this context, Figure 2.1 distinguishes between the types of exception clauses related to national security in international trade agreements. The vertical axis, with the "necessity test"[53] and "good faith standard" at each end,[54] represents the discretionary nature of the necessity element required by the exception. The horizontal axis, with "limitative qualifying clauses" and "expansive security clauses" at each end, represents the scope of situations allowed by the exception. This book argues that although on the face of it multiple exceptions may be available, complex technical and political-economic factors trigger their applicability. On the one hand, in the pre-digital age, "conventional" general exceptions (quadrant III)[55] and security

[53] Please refer to Section 1.4.3 for how the necessity test has been formulated by the Appellate Body in the context of WTO law.

[54] For discussions on good faith as a core principle of interpretation of the WTO Agreement, see, for example, Andrew D. Mitchell, *Legal Principles in WTO Disputes* (Cambridge University Press 2008), at 107–144; Isabelle Van Damme, *Treaty Interpretation by the WTO Appellate Body* (Oxford University Press, 2009), at 19–21; Marion Panizzon, *Good Faith in the Jurisprudence of the WTO: The Protection of Legitimate Expectations, Good Faith Interpretation and Fair Dispute Settlement* (Hart Publishing, 2006).

[55] The General Exceptions, for example, GATT, Article XX; GATS, Article XIV.

exceptions (quadrant II)[56] are too narrowly framed to address cybersecurity objectives. On the other hand, trends to create open-ended or digital sector-specific security exceptions (quadrant I) may also fall short for being excessively unrestrained if due process and good faith are not accorded. The four quadrants are respectively discussed below.

2.3.1 GATT-Type General Exceptions

2.3.1.1 GATT General Exceptions

The exception clauses in quadrants II & III were drafted in the brick-and-mortar age. Therefore, these "pre-digital era exceptions" are not properly formulated to address today's cyber threats. Taking GATS Article XIV General Exception (in quadrant III) as an example, although none of the grounds enumerated under the general exception explicitly refer to cyber risks, a WTO panel may find that the "public morals" exception affords an avenue through which to protect cybersecurity.[57] The parties in dispute, however, must present evidence – most likely involving classified documents – to demonstrate whether alternative measures, such as cybersecurity certifications or conformity assessment procedures, are less intrusive but equally effective. The Panel would have to assess whether such alternative measures should be regarded as WTO-consistent measures that are reasonably available to the responding party. Arguably, the necessity test can serve as a tool that guides states in taking targeted actions necessary to address cybersecurity concerns and refrain from creating unnecessary barriers to international trade.[58]

To be more concrete, the core issue here is the connection between the trade-related cybersecurity measures and the public morals objectives upon which such cybersecurity measures are based. The standard necessity test requires the consideration of alternatives to the measures taken in order to determine whether existing options are "less trade restrictive," while "providing an equivalent contribution to the achievement of the

[56] The Security Exceptions, for example, GATT, Article XXI; GATS Article XIV *bis*.

[57] WTO jurisprudence offers examples of public policies that have been found by panels or the Appellate Body to pertain to "public morals." See Section 1.4.3.

[58] Note that in quadrants III and IV, the TBT Agreement (TBT, Article 2.2) and the CPTPP-type data localization exceptions (CPTPP, Article 14.13) contain a "non-exhaustive" list of policy objectives, under which cybersecurity measures, subject to the necessity test, may be justified.

objective pursued."[59] In litigation, however, it would be unrealistic to expect two hostile states to present their intelligence information for or against the cybersecurity measures at issue. Because the complaining party must present scientific evidence to demonstrate that the proposed cybersecurity alternatives are at least "as good as" the trade measures taken by the responding party, the confidential and politically sensitive nature of security matters makes it particularly difficult for the parties to prove their case to a trade tribunal's satisfaction. It is equally impractical for the tribunal to engage in an evidence-based necessity test.

In any event, it will be a politically and technically challenging task for a trade tribunal to engage in an examination of whether the chapeau of the general exceptions can be satisfied. The two key concepts are "arbitrary or unjustifiable discrimination between countries where the same conditions prevail" and "disguised restriction on international trade," which "prohibit the abusive exercise of rights by states,"[60] and oblige a responding party to "articulate its defense promptly and clearly."[61] Again, such a procedural safeguard, however, poses a fundamental conflict with cybersecurity matters, where intelligence and other classified information are involved.[62] As Cohen argued, trade and security reflect different paradigms. The conflicts between the two competing interests occur not only at the legal technical level, but also at the systems level.[63] As a result, in most cases, the conventional GATT-type general exceptions operate awkwardly when balancing trade and security interests.

2.3.1.2 TBT Legitimate Objectives

In contrast to GATT Article XX and GATS Article XIV, the TBT exceptions, and in particular the "non-exhaustive" list provided in the

[59] See, for example, Panel Report, *European Communities – Measures Prohibiting the Importation and Marketing of Seal Products (EC – Seal)*, WT/DS400/R, June 18, 2014, paras. 5.260–5.264.

[60] Panel Report, *Peru – Additional Duty on Imports of Certain Agricultural Products (Peru – Agricultural Products)*, WT/DS457/R, November 27, 2014, para. 7.94.

[61] *Ibid.*

[62] Shin-yi Peng, "Cybersecurity and Trade Governance" in Julien Chaisse & Cristián Rodríguez-Chiffelle (eds), *The Elgar Companion to the WTO* (Edward Elgar 2023), chapter 3.

[63] Harlan Grant Cohen, "Nations and Markets" (2020) 23(4) Journal of International Economic Law 793, at 811.

TBT Agreement Article 2.2,[64] fall between quadrants III and IV due to their broader scope. As shown in Figure 2.1, unlike the conventional GATT general exceptions, which have a relatively narrow application in terms of the scope of the qualifying conditions, WTO jurisprudence makes it very clear that TBT Article 2.2 provides a "non-exhaustive list of legitimate objectives."[65] In other words, the open and illustrative list under TBT 2.2, which uses the word "inter alia," provides wider policy space for legitimate objectives advanced by the invoking party. Overall, it should be relatively easy to establish that the disputed cybersecurity standards fall within the scope of the exceptions provided under TBT 2.2.[66]

Nevertheless, the necessity requirement remains. TBT exceptions resemble those of the GATT general exceptions in the way that the standard necessity test applies. The key issue here involves whether certain cybersecurity measures, while serving "legitimate objectives," are "more trade restrictive than necessary" to fulfill the legitimate objective. The complaining party bears the burden of establishing that the cybersecurity measures are inconsistent with TBT Article 2.2 because the challenged standards created an "unnecessary" obstacle to international trade.[67] Further, the complaining party must explain why there are reasonably available, less trade-restrictive means of achieving the same

[64] TBT Agreement, Article 2.2: "Members shall ensure that technical regulations are not prepared, adopted or applied with a view to or with the effect of creating unnecessary obstacles to international trade. For this purpose, technical regulations shall not be more trade restrictive than necessary to fulfill a legitimate objective, taking account of the risks nonfulfillment would create. Such legitimate objectives are, inter alia: national security requirements; the prevention of deceptive practices; protection of human health or safety, animal or plant life or health, or the environment. In assessing such risks, relevant elements of consideration are, inter alia: available scientific and technical information, related processing technology or intended end-uses of products."

[65] Appellate Body Reports, *United States – Measures Concerning the Importation, Marketing and Sale of Tuna and Tuna Products (U.S. – Tuna II)*, Recourse to Article 21.5 of the DSU by the US, Second Recourse to Article 21.5 of the DSU by Mexico, WT/DS381/AB/RW/USA, WT/DS381/AB/RW2, January 11, 2019, paras. 7.436–437.

[66] Particular attention should also be accorded to the TBT Preamble, which emphasizes a state's right to protect its "essential security interest." Arguably, the nature of certain cyberattacks, especially those involving critical infrastructure, disrupts "national security" and threatens a state's "essential security interests."

[67] Appellate Body Report, *Australia – Certain Measures Concerning Trademarks, Geographical Indications and Other Plain Packaging Requirements Applicable to Tobacco Products and Packaging (Australia – Tobacco Plain Packaging)*, WT/DS435/AB/R, WT/DS441/AB/R, June 29, 2020, para. 57–65.

level of protection.[68] The confidential, nontransparent nature of the cybersecurity matters once again renders the exercise of the necessity test relatively difficult.[69]

2.3.2 GATT-Type Security Exceptions

Conventional security exceptions (in quadrant II), which can be found in the WTO and many FTAs, represent another form of pre-digital era exceptions that are out of touch with cybersecurity policies. GATT Article XXI(b), as a representative clause, allows a state to take any action "it considers necessary" to protect its "essential security interests," stating the following:

> Nothing in this Agreement shall be construed:
>
> ...
>
> (b) to prevent any contracting party from taking any action which *it considers necessary for the protection of its essential security interests*
>
> (i) relating to fissionable materials or the materials from which they are derived;
>
> (ii) relating to the traffic in arms, ammunition and implements of war and to such traffic in other goods and materials as is carried on directly or indirectly for the purpose of supplying a military establishment;
>
> (iii) *taken in time of war or other emergency in international relations*; or
>
> ... (emphasis added)

Historically speaking, national security exceptions had been utilized in a restrained and cautious manner. China, in both *China – Raw Materials* and *China – Rare Earths*, considered but eventually did not invoke the national security exceptions.[70] In those disputes, despite the fact that the

[68] *Ibid.*, para. 58.

[69] *Cf.*, Gregory Shaffer, "The WTO Tuna-Dolphin II Case (United States – Measures Concerning the Importation, Marketing and Sale of Tuna and Tuna Products)" (2013) 107 American Journal of International Law 192. Shaffer pointed out that, in 2012, the Appellate Body in all three TBT decisions found that the responding party failed to comply with TBT Article 2.1 nondiscrimination obligations. However, the Appellate Body concluded that the responding party did not violate TBT Article 2.2 obligations regarding "unnecessary obstacles to international trade." Although in different context, it can be argued that the trade tribunals are less comfortable about deciding whether a technical standard that pursues a state's legitimate objectives is "unnecessary."

[70] The disputes concerned China's use of export quotas and export duties on various forms of rare earths. Panel Report, *China – Measures Related to the Exportation of Various Raw*

Chinese government repeatedly stressed that China's restrictions were based on important national security concerns surrounding its reliance on foreign suppliers for its military supply chain since rare earth minerals are used in missile and aircraft systems,[71] China nevertheless did not invoke Article XXI(b) of the GATT.[72] In short, before the Panel Report of *Russia – Traffic in Transit* broke the ice, the GATT/WTO consistently avoided issuing findings on the merits of security exceptions for decades. The *Russia – Traffic in Transit* dispute somehow served as a catalyst for WTO members to bring legal challenges against security-based measures, and to invoke the security exception as a defense.

Since *Russia – Traffic in Transit*, WTO panels have clarified how the so-called self-judging clauses operate.[73] In theory, the term "it considers necessary" was drafted to reserve the right to opt out of certain treaty obligations otherwise imposed by the WTO agreements.[74] For decades, it was not clear how the concept of self-judging worked under Article XXI. How much discretion should there be in the determination of a measure's necessity? Should these national security exceptions be construed as entirely self-judging so as to sufficiently preserve the autonomy of a state's security matters? Does this mean that a state is entitled to unilaterally decide on what its essential security interests are, as well as what action is necessary to protect those interests?[75] In this regard, the Panel in *Russia – Traffic in Transit* conceded that Article XXI(b)(iii) "is not totally self-judging."[76] According to the panel, the discretion of a member to designate particular concerns as "essential security interests" is limited by

Materials (China – Raw Materials), WT/DS394/R, February 22, 2012; Panel Report, *China – Measures Related to the Exportation of Rare Earths, Tungsten, and Molybdenum (China – Rare Earths)*, WT/DS431/R, March 26, 2014.

71 Panel Report, *China – Rare Earths*, *ibid.*, paras. 7.398, 7.404, 7.712.

72 This discussion draws upon materials in Shin-yi Peng, "Cybersecurity Threats and the WTO National Security Exceptions" (2015) 18(2) Journal of International Economic Law 449, at 461–462.

73 See *e.g.*, Panel Report, *Saudi Arabia – Measures Concerning the Protection of Intellectual Property Rights (Saudi Arabia – IPRs)*, WT/DS567/R, not yet adopted, para. 7.238.

74 Andrew Emmerson, "Conceptualizing Security Exceptions: Legal Doctrine or Political Excuse?" (2008) 11 Journal of International Economic Law 135, at 139–140; Ryan Goodman, "Norms and National Security: The WTO as a Catalyst for Inquiry" (2001) 2 Chicago Journal of International Law 101, at 119.

75 Stephan Schill and Robyn Briese, "If the State Considers: The Self-Judging Clauses in International Dispute Settlement," in Armin von Bogdandy et al. (eds), *13 Max Planck Yearbook of United Nationals Law* (Martinus Nijhoff Publishers 2009), at 61, 67–69.

76 Panel Report, *Russia – Measures Concerning Traffic in Transit* (*Russia – Traffic in Transit*), WT/DS512/R, April 5, 2019, paras 7.59, 7.78–7.82.

its obligation to apply GATT Article XXI(b)(iii) "in good faith."[77] The panel pointed out that the obligation of good faith requires members not to use the security exceptions as a means to circumvent their WTO obligations.[78] The panel must therefore review whether the security measures have been applied in good faith.[79] In this context, a "plausible link" must be established between the invoking state's "essential security interests" and the trade-restrictive measures in dispute.[80] If we follow the reasoning in *Russia – Traffic in Transit*, an invoking member must demonstrate that the disputed cybersecurity regulations "meet a minimum requirement of plausibility" in relation to the member's national security.[81] In this regard, "plausible link" might be questioned, and "bad faith" might be found, when network security regulations substantially favor domestic goods or services. However, the "good faith" standard will be particularly problematic when the measure at issue is motivated by both "protectionism" and "patriotism," namely, when commercial and security interests are inextricably linked.

More importantly, from *Russia – Traffic in Transit* to *U.S. – Steel and Aluminium Products*, WTO panels have adopted the view that the subparagraphs ("fissionable materials," "traffic in arms," and "war or other emergency in international relations") of Article XXI(b) are exhaustive in establishing the circumstances under which a state may "take the action which it considers necessary for the protection of its essential security interests."[82] In *U.S. – Steel and Aluminium Products*, the panel did not find that the measures at issue were "taken in time of war or other emergency in international relations" within the meaning of GATT Article XXI(b)(iii). In the panel's view, the subparagraphs "form alternative endings to a complete sentence under Article XXI(b)."[83] In other words, the opening terms in each subparagraph qualify the "action" referred to in Article XXI(b), and the three subparagraphs are exhaustive in establishing the circumstances under which a member may take the

[77] *Ibid.*, para. 7.132.
[78] *Ibid.*, para. 7.133.
[79] *Ibid.*
[80] *Ibid.*, paras. 7.131–7.148.
[81] *Ibid.*, para. 7.138.
[82] See, for example, Panel Report, *United States – Certain Measures on Steel and Aluminium Products (U.S. – Steel and Aluminium Products)*, WT/DS544/R, not yet adopted, paras. 6.14–6.16, 7.113–7.114.
[83] *Ibid.*, para. 6.14.

"action" under Article XXI(b).[84] After emphasizing that there is no textual indication that the subparagraphs of Article XXI(b) are merely illustrative,[85] the panel also specifically pointed out – contrary to TBT Article 2.2, which explicitly indicates the illustrative nature of the provisions – that the subparagraphs of GATT Article XXI(b) are exhaustive in establishing the circumstances under which a member may take action to protect its essential security interests.[86]

Thus, trade-restrictive security measures can only be justified under Article XXI(b) if they meet one of the subparagraphs of Article XXI(b), specifically, the existence of an "emergency in international relations" within the meaning of Article XXI(b)(iii). An "emergency in international relations" within the meaning of Article XXI(b)(iii), however, must be "at least comparable in its gravity or severity to a war" in terms of its impact on international relations.[87] In this regard, where cybersecurity risks are routine and unexceptional in modern days, the gravity or severity of an "emergency in international relations," particularly with regard to its impact on international relations, may not be established. Moreover, the phrase "taken in time of" indicates a temporal relationship to the "war or other emergency in international relations."[88] The temporal link that requires cybersecurity measures to be "taken in time of" the "emergency in international relations" is also logically confusing when addressing a long-standing cybersecurity matter that,[89] as Heath observes, is of a permanent nature and must be systematically addressed over time.[90] Evidently, (conventional) security exceptions must be modernized to meet the policy needs of this digital era.

2.3.3 CPTPP-Type Data Localization Exceptions

CPTPP-type exceptions to data localization, which are contextualized in quadrant IV of Figure 2.1, contain a "non-exhaustive" list of policy objectives, under which security measures that are subject to the necessity

84 *Ibid.*, paras. 7.111, 7.116.
85 *Ibid.*, para. 7.113.
86 *Ibid.*, footnote 443.
87 *Ibid.*, para. 7.139.
88 *Ibid.*, para. 7.112.
89 *Ibid.*, paras. 7.112, 7.139–7.149.
90 J. Benton Heath, "The New National Security Challenge to the Economic Order" (2020) 129 Yale Law Journal 1020, at 1046.

test may be justified.[91] To illustrate, Article 14.13 of the CPTPP (Location of Computing Facilities), while recognizing the parties' regulatory autonomy regarding requirements that seek to ensure the security and confidentiality of communications, prohibits parties from adopting data localization measures as a condition for conducting business. The Article also states the following:

> Nothing in this Article shall prevent a Party from adopting or maintaining measures inconsistent with paragraph 2 to achieve a legitimate public policy objective, provided that the measure:
>
> (a) is not applied in a manner which would constitute a means of arbitrary or unjustifiable discrimination or a disguised restriction on trade; and
> (b) does not impose restrictions on the use or location of computing facilities greater than are required to achieve the objective.[92]

Article 14.13 should be understood to mean that parties are allowed to maintain data localization measures to pursue their national security objectives as long as the measure satisfies the anti-protectionism requirements set out in the Article, namely, the procedural safeguard and the necessity test. Although locating computing facilities and storing data in multiple data centers within diverse jurisdictions seem to make more technological sense in managing cybersecurity risks, data localization measures that restrict the ability of companies to transfer data or, more narrowly, require local storage within a particular national border, have been a feature of national security policies. For example, China's Cybersecurity Law, citing national security, requires "critical information infrastructure" operators to store personal information or important data within the territory of China.[93] The Cybersecurity Law of Vietnam, as another example, requires Vietnamese data to be stored locally so as to protect national sovereignty.[94] Similar regulatory initiatives, with different degrees of emphasis on cybersecurity, can be found in various developed and developing countries, including Australia, Brazil, Canada, the EU, India, Peru, Malaysia, New Zealand, Russia, South Korea, and Taiwan, to name just a few.[95]

[91] CPTPP, Article 14.13. For more discussion on data localization, see Section 6.2 of this book.
[92] CPTPP, Article 14.13(3).
[93] China's Cybersecurity Law, supra note 37, Article 37.
[94] The Cybersecurity Law of Vietnam, Decree No. 53/2022/ND-CP, effective August 15, 2022, Article 26.
[95] This discussion draws upon materials in Shin-yi Peng and Han-Wei Liu, "The Legality of Data Residency Requirements: How Can the Trans-Pacific Partnership Help?" (2017) 51:2 Journal of World Trade 183, at 185.

Note that, much like TBT Article 2.2, the CPTPP-type data localization exceptions contain an open-ended list of legitimate objectives and require an initial determination regarding whether, as an objective, the cybersecurity policy is legitimate. Such an approach leaves much ambiguity about how far the exceptions can go in curbing protectionist practices.[96] A CPTPP panel may consider relevant WTO jurisprudence with respect to the general exceptions of the WTO Agreement.[97] Additionally, as previously illustrated, precedent holds that the weighing and balancing exercise under the necessity analysis contemplates a determination as to whether a cybersecurity measure that is less inconsistent with the CPTPP rules is reasonably available.[98] Such alternative measures must provide an equivalent contribution to the achievement of the cybersecurity objectives pursued through the challenged measure. This "trade v. security" balancing exercise is likely to be impractical when confidential national security matters are involved. That being said, a trade tribunal is expected to be cautious when balancing trade and security interests if the localization measures overwhelmingly boost the domestic data industry.[99]

2.3.4 New Generation Trade Agreements' Security Exceptions

Trends in the new generation of international trade agreements suggest that "updated" security exceptions, either via expansive, open-ended formats or through a sectoral approach, are designed to reset the balance between international trade and national security. As shown in quadrant I in Figure 2.1, innovative clauses have been incorporated to reconcile the conflicts between (digital) trade and (cyber) security. The four types of security exceptions in quadrant I represent a dramatically expansive scope and excessively unfettered discretion in security exceptions under the international trade agreements.

2.3.4.1 CPTPP/USMCA-Type Broad Security Exceptions

Contrary to conventional security exceptions, under the CPTPP and USMCA, for example, security exceptions omit the subparagraphs that

[96] *Cf.*, note that several FTAs, such as the USMCA, contain a straightforward ban on data localization. See, for example, USMCA, Article 19.12.

[97] CPTPP, Article 28.12.

[98] See, for example, Panel Report, *EC – Seal*, WT/DS400/R, June 18, 2014, paras. 7.636–639. Appellate Body Report, *EC – Seal*, WT/DS400, paras. 5.260–264.

[99] See generally Neha Mishra, "The Trade – (Cyber)security Dilemma and its Impact on Global Cybersecurity Governance" (2020) 54(4) Journal of World Trade 567.

list the circumstances under which such exceptions could be triggered. By way of illustration, the security exceptions to the CPTPP state that "Nothing in this Agreement shall be construed to ... preclude a Party from applying measures that it considers necessary for the fulfilment of its obligations with respect to the maintenance or restoration of international peace or security, or the protection of its own essential security interests." This type of exception borrows the self-judging element from the WTO security exceptions but contains no limitative qualifying clauses that condition the application of security exceptions,[100] representing an open-ended, broad security clause.

2.3.4.2 DEPA-Type Security Exceptions

Similarly, the security exceptions under the DEPA – a digital sector-specific comprehensive framework – accommodate open-ended exceptions, which are not followed by a closed list of situations.[101] Given the fact that CPTPP is the primary textual source of the DEPA, it is not unusual that the three founding parties of the DEPA – Chile, New Zealand, and Singapore – incorporate the CPTPP-type broad security clauses into the DEPA text. Considering that DEPA is an international trade agreement tailored to the digital economy, and that cybersecurity threats take place across the entire digital ecosystem, such broad and loose security exceptions to the DEPA may mean that there is "no certainty of digital market access."[102] In other words, security interests will easily prevail over economic interests.

2.3.4.3 RCEP-Type Data Localization Exceptions

Another digital sector-specific security clause worth particular attention can be found in the security exceptions to data localization in the Regional Comprehensive Economic Partnership (RCEP). Article 12.14 (Location of Computing Facilities) allows the parties to undertake any data localization measures they consider necessary for the protection of essential security interests.[103] Unlike the CPTPP-type data localization

[100] See, for example, USMCA, Article 32.2; CPTPP, Article 29.2.

[101] See, for example, DEPA, Article 15.2 (Security Exceptions) <www.sice.oas.org/trade/DEPA/DEPA_Module15_e.pdf>.

[102] Dan Ciuriak and Robert Fay, "The Digital Economy Partnership Agreement: Should Canada Join?" (2022) 171 Centre for International Governance Innovation Policy Brief, at 6.

[103] See, for example, RCEP, Article 12.14 (Location of Computing Facilities) <http://fta.mofcom.gov.cn/rcep/rceppdf/d12z_en.pdf>. A similar provision can be found in the

exceptions, which are subject to the standard necessity test, RCEP data localization exceptions, by allowing a party to adopt any measure that "it considers necessary" for the protection of its "essential security interests," impose a lower and softer threshold. This threshold requires the invoking party to substantiate its good faith belief – albeit subjectively – that there is a threat to its "essential security interest," and that data localization measures are necessary for the protection of that essential security interest. It should also be noted that in the RCEP data localization exceptions, the self-judging element has been strengthened with a subparagraph stating that such measures shall not be disputed by other parties.[104]

2.3.4.4 RCEP-Type Critical Infrastructure Security Exceptions

As previously explained, critical infrastructure, such as 5G networks, constitutes the backbone of the functioning of a state. Given that the risk of compromised critical infrastructure can cause massive disruptions to the well-being of citizens, the protection of "critical public infrastructure" – whether publicly or privately owned – has been added to several new generation FTAs as one of the enumerated situations under which security exceptions can be invoked.[105] The textual structure of RCEP Article 17.13, which lists "national/international relations emergency" (Article 17.13(b)(iv)) and "critical infrastructures protection" (Article 17.13(b)(iii)) as parallel circumstances under which the security exceptions could be triggered, indicates that the negotiators of the RCEP intended to distinguish between "national/international emergency" and "critical infrastructures protection." Simply put, the structural separation signals that, when interpreting RCEP Article 17.13 (b) (iii) in

Indonesia-Australia Comprehensive Economic Partnership Agreement (IA-CEPA), Article 13.12 (Location of Computing Facilities) <www.dfat.gov.au/trade/agreements/in-force/iacepa/iacepa-text/Pages/iacepa-chapter-13-electronic-commerce>.

[104] *Cf.*, supra note 92. Note that the CPTPP-type data localization exceptions (CPTPP, Article 14.13) are contextualized in quadrant IV.

[105] RCEP, Article 17.13 (b) (iii) (Security Exceptions) <http://fta.mofcom.gov.cn/rcep/rceppdf/d17z_en.pdf>. Similar provisions can be found in other recently concluded FTAs, such as EU-Singapore Free Trade Agreement and Investment Protection Agreement (EU-Singapore FTA), Article 16.11(Security Exceptions) <https://policy.trade.ec.europa.eu/eu-trade-relationships-country-and-region/countries-and-regions/singapore/eu-singapore-agreement/texts-agreements_en>; IA-CEPA, Article 17.3 (Security Exceptions) <www.dfat.gov.au/trade/agreements/in-force/iacepa/iacepa-text/Pages/iacepa-chapter-17-general-provisions-and-exceptions>.

context, the "emergency" element, which strictly limits the application of the GATT-type security exceptions, does not extend to critical infrastructure security exceptions. The textual structure thus effectively creates a broad and relatively easily satisfied enumerated exception to trade rules – the protection of critical infrastructure.

2.4 National Security and Trade Governance in a Datafied World

2.4.1 Scoping "Essential Security Interests": "Critical Infrastructure" as Touchstone

Taken together, the pre-digital era general and security exceptions are ill-tailored to address today's national security concerns. On the contrary, the new trends, which create open-ended or digital sector-specific security exceptions, are encouraging directions to ensure that the exceptions to international trade rules are aligned with the policy needs of the digital economy. However, the approaches taken in quadrant I may risk the potential for abuse and excessively broad overuse. In particular, the CPTPP/USMCA-Type Broad Security Exceptions – should they become a template for future international trade negotiations – may prove to be a fractious way forward in assessing the concepts of cybersecurity and national security. How can the good faith that requires minimum plausibility curb the potentially expansive interpretations of these types of security exceptions? In this age of digital capitalism, commercial and cybersecurity interests are entangled and often overlap. Most national regulations sit at the intersection of economic and security interests and can serve as both economic and national defense tools. Therefore, two fundamentally difficult issues, legally and technologically speaking, are to what extent cybersecurity concerns are legitimate, and how to distinguish the boundaries of these concerns from illegitimate protectionist measures that primarily stem from considerations surrounding economic competition. Moreover, in terms of sector-specific security exceptions, the questions of what constitutes "critical infrastructure" and how to designate it require due process mechanisms to constrain discretionary abuse.[106] Should social media platforms be considered "critical infrastructure"? How can we ensure non-discrimination in the process of

[106] Gregory Shaffer, "Governing the Interface of U.S. – China Trade Relations" (2022) 115 (4) American Journal of International Law 650, at 655–657.

identification and designation of critical infrastructure? These are the key issues the new generation trade agreements' security exceptions will confront.

It appears that the irreversible regulatory trends are designed to provide greater discretion for states in defining their own national security agenda. The excessively broad definition of "national security," as a result, is challenging the boundary between economic and security concerns. In its 2017 National Security Plan, the US explicitly declared that "economic security is national security."[107] As Claussen stated, the term "economic security" is now the central point, combining various concepts including economic dominance, independence, and hegemony.[108] Converged with the domain of economic security, the term "national security" is now being used in more and more expansive ways, literally including nearly everything – ranging from national broadband, industrial supply chain, and digital trade to steel tariffs, semiconductor export control, etc. This expansion will continue and will lead to an endless list in this digitally connected world. In the context of international economic law, the flexibilities provided under the new generation trade agreements' security exceptions could prove to be an inefficient approach in addressing legitimate security concerns. The overexpansion of the conceptual scope of national security may either mask legitimate objectives or fail to appropriately constrain illegitimate objectives.

What are the possible solutions to the dilemmas surrounding the overly limited quadrants II and III and the overly broad quadrant I approaches to national security? To be sure, there is no such thing as "zero risk" in cybersecurity.[109] In this hyper-connected datafied age,[110] the ever-increasing digital connectivity between computers and devices may mean that vulnerabilities can be introduced at any phase, and in any place.[111] Technical experts agree that a perfectly secure digital

[107] The US Joint Chiefs of Staff, "Trump Announces New Whole-of-Government National Security Strategy" (2017) <www.jcs.mil/Media/News/News-Display/Article/1400686/trump-announces-new-whole-of-government-national-security-strategy/>.

[108] Kathleen Claussen, "Trade's Security Exceptionalism" (2020) 72 Stanford Law Review 1097, at 1116.

[109] Robert O'Harrow, *Zero Day: The Threat in Cyberspace* (Washington Post E-book 2014).

[110] P. W. Singer and Allan Friedman, *Cybersecurity and Cyberwar: What Everyone Needs to Know* (Oxford University Press 2014), at 34; Thomas Mowbray, *Cybersecurity: Managing Systems, Conducting Testing, and Investigating* (Wiley 2013), at 3–14.

[111] Richard Clarke and Robert Knake, *Cyber War: The Next Threat to National Security and What to Do About It* (HarperCollins Publishers 2012), at 69–102.

environment, free of vulnerabilities, is a dream, and "the notion of perfectly secure software almost certainly is a white whale."[112] The core issue turns out to be determining how much "risk" in cyberspace would amount to a danger to a state's "essential security interests."[113] Along a continuum of low to high national security risks, it is all about the relativities. In the context of "trade v. security," however, a borderline must be drawn somewhere, and trade-offs must be made.

That being the case, one possible future direction for trade and cybersecurity governance is to scrutinize the distinction between critical and noncritical infrastructure. Bearing in mind that more and more jurisdictions are now classifying critical infrastructure as a special category that is essential to national security in their domestic legal frameworks,[114] the creation of a commonly accepted definition of "critical infrastructure" would serve as a touchstone in determining the boundaries of "essential security interests." In other words, the protection of critical infrastructure presents a much stronger case than noncritical infrastructure in meeting the minimum requirement of plausibility in relation to a state's "essential security interests." In this regard, Shaffer observes that "the national security risks in the TikTok case are much lower than regarding Huawei's construction of critical infrastructure."[115] All in all, not every infrastructure is judged to be critical,[116] not every good or service from China is of national security concern,[117] and not all issues relating to innovative technology are equated with essential national security.[118] To conclude, "minimum plausibility" within the meaning of international economic law should be relatively easier to establish when it comes to critical infrastructure protection, because such risks, when severe, can disrupt the operations of a state's vital services, resulting in significant

[112] *Ibid.* See also Jane Chong, "Why Is Our Cybersecurity So Insecure?" (*The New Republic*, October 11, 2013).

[113] Peng, supra note 72, at 470.

[114] The UK National Protective Security Authority, supra note 15.

[115] Shaffer, supra note 106, at 650–654, 670.

[116] The UK National Protective Security Authority, supra note 15.

[117] In this regard, Kho pointed out that "taking the view that everything that China does is of national security concern ignores how best to address some of the key concerns that are in fact economic and competitiveness based." Stephen Kho and Yujin K. McNamara, "Focus on China: The Expansive Use of National Security Measures to Address Economic Competitiveness Concerns" (2022) 17 University of Pennsylvania Asian Law Review 368, at 375.

[118] Similar assertions have been made by the Chinese delegation in WTO meetings. See WTO, "Minutes of the Committee on Market Access" G/MA/M/70 (May 28, 2019).

loss of life and detrimental economic and social impacts. In this way, the concept of critical infrastructure may serve as a useful tool in filtering out the overgeneralization of national security claims. Ultimately, a more proper balance may be sustained between free trade and national security, and, in particular, cybersecurity.

2.4.2 Risk Assessment and Technical Standards

Another important direction for trade and cybersecurity governance is to prevent unfettered administrative discretion in security matters. This is particularly important in view of the fact that governments are moving toward risk-based approaches to protect national security and cybersecurity.[119] Instead of adopting prescriptive, one-size-fits-all rules, states assess cyber risks and exercise discretion to reduce them in a timely and proactive manner. It can be said that the most significant difference between ancient and modern security infrastructure is the rapid pace of change in security threats. The Great Wall of China was built across the northern border to protect imperial China against security threats. It took hundreds of years for ancient China's security situation to change. On the other hand, the modern security landscape has been measured in mere months, or even days. Literally, the perception of risks is in real time. In light of the dynamic nature of national security in modern days, it makes more sense for national regulators to take a risk-based approach rather than laying down prescriptive rules.

In this regard, several FTAs such as the Digital Trade Chapter of the USMCA include recognition of "the evolving nature of cybersecurity threats"[120] and the importance of taking risk-based approaches instead of adopting prescriptive regulations in addressing those threats.[121] On the one hand, a risk-based approach provides national regulators with some extent of flexibility to encourage innovation that may otherwise be constrained under a catch-all approach. Rather than a uniform set of

[119] In the author's view, US export controls that block access by China to advanced semiconductors used in artificial intelligence and quantum computing can be seen as an example of a "risk-based approach" to security management. Arguably, the so-called "small yard, high fence" strategic policy that precisely defines what technologies are key to US national security interests represents a tailored and targeted risk-based approach.

[120] See, for example, USMCA, Article 19.15, which promotes risk-based approaches rather than prescriptive regulation in addressing cyber threats.

[121] Similar text can be found in the consolidated negotiating text of the WTO JSI on E-Commerce, INF/ECOM/62/Rev (December 2020), at 58.

blanket prohibitions that apply to all in the same manner, the risk-based approach recognizes variances across or within critical sectors, allows for individual assessments, more efficiently targets implementation efforts in those sectors that pose the highest risk, and, at the same time, minimizes the regulatory impact on the critical industry and avoids unintended side effects of regulation.[122] In short, because digital technologies are rapidly evolving, any overly specific or rigidly prescriptive rules governing cybersecurity will either become quickly outdated or hinder innovation in the digital market.

On the other hand, the risk-based approach to cybersecurity comes with the danger of abuse of decision-making powers. Instead of applying the same rules in an equal way, irrespective of the level of risk or harm, the risk-based approach provides tailored protection, depending upon the level of risk at stake under each specific situation. Rather than imposing any kind of inflexible rules, national regulators exercise a degree of discretion when weighing cybersecurity risks, cyberattack harms, and regulatory benefits.[123] Because the approach relies on policy judgements rather than detailed prescriptions, the cybersecurity regulatory scheme leaves national regulators with broad discretion when conducting risk assessments. After all, at the core of the risk-based approach is a regulatory strategy through which regulators target resources toward sectors or activities that present the highest risk and, at the same time, reduce resources in those sectors or activities with relatively low risk. These decision-making processes designed to achieve the "right" balance between lower and higher risks "are all matters of judgement that regulators have to confront along the way," according to Black and Baldwin.[124] In many jurisdictions, cybersecurity measures will only be proposed where a need has been identified, namely, the regulatory targets. The danger of a risk-based approach, therefore, is discretionary abuse.

In this regard, there are rules that provide due process and other procedural safeguards at both the national and international levels to constrain discretionary power when assessing cybersecurity risks.

[122] Australian Government, Attorney-General's Department, "Submission to the Parliamentary Joint Committee on Intelligence and Security" (2017).

[123] See generally Raphaël Gellert, *The Risk-Based Approach to Data Protection* (Oxford University Press 2020), at 1–25.

[124] Julia Black and Robert Baldwin, "When Risk-Based Regulation Aims Low: A Strategic Framework" (2012) 6(2) Regulation & Governance 131, at 144.

In particular, international economic law is increasingly designed to constrain domestic regulation where the application of these regulations has external effects on other states. At the multilateral level, the obligations of GATT X:3(a) and GATS Article VI:1,[125] which allow challenges to the administration of domestic regulations that are otherwise consistent with the GATT or GATS, were designed to be an important tool in tackling situations in which a general scheme does not make any distinction between foreign and domestic service suppliers, but the administration of this scheme is not "reasonable, objective, or impartial."[126] Admittedly, GATT X:3(a) and GATS Article VI:1 may not be sufficiently forceful in a manner that safeguards due process and counters the potential abuse of administrative power in the process of risk assessment.[127] That said, as Chapters 3 and 5 will continue to address, the "good regulatory practices" agenda in the new generation FTAs, which seeks to enhance due process, transparency, legal clarity, and judicial review of administrative decisions, may shed light on how international trade agreements might prove helpful in preventing irrational, biased, or arbitrary cybersecurity risk assessments. Moreover, the adoption of international cybersecurity standards can mitigate concerns surrounding discretionary abuses in risk assessment. In this regard, the TBT Agreement can assume a substantial role in promoting international standards on cybersecurity, which can in turn facilitate the global development of common security approaches. At the end of the day, a nonregulatory approach and international soft law play important roles in governing cybersecurity and reshaping international economic order in the age of datafication. Chapter 6 will dive deeper into this aspect.

[125] See, for example, GATS, Article VI:1, which states "[i]n sectors where specific commitments are undertaken, each Member shall ensure that all measures of general application affecting trade in services are administered in a reasonable, objective and impartial manner."

[126] Padideh Ala'i, "From the Periphery to the Center? The Evolving WTO Jurisprudence on Transparency and Good Governance" (2008) 11(4) Journal of International Economic Law 779, at 795.

[127] Shin-yi Peng, "The Rule of Law in Times of Technological Uncertainty: Is International Economic Law Ready for Emerging Supervisory Trends?" (2019) 22(1) Journal of International Economic Law 1, at 23. In this regard, van Aaken proposed that one possible procedural solution is establishing a special council on cybersecurity. Anne van Aaken, "Introduction to the Symposium on Digital Trade" (2023) 117 AJIL Unbound 94, 98.

2.5 Conclusion

This chapter addresses the data network in the context of the cybersecurity threat landscape, which is increasingly perceived as a national security issue, especially when critical infrastructure is directly involved. Before we shift the focus to digital applications that drive datafication, it is worth reiterating that data networks have become strategic political and economic assets of a state. As the backbone infrastructure, 5G networks literally resemble interactive central nervous systems in the data-driven economy. The weaponization of 5G networks has brought about further challenges to international economic legal order. In Chapters 1 and 2, we explored two important dimensions of the broadband infrastructure – "trade and development" and "trade and security" – both of which are the foundations for a platform-driven, data-fueled world. The chapters in Part II will zoom in on digital applications, analyze the phenomenon of platformization, and explore considerations pertaining to the regulation of digital platforms.

PART II

Driving Datafication

Digital Platform

3

Data-Driven Platform as Service

Classification, Market Access, and Digital Sovereignty

3.1 Introduction

At the platform level, our daily lives are increasingly transformed into structured data flows. Looking back to the negotiating history of the WTO, however, today's platform economy was an unknown market phenomenon when the WTO was established in the early 1990s. At the time of the Uruguay Round negotiations, Mode 1 (cross-border) trade was considered insignificant or even "irrelevant" to most of the services sectors.[1] Such an understanding was reflected in the distribution of the commitments by mode of supply under the GATS. Some 30 percent of all members' market access commitments on Mode 1 services trade are unqualified, that is, without limitations, as compared to only 15 percent of the commitments on Mode 3 (commercial presence).[2] Furthermore, the level of obligations for Mode 1 services trade does not differ in an obvious way between developed and developing countries.[3] Evidently, the GATS negotiators could not have been aware of the future existence and influences of digital platforms. Those pro-liberalization market access commitments on Mode 1 were based on the brick-and-mortar business models in the pre-Google days.

Technological innovations have brought about exponential growth in data generation, analysis, and use. This raises the question of whether the GATS market access commitments, which were made decades ago, remain tenable in this datafied world.[4] From geopolitical perspectives,

[1] GATS, Article I. "Mode 1" refers to services supplied cross-border.

[2] WTO Secretariat, *Guide to the GATS: An Overview of Issues for Further Liberalization of Trade in Services* (Kluwer Law International 2001), at 598, 602.

[3] Mirelle Cossy, "Cross-Border Supply of Services – Pattern of Specific Commitments" (April 28–29, 2005), WTO Symposium on Cross-Border Supply of Services.

[4] Dan Ciuriak, "The Challenge of Updating Institutions for Digital Trade" (2021) Opinion, Centre for International Governance Innovation <www.cigionline.org/articles/the-chal

as discussed in Chapter 2, issues surrounding national security now represent the most challenging battlefield facing international economic legal order. Digital transformation calls into question whether existing market access commitments, which are the result of "bargains" struck in a "previous technological era," can be reasonably sustained,[5] especially when considering the national security risks addressed above.[6] One notable example is when the Trump administration in 2020 decided to bar people in the US from downloading TikTok and WeChat, two social media platforms owned by Chinese companies.[7] China maintained that the services provided by the two platforms are covered by the US' GATS Schedule of Commitments on advertising services, computer-related services, telecommunications, audio-video services, and entertainment services.[8] The dispute over TikTok and WeChat demonstrates the key problems this chapter attempts to address: How are digital platforms covered by the GATS market access obligations? Are trade commitments "resilient" enough to outlive "technological generations?"

Even for services sectors that are less security-sensitive, classification nevertheless matters, as it decides to what extent GATS applies. To illustrate, there are two different groups of obligation under the GATS – "general obligations," such as most-favored-nation treatment and transparency, which are applied across all sectors, and "specific commitments," such as market access and national treatment, which are only applied to those sectors a member inscribes in its Schedule of Commitments. The flexible nature of the latter, as stressed by GATS drafters, was designed to allow each member to adjust the market entry

lenge-of-updating-institutions-for-digital-trade/>. For more discussions, See Shin-yi Peng, "The Uneasy Interplay between Digital Inequality and International Economic Law" (2022) 33(1) European Journal of International Law 205, at 213–215.

5 Ciuriak, *Ibid.*

6 See Section 2.2.1 of this book.

7 The US White House, "Executive Order on Addressing the Threat Posed by WeChat" (August 6, 2020) <https://trumpwhitehouse.archives.gov/presidential-actions/executive-order-addressing-threat-posed-wechat/>.

8 Inside US Trade, "China Accuses U.S. of Violating WTO Rules in TikTok, WeChat Moves" (October 2, 2020). The Trump administration imposed restrictions on Chinese-owned social media platforms TikTok and WeChat. China claimed that the US actions violate its commitments under the GATS. China maintained that the two platforms provide services covered under GATS obligations, for example, advertising services, computer-related services, telecommunications, audio-video services, and entertainment services. As discussed in Chapter 2, the Biden administration has issued an Executive Order redirecting scrutiny of the Chinese apps.

conditions pursuant to its sector-specific policy concerns and objectives.[9] By scheduling the specific commitments, which have been individually and uniquely exercised by each member "on their own pace,"[10] a member is legally obliged to open a services market pursuant to its GATS Schedule.[11] In other words, market access applies under the GATS on a sector-by-sector basis. Sectoral classification, therefore, is the basis for identifying the scope of market access commitments under the GATS architecture.

Specific commitments have been scheduled based upon classification guidance W/120, prepared by the GATT Secretariat during the Uruguay Round negotiations. W/120 primarily relied upon the United Nations' Provisional Central Product Classification (CPC), dating back to 1991.[12] It goes without saying that services sectors have undergone significant changes since then. Today's commercial realities mean that W/120 classifications have become inadequate, and their correspondence with the CPC is out of date, leading to unreliable segmentations. More and more digital-related services identified in the W/120 and the CPC, such as facsimile services (7521**, 7529**), no longer make modern business sense. At the same time, more and more "new" services are not explicitly covered by the W/120 and the CPC with legal certainty.[13] At the heart of the issue is the scheduling logic of the GATS architecture. The GATS was introduced as a positive-list agreement, in which there is no market access for services trade unless it has been positively inscribed in a member's GATS Schedule.[14] Such a positive-list architecture creates problems for any digitalized service that currently exists in the markets but was not explicitly "described" in the CPC.[15] In this regard, much ink

[9] WTO Secretariat, supra note 2, at 591–592.

[10] Scott Sinclair and Jim Grieshaber-Otto, *Facing the Facts: A Guide to the GATS Debate* (Canadian Center for Policy Alternatives 2002), at 26.

[11] These specific Commitments guarantee minimum levels of treatment. However, note that they do not prevent WTO members' services markets from being more liberal in practice.

[12] United Nations, "Provisional Central Product Classification (CPC)" (1991) <https://unstats.un.org/unsd/classifications/Econ/Download/In%20Text/CPCprov_english.pdf>.

[13] Rolf H. Weber and Mira Burri, *Classification of Services in the Digital Economy* (Springer 2012), at 17–20.

[14] *Ibid.*, at 45. The GATS adopted a hybrid approach to scheduling commitments, with a positive list of sectors in which a member is willing to make binding market access commitments, together with a negative list of nonconforming measures regarding market access and national treatment that are retained in scheduled sectors.

[15] WTO, "Note by the Secretariat" MTN.GNS/W/120 (July 10, 1991). For the purposes of the Uruguay Round negotiations, the WTO Secretariat developed the GATS Services Sectoral Classification List ("the W/120") to enhance the consistency of the commitments

has been spilled surrounding whether search engines like Google are covered by GATS commitments, since China blocked Google.com and redirected traffic to local search engines. Are Google services already accommodated by the existing CPC? Commentators have argued both for and against with respect to the question of whether the W/120 and CPC subsectors "online information retrieval," "value-added telecommunications service," "data processing services," "online hosting and publication services," "advertising services," and "database services" include search engines such as Google.[16] In any event, Google cannot perfectly satisfy any definitions or conditions described in the existing CPC system, and as a result, classifying Google in either subsector seems illogical from a legal perspective. Likewise, how might chat applications such as WhatsApp best be defined? How might virtual meeting services such as Zoom be classified? Similar questions can be raised regarding the classification of endless lists of data-driven activities.

3.2 The "Renewal" of Trade Commitments

3.2.1 Services Digitalization: Technological Neutrality

Market access to data-related services has been the primary litigated area under the GATS. The first WTO ruling concerning e-commerce was on US restrictions over Internet gambling services. Antigua and Barbuda initiated a WTO dispute settlement case against the US,[17] claiming that US Internet gambling restrictions at both the federal and state levels violated its market access commitments to "Entertainment Services" under the GATS. This dispute concerned various US domestic measures

undertaken by members. Although it is optional, most members follow the W/120 classification system, whose 160 subsectors are defined by more detailed descriptions in the CPC. Thus, CPC categories help clarify the scope of the commitments actually undertaken under the GATS, and most members list the corresponding CPC numbers when scheduling their GATS commitments.

16 See, for example, Henry Gao, "Google's China Problem: A Case Study on Trade, Technology and Human Rights under the GATS" (2011) 6 Asian Journal of WTO & International Health Law & Policy 349, at 364; Tim Wu, "The World Trade Law of Censorship and Internet Filtering" 7(1) Chicago Journal of International Law (2006) 263, at 265.

17 Appellate Body Report, *United States – Measures Affecting the Cross-Border Supply of Gambling and Betting Services (U.S. – Gambling)*, WT/DS285/AB/R, April 20, 2005, paras. 6.19–6.40.

relating to gambling and betting services.[18] The complaining party pointed out that the US measures in dispute constitute a "total prohibition on the cross-border supply of gambling and betting services."[19] It further claimed that the prohibition violated Article XVI:1 of the GATS because, despite having scheduled a "full market access" commitment for the cross-border supply (*i.e.*, Mode 1) of gambling and betting services, the US "maintains and enforces measures prohibiting the cross-border supply" of those services.[20]

In its submission, the US government was of the view that "new technologies, including high-speed telecommunications and the Internet" have brought about explosive growth in online gambling, and such a dramatic increase has raised serious regulatory and law enforcement concerns in the country.[21] The US stressed that throughout its history, the country has consistently imposed tight regulations on the remote supply of gambling.[22] According to the US submission, gambling has been regulated in the US back to the earliest years of the Colonial era,[23] and the country has expanded the relevant regulatory regime for the remote supply of gambling so that it addresses modern threats and, in particular, criminal activities on the Internet.[24] To illustrate the regulatory characteristics of Internet gambling, the US elaborated at length regarding how, compared with nonremote gambling services (*i.e.*, traditional casinos), Internet gambling (*i.e.*, virtual casinos) poses greater threats of organized crime, money laundering, fraud, and youth gambling.[25] The US therefore claimed that a proper interpretation of its GATS

[18] In subsector 10.D of the U.S. GATS Schedule of Specific Commitments, the US inscribed the following entry: "Other Recreational Services (except sporting)." Then, next to that column, in the column titled "Limitations on Market Access," the US listed the four modes of supply, and for Mode 1, the US inscribed the word "None." Based on this entry, Antigua argued that the US has made a full market access commitment to Mode 1 of gambling and betting services.

[19] In this case, the Antiguan gambling and betting services at issue were supplied through the online mode, which, as argued by Antigua, is defined in Article I:2(a) of the GATS and involves a service "delivered within the territory of the member, from the territory of another member."

[20] Panel Report, *U.S. – Gambling*, WT/DS285/R, April 20, 2005, paras. 5.21–5.24.

[21] First Written Submission of the United States, *U.S. – Gambling*, WT/DS285, November 7, 2003, para. 2.

[22] *Ibid.*, para. 8.

[23] *Ibid.*

[24] *Ibid.*, paras. 8–9.

[25] Second Written Submission of the United States, *U.S. – Gambling*, WT/DS285, January 9, 2004, paras. 46–56.

Schedule would show that it had never opened its market to online gambling.

WTO jurisprudence makes clear that "a member's intent is not relevant" in determining whether the member has a commitment with respect to digital-enabled delivery.[26] Instead, under WTO law, the only relevant issue is whether the responding member in this particular dispute has explicitly excluded electronic means of service delivery from the market access commitments in its GATS Schedule.[27] The panel in *U.S. – Gambling*, by citing the "Progress Report of the Work Programme on Electronic Commerce,"[28] indicated that "[it] was the general view that the GATS is technologically neutral in the sense that it does not contain any provisions that distinguish between the different technological means through which a service may be supplied."[29] Noting the principle of "technological neutrality," which, according to the panel, "seems to be largely shared among WTO members," the panel stressed that "where market access and national treatment commitments exist, they encompass the delivery of the service through electronic means."[30] In short, by pointing out that "the GATS does not limit the various technologically possible means of delivery under Mode 1,"[31] the panel considered transactions via electronic media one of the "inherent means of delivery" of Mode 1 trade. Thus, the panel concluded that a market access commitment for Mode 1 implies the right of foreign companies to supply services through all means of delivery, including the Internet.[32]

[26] Panel Report, *China – Measures Affecting Trading Rights and Distribution Services for Certain Publications and Audiovisual Entertainment Products (China – Publications and Audiovisual Products)*, WT/DS363/R, January 19, 2010, para. 4.223.

[27] It should be clarified that market access commitments to a particular sector do not prevent states from regulating that sector for legitimate public objectives. See Section 3.5 for more on the relationship between market access and domestic regulation.

[28] Council for Trade in Services, Submission by the United States, "Work Programme on Electronic Commerce" WT/GC/16 (February 12, 1999), para. 4.

[29] Panel Report, *U.S. – Gambling*, adopted April 20, 2005, para. 6.285, footnote 836. The same paragraph also states "[M]ode 1 implies the right for other Members' suppliers to supply a service through all means of delivery, whether by mail, telephone, Internet, etc."

[30] *Ibid.*

[31] *Ibid.*, para. 6.281.

[32] *Ibid.*, paras. 6.285–6.287. Note that the US' appeal focused on the Panel's interpretation of Article XVI:2 (a)(c) of the GATS. The Appellate Body therefore did not review the Panel's finding regarding the means of delivery under Mode 1.

3.2.2 *Services Platformization: Evolutionary Interpretation*

The case of *China – Publications and Audiovisual Products* is another compelling example of how digital technologies have disrupted the traditional understanding of market access commitments.[33] In its GATS Schedule, China opened its market to "sound recording distribution services"[34] and listed no national treatment limitations under Mode 3 (commercial presence) for Chinese-foreign contractual joint ventures. Given these commitments, Chinese-foreign contractual joint ventures, including the majority of foreign-owned joint ventures, should enjoy national treatment in terms of sound recording distribution. The Chinese domestic legal framework,[35] however, limits the ability of foreign-invested enterprises to engage in the distribution of sound recordings by prohibiting these enterprises from "electronically distributing" their music services via online platforms such as iTunes. The US therefore claimed that China's measures were inconsistent with the GATS obligations.[36]

China in turn asserted that online music platforms are not covered by China's GATS market access commitments.[37] China argued that the music industry landscape has been undergoing major structural changes since its WTO accession negotiations. At the time of the negotiation of China's GATS commitments, the legal framework governing the recorded music market exclusively addressed the distribution of sound recordings in their traditional, hard copy format.[38] China submitted several pieces of evidence to support its position that online music services did not constitute an established business operating within the Chinese legal framework during its GATS negotiations, and that China

[33] Appellate Body Report, *China – Publications and Audiovisual Products*, WT/DS363/AB/R, January 19, 2010. This dispute concerns China's national treatment limitations under "Mode 3."

[34] Panel Report, *China – Publications and Audiovisual Products*, paras. 7.1300–7.1311. China committed to allowing foreign services suppliers to establish contractual joint ventures with Chinese partners to engage in sound recording distribution.

[35] First Written Submission of the United States of America, *China – Publications and Audiovisual Products*, WT/DS363, May 13, 2008, para. 357.

[36] More specifically, this refers to China's national treatment commitments under "Mode 3." *Ibid.*, paras. 140–155, 357.

[37] First Written Submission of the People's Republic of China, *China – Publications and Audiovisual Products*, WT/DS363, June 20, 2008, paras. 389–403. The Chinese government argued that electronic distribution of sound recordings was a new phenomenon that emerged fully after China acceded to the WTO.

[38] *Ibid.*, paras. 446–448.

was not aware music was being electronically distributed when it joined the WTO.[39] According to China, the first online music service platforms in China were launched in the early 2000s. In other words, such digital platforms are a new phenomenon that did not exist at the time of China's WTO accession.[40] China therefore claimed that online music platforms, which were not offered for liberalization at the time of its WTO accession, "cannot be committed post hoc through the dispute settlement process."[41]

On this issue, the principle of technological neutrality was central to the US' arguments against China.[42] The US relied on the principle to point out that the differences between physical and digital distribution are not relevant to the interpretation of the scope of a GATS commitment unless specified in a member's schedule.[43] In the view of the US, the electronic distribution of services merely constitutes "a new means of delivery for an existing service," and the GATS is sufficiently dynamic to cover new technological innovations "affecting the delivery of services."[44] The US rebutted that China's position, if accepted, would result in "an unworkable outcome,"[45] simply because in that case, GATS commitments "must be renegotiated each time a new technology results in a new means of supplying a service."[46] The US stressed that by this logic, WTO members could invoke such reasoning to "evade [market access] services commitments" whenever a new form of service delivery technology was developed.[47]

The most important implication of this dispute is the Appellate Body's ambiguous stance on the (in)significance of "technical possibility" and the (ir)relevance of "commercial reality" – namely, the state of technology and the market that existed at the time of the treaty negotiations. The Appellate Body emphasized that, at least in this dispute, the technical and

[39] Panel Report, *China – Publications and Audiovisual Products*, paras. 7.1161–7.1167.

[40] First Written Submission of the People's Republic of China, *China – Publications and Audiovisual Products*, paras. 443–448.

[41] *Ibid.*, para. 509.

[42] Oral Statement of the United States of America at the First Substantive Meeting of the Panel, *China – Publications and Audiovisual Products*, WT/DS363, July 22, 2008, para. 56.

[43] *Ibid.*, para. 51.

[44] *Ibid.*, paras. 72–73.

[45] *Ibid.*, para. 56.

[46] *Ibid.*

[47] *Ibid.*, para. 73.

commercial factual situations are not the central considerations.[48] In this regard, the Appellate Body stated that GATS Schedules constitute a part of the multilateral trade agreements, with "continuing obligations" entered into by WTO members "for an indefinite period of time."[49] The Appellate Body drew attention to the treaty interpretation approach taken in *U.S. – Shrimp*,[50] where the term "exhaustible natural resources" in Article XX(g) of the GATT was read "in the light of contemporary concerns of the community of nations about the protection and conservation of the environment."[51] To summarize, under the concept of evolutionary interpretation, the Appellate Body in *U.S. – Shrimp* reasoned that the GATT was crafted more than fifty years ago, and the generic term "natural resources" in Article XX(g) is not "static" in terms of its content or reference, but is, rather, "evolutionary."[52] Likewise, the Applegate Body in *China – Publications and Audiovisual Products* concluded that the Chinese commitments in the dispute are "generic terms" whose content may "change over time,"[53] namely, from physical to digital.[54]

3.3 Classifying Data-Driven Platforms

3.3.1 Rapidly Changing Markets: Technologically Future Proof?

Answering the question raised earlier – whether international trade commitments are sufficiently resilient to outlive technological generations, in particular, from physical to digital – the position of the GATS Council on Services is that the GATS applies even as technology changes a service's delivery method.[55] Therefore, "much of e-commerce

[48] Appellate Body Report, *China – Publications and Audiovisual Products*, paras. 407–410.
[49] *Ibid.*, para. 396.
[50] *Ibid.*, para. 397; Footnote 705.
[51] Appellate Body Report, *United States – Import Prohibition of Certain Shrimp and Shrimp Products* (*U.S. – Shrimp*), WT/DS58/AB/R, November 6, 1998, paras. 129–130.
[52] *Ibid.*, para. 130.
[53] Appellate Body Report, *China – Publications and Audiovisual Products*, para. 396.
[54] This discussion draws upon materials in Shin-yi Peng, "Digital Trade" in Daniel Bethlehem et al. (eds), *The Oxford Handbook of International Trade Law* (Oxford University Press 2022), chapter 29; Shin-yi Peng, "Renegotiate the WTO Commitments? Technological Change and Treaty Interpretation" (2012) 45(2) Cornell International Law Journal 403–430.
[55] See Susan Ariel Aaronson and Patrick Leblond "Another Digital Divide: The Rise of Data Realms and its Implications for the WTO" (2018) 21(2) Journal of International Economic Law 245, at 252.

falls within the GATS' scope," and "GATS obligations cover measures affecting the electronic delivery of services."[56] As discussed above, WTO case law has further confirmed that GATS disciplines and obligations extend to services supplied electronically. The reach of existing GATS commitments applies to digital means of service delivery that have emerged since the GATS was concluded in 1994. WTO members need not renegotiate their market access commitments "in the face of ever-changing technology."[57]

If we follow the logic of the Appellate Body in *China – Publications and Audiovisual Products,* when a term in a WTO member's market access schedule is sufficiently "generic," the commitment would be a "timeless" WTO obligation; on the other hand, when the term is sufficiently specific, the commitment would be a "time-bound" obligation that applies to a specific "technological status quo." Under such an interpretive approach, virtually all GATS-specific commitments are made in a "sufficiently generic" way and are therefore open-ended and able to accommodate any possible future means of delivery. For example, Taiwan opened its "Cellular Mobile Phone Services" in its GATS Schedule when it joined the WTO in 2002. What the Taiwanese trade negotiators had in mind at the time of the trade negotiations was the state-of-the-art – namely, 2G – technology. The negotiators were of course unaware of how the powerful 5G technology of today would enable the IoT and AI, as well as how these 5G-enabled applications would change the way we live and work. However, since Taiwan did not specify "2G" in its GATS Schedule, the market access concessions of "Cellular Mobile Phone Services" would automatically evolve into the "new" context as time passes – from 2G to 3G, 4G, 5G . . . and xG. At the core of the issue are the "temporal variations" in human language. Our language meanings are under "constant flux" according to social, cultural, and technological contexts.[58] Should we interpret a GATS market access commitment using the "ordinary meaning" at the time of its treaty conclusion (*i.e.*, historical language) or the "ordinary meaning" at the time of interpretation (*i.e.*, modern language)?[59]

[56] Council for Trade in Services, supra note 28.

[57] Oral statement of the United States of America at the First Substantive Meeting of the Panel, *China – Publications and Audiovisual Products,* para. 75.

[58] Ulf Linderfalk, *On the Interpretation of Treaties* (Springer 2007), at 73.

[59] For more detailed discussions in this regard, see Shin-yi Peng, supra note 54, at 403.

In *China – Publications and Audiovisual Products*, China repeatedly stressed in its written submissions that the only viable way to address the issue of technological and social evolution should be via trade (re)negotiations, rather than via the "fast track" of WTO dispute settlement procedures.[60] If a member wants online services to be liberalized, then it must pursue such liberalization by undertaking new negotiations with other members.[61] In China's view, the WTO tribunals should refrain from anticipating the results of future trade negotiations.[62] The Chinese government pointed out that unduly extending the scope of members' existing GATS commitments would be antithetical to the principle of "progressive liberalization," as reflected in both the GATS Preamble and Article XIX, which indicates that the GATS is aimed at establishing a multilateral framework for the expansion of services trade under conditions of transparency and progressive liberalization.[63] According to China, such a principle shapes the structure of the GATS, which allows members to undertake specific commitments through successive rounds of multilateral negotiations with a view toward incrementally liberalizing their services markets rather than doing so immediately and completely at the time of their WTO accession.[64] China therefore asserted that the same principle requires the panel to base its analysis of the relevant terms in a member's GATS Schedule on their meaning at the time of trade negotiations, so as to prevent the extension of the scope of market access commitments based on "temporal variations in language."[65]

In light of the Appellate Body's evolutionary approach to interpretation, key questions remain: Is the GATS "sufficiently dynamic," as framed by the US in *China – Publications and Audiovisual Products*, to cover every new technological innovation affecting trade in services?[66] Digital technologies and data markets are changing rapidly and

60 First Written Submission of the People's Republic of China, *China – Publications and Audiovisual Products*, para. 448.

61 *Ibid.*, para. 510.

62 *Ibid.*, paras. 512–514.

63 GATS, the Preamble: "Members . . . Recognizing the right of Members to regulate, and to introduce new regulations, on the supply of services within their territories in order to meet national policy objectives and, given asymmetries existing with respect to the degree of development of services regulations in different countries, the particular need of developing countries to exercise this right . . . ."

64 Appellate Body Report, *China – Publications and Audiovisual Products*, para. 394.

65 *Ibid.*, para. 47.

66 Oral Statement of the United States of America at the First Substantive Meeting of the Panel, *China – Publications and Audiovisual Products*, para. 75.

disruptively. Technically, how can we distinguish between "new service supply modalities" and "new services?" Does it make economic and legal sense that the former is already covered by the existing market access commitments, while market access for the latter is subject to future trade negotiations? Relying on concepts such as "technological neutrality" or "evolutionary interpretation" to expand the scope of market access commitments under the GATS, if applied to an extreme, may mean that international trade commitments are future-proof and are therefore "auto-renewed" across technological generations.

3.3.2 *Innovative Business Models: Case-by-Case Approach?*

Classification with definition matters in every legal instrument – it decides the scope of each legal obligation, and it defines the boundary of each regulation. To a large degree, technological uncertainty causes equal challenges to both international trade law and domestic regulation in this regard. After all, "treating like services alike" is a commonly shared regulatory principle. In the context of domestic regulation, classification issues arise along every step of digitalization and datafication. For example, should a "traditional service" and a "platform-based new service" be classified in the same manner for regulatory purposes? City authorities should enforce existing taxi regulations over Uber if it is classified as a transport service, like the traditional taxi. Similarly, Airbnb hosts should be required to obtain licenses if they are classified as real estate agents. For sectoral regulators, the decision on whether the two types of services – one in physical form and the other online – fall within the same regulatory category is dependent upon the characteristics of the services at issue. The central question always surrounds whether the digital platform is "similar to" or "different from" its off-line analogues.[67]

The approaches taken by the European Court of Justice (ECJ) serve as an interesting reference here.[68] On the question of whether Uber should be classified as a "transport services supplier" and should therefore be

[67] This discussion draws upon materials in Shin-yi Peng, "Levelling the Playing Field between Sharing Platforms and Industry Incumbents: Good Regulatory Practices?" in Anupam Chander and Haochen Sun (eds), *Data Sovereignty* (Oxford University Press 2023), chapter 7.

[68] The key legal issue was whether the sharing platforms in question should be classified as "information society services," which could therefore enjoy the benefits of free movement.

required to seek prior regulatory approval, the ECJ decided that the services offered by Uber should not be regarded as an "Information Society Service" under the EU's E-Commerce Directive. Rather, Uber should be legally equated with traditional transport services (*i.e.*, taxi services) that must be regulated.[69] However, the ECJ ruled that Airbnb must be classified as an "Information Society Service" as defined in the E-Commerce Directive. In other words, the ECJ held that Airbnb and Uber should be treated differently.[70] According to the ECJ rulings, the commercial offering provided by Uber is in itself "more than an intermediary service."[71] Overall, Uber's activities should be classified as "intermediation services forming an integral part of an overall service," and "the main component of which is a transport service."[72] In this regard, Uber must comply with the domestic regulations of each EU member state pertaining to "transport services."[73] However, the ECJ stressed that a similarly decisive influence of Airbnb, in terms of its power over the transactions of the accommodation services, could not be identified.[74] The ECJ thus classified the intermediation service offered by Airbnb as an "information society service" that is entitled to the benefits of free movement.[75] In short, different legal classifications trigger the implementation of different sets of rules.

In the above ECJ rulings, the different treatment of the two data-driven platforms is primarily attributable to two factors: first, the ability of users to successfully operate without the platform, and second, the ability of the platforms to control transactions. According to the ECJ's assessment, Airbnb's business model is not comparable to that of Uber, in the sense that "Airbnb's intermediation service is in no way indispensable to the provision of accommodation services."[76] In addition, Uber had exercised "decisive influence" over conditions that are "economically significant aspects of the service," while Airbnb had not.[77] In brief, the technical features and business models of a digital platform are complex

69 Case C-434/15, Association Professional Elite Taxi v. Uber Systems Spain, SL, 2017 E.C.R. 981.
70 *Ibid.*
71 *Ibid.*
72 *Ibid.*
73 *Ibid.*
74 Case C-390/18, Airbnb Ireland, 2019 E.C.R. 1112.
75 *Ibid.*
76 *Ibid.*
77 *Ibid.*

and involve a great number of variables.[78] The ECJ approaches to classifying the commercial nature of a platform are dynamic and pragmatic. Various conclusions can be drawn as to whether a specific platform qualifies as an "information service." The nature of a platform is therefore legally unsettled. In the wake of the ECJ judgments, it would seem that the answer to the question of how to determine the exact nature of the services provided by platforms is dependent upon a case-by-case assessment of the characteristics of a particular platform. This, however, begs the question of relevant criteria, as well as their weighting.

The ECJ's practice of platform classification demonstrates that the WTO is not alone in this "digital dilemma." On the one hand, legal certainty and predictability are valuable attributes in any legal system, and consistency in the application of rules is an important source of legitimacy for any dispute resolution mechanism. It remains difficult to predict how a digital platform will be classified by the ECJ, thereby rendering such platforms subject to either a "light touch" or a "heavy hand" in terms of regulation. This case-by-case uncertainty may invite endless disputes. On the other hand, in light of the unpredictable nature and incredible pace of technology, judicial discretion is becoming a "necessary evil." Judicial activism inheres in the incompleteness of rules. If the definition is sufficiently precise, there is less room for judicial judgments. However, in situations where a classification system does not provide clear-cut definitions, there are opportunities for the tribunals to operate in a reactive manner and engage in dynamic interpretation. Indeed, the classification systems under both the GATS Schedules and the EU E-Commerce Directive are outdated.[79] The WTO and the ECJ will need to continue to classify digital platforms in a judicially active way if the relevant definitions in the legal instruments are disconnected from rapidly changing technologies.

In this context, the EU's Digital Services Act (DSA),[80] which aims to upgrade the more than twenty-year-old EU E-Commerce Directive, applies to a broad category of online players, including "mere conduit" services,

[78] For example, under the EU's Digital Services Act (DSA), core platform services include: online intermediation services (*i.e.*, marketplaces, app stores), online search engines, social networking, cloud services, and advertising services. Regulation (EU) 2022/2065 of the European Parliament and of the Council of October 19, 2022 on a Single Market For Digital Services and amending Directive 2000/31/EC (Digital Services Act).

[79] Note that the DSA is intended to modernize the EU's E-Commerce Directive, which dates back to 2000.

[80] The DSA was first proposed in December 2020 along with another landmark piece of legislation from the EU – the Digital Markets Act (DMA) – to shape the legal order of the digital economy. See Chapters 4 and 5 for further discussion.

"caching" services, hosting services, online platforms, very large online platforms (VLOPs), and very large online search engines.[81] Among other terms, "online platform" is defined in Article 3 (i) of the DSA as follows:

> . . . a hosting service that, at the request of a recipient of the service, stores and disseminates information to the public, unless that activity is a minor and purely ancillary feature of another service or a minor functionality of the principal service and, for objective and technical reasons, cannot be used without that other service, and the integration of the feature or functionality into the other service is not a means to circumvent the applicability of this Regulation. . .[82]

It takes time to determine if such a broad definition can solve the practical issue of legal uncertainty present in the EU E-Commerce Directive. At first glance, the taxonomies offered by the DSA, to a certain extent, overlap and create uncertainty in determining if a regulation is applicable to a particular case. Admittedly, there is no "one-size-fits-all definition" of a digital platform.[83] It is necessary to create multiple taxonomies, as the DSA does, to classify the different kinds of data-driven activities depending on their primary functions, the actors involved, the ways in which they exploit data, the sources of revenue, and the level of control they exercise over users' activities.[84] Logically, the same digital platform may also be classified into multiple categories simply because of the multiple functions it features.[85] In any event, the DSA intends to cover very broad and diversified sets of services offered on the Internet. The definitions therein are functionally constructed, allowing regulators to map the business practices to policy issues. In conclusion, will the approach taken by the DSA end the legal uncertainty? Probably not. However, the approach offers a high degree of generality, which is key in reducing the risk of regulatory disconnection.

3.4 Future Market Access for Data-Driven Platforms

3.4.1 *The WTO: Reforms and Renegotiations Needed*

Turning back to the international trading regime, what lessons and reflections can we draw from the EU's regulatory experience? This book

[81] DSA, Article 3 (Definitions).
[82] *Ibid.*
[83] European Parliament, "Liability of Online Platforms" (2021) <www.europarl.europa.eu/RegData/etudes/STUD/2021/656318/EPRS_STU(2021)656318_EN.pdf>, at 17.
[84] *Ibid.*, at 17–22.
[85] *Ibid.*, at 16–17.

contends that trade negotiators in this age of datafication must be aware of the impossibility of drafting trade rules that speak directly to every situation and must also recognize the need for constant adaptation to technological advancements. By the same token, some sort of functional approach to market access commitments must be incorporated into trade negotiations. When opening a market to an innovative sector, international trade agreements should employ flexible language so as to allow reasonable room for technological changes, and to prevent market access commitments from becoming quickly overtaken by subsequent events. One example is the functionally simplistic approach to the telecom services sector classification proposed by the EU. Inscribing a simple entry, "any service consisting of the transmission and reception of signals by any electromagnetic means," as suggested by the EU, would seem to end classification uncertainty in the telecom sector.[86] At the end of the day, it is not possible to have a precise and clear-cut definition for market access commitments in the data-driven sectors.

Looking toward the future, substantial reforms and renegotiation are needed in the WTO, assuming it is politically feasible someday. Although both *U.S. – Gambling* and *China – Publications and Audiovisual Products* raised the question of how a schedule of commitments is to be interpreted to include a new service not in existence at the time of negotiations,[87] WTO case law is not entirely clear regarding in what situation and to what extent the "state of technology" that existed at the time of the market access negotiations is relevant in determining the scope of the commitments. On the one hand, digital technology is organic and technologically innovative, and we must read the existing trade commitments in a dynamic and evolutionary way. On the other hand, judicial interpretation may not be the most appropriate method of clarifying whether the W/120 and the CPC cover certain digital trade-related services. What is covered and what is not covered by members' GATS Schedules is an

[86] Communication from the European Commission, "Classification in the Telecom Sector under the WTO-GATS Framework" TN/S/W/27, S/CSC/W/44 (February 10, 2005); As suggested by Brownsword and Somsen, "the more the law strives to be precise and comprehensive, the sooner it is likely to become disconnected from rapidly changing technologies that are its regulatory targets." Roger Brownsword and Han Somsen, "Law, Innovation and Technology: Before We Fast Forward – A Forum for Debate" (2009) 1 Law, Innovation and Technology 1, at 3.

[87] See Sondre T. Helmersen, "The Evolutionary Treaty Interpretation by the WTO Appellate Body" in Georges Abi-Saab et al. (eds), *Evolutionary Interpretation and International Law* (Hart Publishing 2019), at 210–212.

issue that should be (re)negotiated by WTO members, not by litigation.[88]

In conclusion, there is an urgent need for the W/120 scheme to be replaced or revised.[89] Negotiating proposals, including technical discussions regarding how to classify platforms for cloud computing services,[90] have been submitted to address necessary adjustments, and to ensure that services classification and scheduling can accommodate modern commercial and technological developments. The GATS classification/scheduling system must be reformed in light of innovative advances and trends toward a datafied world.[91] From iTunes and Google to TikTok and WeChat, the legal certainty of market access for digital trade cannot be ensured until classifications can be unambiguously defined. Moreover, renegotiations are needed to curb the notion that the GATS Schedules are "future proof" – covering all platform-based, data-driven e-commerce.[92] At the time of this writing, it remains to be seen to what extent the WTO JSI on E-commerce will be able to clarify issues surrounding the market access of digital platforms.

3.4.2 *The FTAs: Data Flows as both the Means and the End*

Under the FTAs concluded in more recent years, the E-Commerce/Digital Trade Chapters can be seen as a flipped governing approach that creates "*de facto* market access" for cross-border services trade. Essentially, the concept underlying the E-Commerce/Digital Trade Chapters was that rather than the "services," the "data flows used to

[88] Shin-yi Peng, "Regulating New Services through Litigation? Electronic Commerce as a Case Study on the Evaluation of Judicial Activism in the WTO" (2014) 48(6) Journal of World Trade 1189, at 1222; Wu, supra note 16, at 283; Gao, supra note 16, at 361–367.

[89] See for example, Communication from Australia and Canada, "Understanding on the Scope of Coverage of CPC 84 – Computer and Related Services" TN/S/W/60, S/CSC/W/51 (January 26, 2007). See also Non-Paper for the Discussions on Electronic Commerce, "Work Programme on Electronic Commerce" JOB/GC/100 (July 25, 2016).

[90] See, for example, Communication from the United States, "Work Program on Electronic Commerce: Ensuring that Trade Rules Support Innovative Advances in Computer Applications and Platforms" S/C/W/339 (September 20, 2011); Communication from the European Commission, "An Enabling Environment to Facilitate Online Transactions" TN/S/W/64 (May 23, 2017).

[91] Lee Tuthill and Martin Roy, "GATS Classification Issues for Information and Communication Technology Services" in Mia Burri and Thomas Cottier (eds), *Trade Governance in the Digital Age* (Cambridge University Press 2012), at 157.

[92] Gao, supra note 16, at 364 (discussing the most appropriate classification for Google's search services); Peng, supra note 54 (discussing whether the GATS is sufficiently dynamic to cover every new technological innovation given its positive-list architecture).

supply the services" require legal protections under an international trade agreement.[93] Under the CPTPP's E-Commerce Chapter and the USMCA's Digital Trade Chapter, as examples, parties have agreed to allow the "cross-border transfer of information . . . by electronic means" when the activity is for the conduct of the business of a covered person under the respective FTA.[94] Therefore, by securing the free flow of data, the E-Commerce/Digital Trade Chapters themselves open the market for data-driven sectors.

At the crux of the matter is the relationship between Cross-Border Trade in Services (*e.g.*, Chapter 10 of the CPTPP, Chapter 15 of the USMCA), on the one hand, and E-Commerce/Digital Trade (*e.g.*, Chapter 14 of the CPTPP, Chapter 19 of the USMCA), on the other hand. To what extent does the latter expand market access for the former? Would the latter be construed as overriding the nonconforming market access measures reserved by parties under the former? Or is it the other way around? How might the regulatory disciplines surrounding data transfer provided in the latter affect the market access commitments of the former? Indeed, when read together, there is an overlap in the scope of application of the Cross-Border Trade in Services Chapter and the E-Commerce/Digital Trade Chapter. For example, a domestic measure restricting health-related data transfer directly involves the obligations on the free flow of data in the E-Commerce/Digital Trade Chapter, and at the same time amounts to a trade barrier to market access for cross-border health services. Therefore, the rules from both chapters simultaneously apply when a domestic measure restricts cross-border data flows. To summarize, when data flow is considered a "means" for the supply of a service, it falls within the scope of the Cross-Border Trade in Services Chapter; when data flow itself is an "end," it is regulated under the E-Commerce/Digital Trade Chapter.[95]

Taking the CPTPP as an example, Cross-Border Trade in Services under the CPTPP, as defined in Article 10.1, contains three modes: cross-border supply (the same as Mode 1 under the GATS), consumption abroad (the same as Mode 2 under the GATS), and the presence of

[93] Thomas Streinz, "International Economic Law's Regulation of Data as a Resource for the Artificial Intelligence Economy" in Shin-yi Peng et al. (eds), *Artificial Intelligence and International Economic Law: Disruption, Regulation, and Reconfiguration* (Cambridge University Press 2021), at 175, 185–186.

[94] CPTPP, Article 14.11(1); USMCA Article 19.11(1).

[95] Streinz, supra note 93, at 185–187.

natural persons (the same as Mode 4 under the GATS). Chapter 10 mirrors similar core obligations in the GATS, including market access. The language of Article 10.5 (Market Access) is to a large extent borrowed from GATS Article XVI, which provides that no party may adopt quantitative limitations on the supply of services. In general, the CPTPP parties take a broad approach to cross-border trade in services, with services covered unless specifically listed in a party's schedule of nonconforming measures. Such a negative-list approach to services market access has in recent years been adopted by a large number of FTAs.[96] According to Article 10.7, the market access obligations under Article 10.5 shall not apply to any measure a party maintains with respect to sectors or activities, as excluded by that party in its Schedule to Annex II.[97] In other words, parties commit to opening the services market except in sectors where the "non-conforming measures" are listed in parties' schedules. Such a modality allows CPTPP parties to reserve the right to maintain or adopt restrictions for a particular sector, namely, to apply any measures that are inconsistent with certain obligations.[98] In short, a party-specific list of reservations enables a party to have full discretion to maintain existing nonconforming domestic regulations or to adopt new regulations without any legal consequences under the CPTPP.

It is important to note that to the extent Chapters 10 (Cross-Border Trade in Services) and 14 (Electronic Commerce) overlap, the former trumps the latter. To illustrate, there are two provisions dealing with the Chapters 10/14 overlap. First, Article 14.2(4) of the CPTPP states that measures affecting the cross-border supply of a service that is delivered electronically are subject to the obligations, nonconforming measures, and exceptions applicable to Chapter 10.[99] Second, Articles 14.2(5) and 14.2(6) of the CPTPP further clarify that any market access-related obligations in Chapter 14 – in particular, Article 14.11 (Cross-Border Transfer of Information by Electronic Means) and Article 14.13 (Location of Computing Facilities) – are subject to the relevant

[96] Unlike the GATS, a negative-list approach is essentially a "top-down" scheduling modality, under which all services sectors are to be opened for market entry unless otherwise specified by parties in their reservation lists appended to the FTA. See Aaditya Mattoo and Pierre Sauvé, "Regionalism in Services Trade" in Aaditya Mattoo et al. (eds), *A Handbook of International Trade in Services* (Oxford University Press 2008), at 256.

[97] CPTPP, Article 10.7.

[98] *Ibid.*

[99] CPTPP, Article 14.2(4).

provisions, exceptions, and nonconforming measures of Chapter 10.[100] For example, in its Annex II of the CPTPP, Australia listed nonconforming measures concerning the market access of distribution services. More specifically, it reserves the right "to adopt or maintain any measure with respect to wholesale and retail trade services of tobacco products, alcoholic beverages or firearms."[101] Assuming that Australia maintains a ban on online tobacco advertising, the marketing restrictions on digital platforms would fall within the Chapters 10/14 overlap. In that case, Article 14.11 (Cross-Border Transfer of Information by Electronic Means) would not apply because Australia did not forgo the right to introduce any market access-impairing tobacco measures in the future.

Much ink has been spilled by commentators regarding how the E-Commerce/Digital Trade Chapter can facilitate the free flow of data and thereby open the digital market. A strict focus on the E-Commerce/Digital Trade Chapter, however, might be too narrow to grasp the full picture.[102] As illustrated above, the Chapter on Cross-Border Trade in Services covers the data flows required to supply the specified services. At the same time, the Chapter on E-Commerce/Digital Trade, although it primarily concerns the regulatory disciplines on data flows, contains market access-related provisions that aim to protect data movement against cross-border data transfer restrictions.[103] When the obligations of the two chapters are in conflict, the obligations in the Cross-Border Trade in Services Chapter prevail.

Turning back to data-driven platforms, the overlapping provisions in the two chapters of the FTAs complicate their global market access. The commitments on "cross-border data flows" would not apply when parties do not allow "cross-border trade in services." In this regard, listing nonconforming measures under the Cross-Border Trade in Services Chapter would represent the most critical step in reserving the right to regulate the digital economy.[104] In the case of the CPTPP, several parties

[100] CPTPP, Article 14.2(5); Article 14.2(6).

[101] CPTPP, Annex II – Australia – 13.

[102] Deborah Elms, "The Comprehensive and Progressive Trans-Pacific Partnership Policy Innovations and Impacts" (2018) Global Economic Dynamics Focus Paper, at 14 (pointing out that "digital economy provisions can be found throughout the [CPTPP] agreement").

[103] Andrew Mitchell, "Brief of Evidence of Andrew David Mitchell in the Matter of the Trans-Pacific Partnership Agreement Inquiry before the Waitangi Tribunal" (2020), para. 96.

[104] See Section 4.4.2 of this book for more discussions.

have carefully safeguarded the boundaries of the services markets. New Zealand, for example, has circumscribed the scope of its CPTPP market access commitments on cross-border trade in services to exclusively match its GATS commitments.[105] Japan, as another striking example, has listed nonconforming market access measures for "all unrecognized or technically unfeasible services" as follows:

> **Cross-Border Trade in Services:**
> Japan reserves the right to adopt or maintain any measure relating to services *other than those recognized or other than those that should have been recognized* by the Government of Japan owing to the circumstances at the date of entry into force of this Agreement. (emphasis added) . . .
> Japan reserves the right to adopt or maintain any measure relating to the supply of services in any mode of supply in which *those services were not technically feasible at the date of entry into force of this Agreement* (emphasis added).[106]

Obviously, the Japanese inscription was inspired by the *China – Publications and Audiovisual Products* dispute. Considering that the negative-list approach adopted by the CPTPP would allow "new services" to be automatically included in the trade agreement and therefore entitle such services to be traded across borders in the CPTPP markets, Article 10.7 serves as a safety valve, allowing Japan to block not only "all unrecognized or technically unfeasible services," but also the means to deliver such services. Put simply, the inscription ensures that Japan does not risk committing to future services and associated delivery means that do not yet exist.

3.5 The Relationship between Market Access and Domestic Regulation

3.5.1 The Right to Regulate: Digital Sovereignty

Of course, market access obligations under international trade agreements do not prevent countries from adopting or implementing domestic regulations in pursuit of legitimate national policies. The GATS explicitly recognizes the right of members to pursue policy objectives through regulation, even in sectors where they have undertaken full commitments

[105] CPTPP, Annex II – New Zealand – 14.
[106] CPTPP, Annex II – Japan – 5.

to market access.[107] Once a state opens the international trade market of a specific sector, there might be a new need for domestic regulatory interference in the market to accomplish economic objectives such as market competition, or noneconomic social goals such as consumer protection.[108] In a nutshell, domestic regulation is essential to achieve legitimate policy objectives intertwined with trade in services, because the markets do not always work perfectly and cannot always bring about socially desired results by themselves.[109]

A sovereign's right to regulate in the age of datafication has been conceptualized into the notion of "digital sovereignty."[110] In Europe, as the most striking illustration, internal political supports have been overwhelming in shaping policy approaches to enhance Europe's "strategic autonomy" in the digital age.[111] The concept of "digital sovereignty" is thus becoming more and more common in the policy and academic literature, although there are divergent interpretations of it.[112] Various meanings have been attached to the concept. It is often used to denote "the ability of nation states to control the digital infrastructure on their territory and the data of their citizens."[113] The terminology, however, is increasingly used in a much broader context and almost always refers to the digital dimensions of a nation's autonomy,[114] including the ability of states to take action, both proactively and offensively, in the construction of digital infrastructure systems themselves, as well as the production, storage, processing, and analysis of the data of their citizens.[115] We can say that the unprecedented economic and social influence of big tech has

[107] Moreover, a violation of market access obligations might also be justified under exceptions contained in the WTO, such as Articles XIV (General Exceptions) and XIV *bis* (Security Exceptions) of the GATS, as well as in the FTAs, such as Articles 14.11(3) (Legitimate Public Policy Exceptions) and 29.1(3) (General Exceptions) of the CPTPP.

[108] Panagiotis Delimatsis, *International Trade in Services and Domestic Regulations: Necessity, Transparency and Regulatory Diversity* (Oxford University Press 2007), at 87–91.

[109] *Ibid.*, at 87.

[110] European Parliament, "Digital Sovereignty for Europe" (2020) <www.europarl.europa.eu/thinktank/en/document/EPRS_BRI(2020)651992 > .

[111] *Ibid.*

[112] The term is often used interchangeably with "data sovereignty."

[113] Lokke Moerel and Paul Timmers, "Reflections on Digital Sovereignty" (2021) EU Cyber Direct <https://eucyberdirect.eu/research/reflections-on-digital-sovereignty>.

[114] European Parliament, "Europe's Digital Decade and Autonomy" (2021) <www.europarl.europa.eu/RegData/etudes/STUD/2021/695465/IPOL_STU(2021)695465_EN.pdf>, at 59.

[115] *Ibid.*

served as the catalyst for the concept of "digital sovereignty," which is rooted in the need to safeguard regulatory authority in a data-driven world.

To summarize, there are growing concerns that individuals are losing control over their data, and that regulators are losing power to shape the legal framework of the digital sphere. Against this context, digital sovereignty has become a common concept to describe a broader range of digital policies and justify related regulation designed to defend a state's interests and values. Nonetheless, as the following chapters will continue to explore, domestic regulations are subject to disciplines under international economic law to safeguard the benefit of market access commitments, ensure that existing market entry is not nullified by unnecessary regulatory requirements, and reduce the likelihood of biased implementation of regulations.[116] In the context of digital trade, governments are free to regulate platforms but must do so in a way that does not constitute unnecessary barriers to trade. After all, the ability of services suppliers to engage in international trade is particularly affected by domestic regulation, including measures related to licensing and qualification requirements and procedures, as well as technical standards. Regulatory protectionism may impose disadvantages on platform services in a manner that is not necessary for the fulfilment of a genuine public policy objective. Domestic regulation adopted without adequate prior notification may prevent foreign services suppliers from competing on a level playing field. Excessive standards may also significantly distort international trade. Therefore, international trade rules should be in place to decide when and under what conditions legitimate policy objectives prevail over digital trade interests. As argued by Delimatsis, market access of the services trade "is only useful when it goes hand in hand with the promotion of sound domestic regulation."[117]

Domestic regulations that are not trade restrictions per se can still have unnecessary trade-restrictive effects. Article VI:4/5 of the GATS itself, however, is too weak to promote best regulatory approaches in an international context.[118] For this reason, Article VI:4 of the GATS

[116] See Section 5.4.2.

[117] Panagiotis Delimatsis, "Concluding the WTO Services Negotiations on Domestic Regulation: Hopes and Fears" (2020) 9(4) World Trade Review 643, 672.

[118] Markus Krajewski, *National Regulation and Trade Liberalization in Services* (Kluwer Law International 2003), at 140; Pierre Sauvé, *Trade Rules Behind Borders: Essays on Services, Investment and the New Trade Agenda* (Cameron May 2003), at113–115.

mandates the development of disciplines to ensure that domestic measures pertaining to licensing and qualification requirements and procedures and technical standards do not constitute unnecessary barriers to the services trade. The conclusion of the WTO JSI on Domestic Regulation, which sets out common rules requiring good regulatory practices, was a significant step in the multilateral trading regime to ensure that "existing liberalization commitments are not nullified by opaque and complex authorization procedures."[119] At the same time, more and more FTAs contain GATS-plus regulatory obligations, especially the trends to include a Regulatory Coherence/ Good Regulatory Practice Chapter in the FTA. This book will take a deep dive into this issue in Chapter 5.

3.5.2 The Quantity/Quality Dichotomy

Before we further address issues surrounding platform regulations in Chapters 4 and 5, a central, preliminary question lies in the relationship between market access and domestic regulation. Arguably, the structure of the GATS is based on a separation between domestic measures identified as "limitations on market access" (which fall under Article XVI)[120] and measures adopted to ensure the quality of the service (which fall under Article VI:4/5). Such a structural separation and distinction is based on the rationale that the regulatory intervention cannot be considered as "trade restrictiveness." Pursuant to the Scheduling Guidelines (S/L/92),[121] the market access column in a member's schedule must be confined to specifying the "terms, limitations and conditions of market access" listed in Article XVI:2(a)-(f), which essentially refer to limitations on (a) the "number" of services suppliers; (b) the "value" of transactions or assets; (c) the "number" of service operations or quantity of output; (d) the "number" of natural persons; (e) the legal form of establishment, such as "joint venture" requirements; and (f) foreign

[119] WTO, "Services Domestic Regulation: Rationale and Content, Potential Economic Benefits, and Increasing Prevalence in Trade Agreements" (2022) <www.wto.org/english/tratop_e/serv_e/sdr_factsheet_e_oct21.pdf>, at 2.

[120] Article XVI:1 of the GATS obliges WTO members to accord services and services suppliers of other members "no less favourable treatment than that provided for under the terms, limitations and conditions agreed and specified in its Schedule." Article XVI:2 defines measures that a member should not adopt or maintain, unless otherwise specified in its Schedule.

[121] WTO, "Guidelines for the Scheduling of Specific Commitments Under the General Agreement on Trade in Services" Council for Trade in Services, S/L/92 (March 28, 2001).

"capital participation." S/L/92 further clarifies that "approval procedures or licensing and qualification requirements" should not be scheduled under Article XVI "as long as they do not contain any of the limitations specified in Article XVI."[122] Regarding the distinction between Article XVI (market access) and Article VI:4/5 (domestic regulation), paragraph 11 of the S/L/92 states that the former refers to "maximum limitations," while the latter applies to "minimum requirements." A measure that does not conform to the latter "cannot be scheduled."[123]

In fact, during the Doha Round of negotiations, several members advocated for the "numerical target" as a complementary approach to the services market access negotiations that are "quantitative" in nature.[124] It is therefore reasonable to state that the negotiating modalities and the scheduling technology of GATS market access commitments are numerically oriented and quantity-driven. However, the dichotomy of quality vis-à-vis quantity may not always operate well in the real world. The quantity/quality distinction became blurred in WTO jurisprudence, and the problem of identifying the line between market access and domestic regulation is most acute in the broad interpretation of the concept of "zero quota." In *Mexico – Telecom,*[125] Mexico submitted that the "permit requirement" establishes a "zero quota" for Mode 3 market access.[126] According to Mexico, the permit requirement is qualified by the paragraph indicating the following: "[t]he establishment and operation of commercial agencies is invariably subject to the relevant regulations."[127] Mexico was of the view that nothing in its entry committed it to issuing the corresponding regulations, which is "equivalent to a zero quota."[128] Mexico's arguments point to the confusing boundary

[122] *Ibid.*, para. 11.
[123] *Ibid.*
[124] Communication from the European Commission, "Elements for Complementary Approaches in Services" TN/S/W/55 (October 27, 2005).
[125] Panel Report, *Mexico – Telecom*, para. 4.105.
[126] Mexico's Answer to Question No. 2(a) of the Panel, *Mexico – Telecom* (December 19, 2002).
[127] Panel Report, *Mexico – Telecom*, para. 7.349.
[128] However, the Panel stated that "[i]f the meaning of Mexico's entry is that Mexico has full discretion [regarding] whether or not to issue regulations [governing the granting of licenses], then it follows that Mexico has indeed not undertaken any commitment on the number of suppliers." Panel Report, *Mexico – Telecom*, para. 7.356. The Panel further stated that "subparagraph (d) [of Article XX:1] requires that a schedule shall specify . . . where appropriate the time-frame for implementation of such commitments . . . We therefore consider that subparagraph (d) of Article XX:1 requires the specification of a time-frame for implementation, should a Member wish to implement a

between Articles XVI (market access) and VI (domestic regulation) of the GATS. Unfortunately, the concept of "zero quota" since then has become rooted in WTO jurisprudence. The leading case in this issue is *U.S. – Gambling*. The US argued that regulations on online gambling services are not "quantitative limits" within the meaning of Article XVI:2, and that a commitment under XVI only prohibits "quantitative measures" included in XVI:2.[129] As claimed by the US, "there is no reason why a Member's imposition of nationality-neutral limitations" could violate GATS Article XVI "so long as the particular measures in question do not take the form of numerical quotas or any other form prohibited by Article XVI:2."[130] The Appellate Body in this particular issue ruled that the US measures in the dispute should be considered a limitation within the ambit of Article XVI:2(c) for the reason that it "totally prevents the services operations and output" through one or more or "all means of delivery that are included in Mode 1."[131] Such a ban, according to the panel and the Appellate Body, amounts to a "zero quota," and this constitutes a quantitative limitation within the meaning of Article XVI:2(a) and (c).[132]

As Pauwelyn pointed out,[133] the implication of this confusing ruling is the risk of equalizing the "zero quota effect" of a licensing or qualification requirement (that is a nonquantitative restriction) with a numerical quota (that is a real quantitative limitation). To be sure, the concept that market access and domestic regulation are "mutually exclusive" is overly simplified and at odds with administrative operations in the real world. The key, as commentators have suggested, is to make a distinction between the US regulations in *U.S. – Gambling*, that is, a blanket prohibition that bans gambling services suppliers to zero with respect to all cross-border trade, and other situations under which domestic regulation is of a "less drastic quantitative effect."[134] To conclude, recognizing the

commitment after its entry into force." In the view of the Panel, if a Member does not specify a time-frame, "implementation must be deemed to be concurrent with the entry into force of the commitment." Panel Report, *Mexico – Telecom*, para. 4.137.

129 Appellate Body Report, *U.S. – Gambling*, para. 83.

130 *Ibid.*

131 *Ibid.*, paras. 257–265.

132 *Ibid.*

133 Joost Pauwelyn, "Rien ne va plus? Distinguishing Domestic Regulation from Market Access in GATT and GATS" (2005) 4 World Trade Review 131, at 133.

134 *Ibid.*, *Cf.*, Panagiotis Delimatsis, *International Trade in Services and Domestic Regulations: Necessity, Transparency, and Regulatory Diversity* (Oxford University Press 2007), at 140.

"zero quota" interpretation will be potentially problematic for every domestic regulation that has the "effect" of restricting market access. Therefore, "zero quota" arguments should be used in very limited cases in which the quantitative impact of a licensing/qualification requirement is extreme.

3.5.3 "Market Access Commitments" Matter

Focusing on the rulings from the *U.S. – Gambling* case, to what extent can a WTO member regulate digital platforms assuming, *arguendo*, that such a service is covered by the member's GATS Schedule of Commitments? If the standard of review set by *U.S. – Gambling* remains the precedent-setting case on the quantity/quality dichotomy,[135] how far can domestic regulation go without causing the "zero quota effect" and therefore falling within the scope of Article XVI of the GATS? The following two scenarios related to Teleland and Digiland – both of which are WTO members – demonstrate the relationship between market access and domestic regulation when it comes to platform regulations.

> Scenario one: Teleland decided to prohibit transactions with Digiland-originated mobile apps, referring to them as significant threats to national security and privacy protection. Among the most popular of the banned apps was Let'sTalk, the messaging service owned by Digiland's Superdigital Holding. The government overseeing Teleland cited national security concerns as the justification for the bans, flagging the data-collecting activities of Let'sTalk and the potential for the Digiland government to obtain Teleland citizens' personal information. Let'sTalk was removed from the app stores and was no longer available for download in Teleland. In addition, the Ministry of Information Technology of Teleland issued a blocking order directing telecommunications companies, including the 5G operators and other ISPs, to block access to Let'sTalk.

> Scenario two: Amid COVID-19, the considerable increase in demand for digital services, including e-education and e-health, led to an equivalent increase in data volumes in Teleland. At the same time, the social distancing policy dramatically boosted the demand for streaming entertainment content, which strained the telecommunications infrastructure in Teleland. Netfly, which is owned by Digiland's Techmedia Holding, is

135 Note that many recent FTAs require their dispute settlement panels to "take into account relevant interpretations in reports of WTO panels and the WTO Appellate Body." See, for example, Article 26.22 (Rules of interpretation) of the EU–NZ FTA.

the dominant subscription streaming TV service in Teleland. In order to alleviate network congestion, the telecom regulator of Teleland issued an order requiring ISPs to prioritize traffic associated with e-education and e-health over traffic from streaming TV services. The order effectively reduced Netfly's network traffic in Teleland by 40 percent, which affected its quality of service and led to a substantial drop in subscribers.

Suppose that Teleland's GATS Schedule of Specific Commitments includes full market access commitments in the relevant sectors on Modes 1 and 3. In these hypothetical cases, the critical question is whether the two measures in dispute – the blocking in scenario one and the throttling in scenario two – constitute market access limitations to cross-border supply pursuant to Article XVI:2 of the GATS. Following the approach of the Appellate Body, Digiland could argue that the ban on Let'sTalk, which amounts to a "zero quota," constitutes a "limitation on the number of services suppliers in the form of numerical quotas" within the meaning of Article XVI:2(a). The issue in scenario two, on the other hand, is less straightforward. Although Teleland's network management has reduced Netfly's network traffic by 40 percent, it does not result in the "zero quota," as the streaming TV service may still operate in Teleland.

To conclude, market access commitment matters. Once full market access commitments are made, the quantitative impact of a member's domestic regulation, if it cannot be justified under general or security exceptions, should not be too extreme. Domestic regulation might be considered a market access limitation simply because it has a substantial "quantitative effect." The broad reading of Article XVI of the GATS in WTO jurisprudence has to some extent intruded upon the regulatory autonomy of WTO members.

3.6 Conclusion

Digitalization, datafication, and platformization were unforeseen phenomena when WTO members made the GATS market access commitments. However, as evidenced by the *U.S. – Gambling* and *China – Audiovisual Services* disputes, these decades-old commitments have certainly played more than a marginal role in the story of the evolution of global datafication. Regardless of whether or not it is a "historical accident," members have undertaken the obligations through the GATS market access commitments, effectively leaving the door open for big tech companies. In view of those market access commitments, international trade liberalization must be accompanied by the introduction of new domestic regulation to address the potential risks and harms. As explained by Cohen,[136] "the emergence of platform-based business models has reshaped ... the consumption of goods and services." Chapters 4 and 5 will continue to address how platformization may have caused problems – including information manipulation, data capitalism, and algorithm discrimination – that a state cannot easily police.

[136] Julie E. Cohen, "Law for the Platform Economy" (2017) 51 U.C. Davis Law Review 133, at 137.

4

Data as Speech and Expression

Trade Aspects of Media Content Regulation

4.1 Introduction

Digital media content regulation represents a striking aspect of the dilemmas facing governments in the age of datafication. For decades, the audiovisual sector has traditionally been heavily regulated.[1] Given the high social and cultural importance of the sector, sector-specific audiovisual measures usually include, among others, free speech safeguards, cultural diversification screen quotas, regulations concerning the protection of minors, content controls, must-carry rules, advertising restrictions, product placement rules, public service obligations, production subsidization rules, foreign ownership limitations, and taxation policies.[2] In conjunction with the trends toward datafication and platformization, debates surrounding media policy are now shifting to the ambit of digital content governance.

Given their power to datafy a social phenomenon, digital platforms have become important gateways – and the main gateway in most places of the world – through which the public accesses and disseminates media content. How, then, can we regulate the "media sector" in a digital world? At this moment, regulators all over the world are struggling with whether to impose more responsibilities on online platforms, so as to create a fairer and safer digital space where the "new media" on the Internet can fulfill its broader democratic and cultural functions. Moreover, a closely related technologically challenging issue is how to address the jurisdiction problem and ensure that "domestic" regulation of "global" digital platforms can be effectively enforced.

1 Communication from Switzerland, "GATS 2000; Audio-visual Services, Council for Trade in Services" S/CSS/W/74 (4 May 2001).

2 Shin-yi Peng, "GATS and the Over-the-Top Services: A Legal Outlook" (2016) 50 (1) Journal of World Trade 21, at 40.

This chapter focuses on two angles – speech regulation and cultural policy – to explore the interplay between digital media content regulation and international economic law. First, when "data" is regarded as "speech," the interface between domestic media regulation and international trade rules is transformed into a highly political or even sensational topic, as it involves the national constitutional discourse against disproportionately regulating "speech." In many jurisdictions, speech must be narrowly regulated, and any speech regulation will inevitably involve complex policy questions surrounding to what extent it intrudes upon freedom of expression. That said, the proliferation of cyberbullying, hate speech, misinformation/disinformation,[3] fake news, and other harmful or illegal content on social media has become a major societal concern, which has apparently been shown to impact public interests. To what extent should platforms be accountable for such "speech" generated by individuals? At the same time, how can we prevent excessive blocking of user-generated content (UGC) such as Twitter (now called X) tweets and Facebook posts? The central concern of this chapter is to explore how international trade agreements interact with domestic platform regulations that address these problems.

Second, digital media content is of cultural significance, and the "culture v. trade" debate reaches another level of controversy when "data" is regarded as "cultural expression." Traditionally, the audiovisual sector – primarily television, film, and music – has been considered a venue reflecting the cultural and social characteristics of a nation and its people, as well as a means through which to present a nation's unique identity to the rest of the world.[4] Due to its cultural components,[5] the audiovisual sector has long played an important role in shaping the identity of heritage, promoting linguistic diversity, and contributing to

[3] The terms "misinformation" and "disinformation," although frequently used interchangeably, vary in the sense of the intent of the speaker/publisher. "Misinformation" refers to a situation in which the speakers/publishers do not know for certain that the information being spread is erroneous, while "disinformation" generally refers to misleading information that the speakers/publishers intentionally and maliciously spread to deceive audiences. See Canadian Center for Cyber Security, "How to Identify Misinformation, Disinformation, and Malinformation" (February 2022) <https://cyber.gc.ca/en/guidance/how-identify-misinformation-disinformation-and-malinformation-itsap00300>.

[4] See generally Joel Richard Paul, "Cultural Resistance to Global Governance" (2000) 22 Michigan Journal of International Law 1.

[5] Council for Trade in Services, Communication from United States, "Audiovisual Services" S/C/W/78 (December 8, 1998).

cultural diversity.[6] Today, video streaming services (VSS) are fast becoming a substitute for traditional "television" and have brought about tremendous challenges to media regulators. Policy debates include whether and to what extent VSS such as Netflix should be subject to existing television regulation, and in particular, the screen quota requirement that has been the main tool in cultural policy to guarantee market share for local content output and thus protect local culture.[7]

From the aspects of international economic law, questions regarding how a state regulates speech and promotes culture also involve a broad set of issues that may be subject to trade negotiations or dispute settlement. When data is generated as the by-product of other services, it can be a mere digital footprint; but when data communicates to affect opinions and change others' minds, it becomes speech and expression.[8] On the path toward a datafied world, currently UGC and VSS have become targets of national regulations that intend to protect free speech and culturally diverse expression. At the same time, they are at the crux of international trade negotiations that aim to promote the free flow of data.

4.2 Regulating UGC: Trade Aspects of Speech Regulation

4.2.1 Social Media Platforms: "Digital Town Square?"

UGC refers to "media content that is produced by users of that medium."[9] Today, UGC is primarily associated with the text, comments, images, and videos users have created and directly uploaded to digital platforms. Given its focus on openness and decentralization, UGC is essentially a form of self-expression, social participation, and democracy engagement,[10] which greatly differs from the "traditional" one-way

6 See Janet Blake, *International Cultural Heritage Law* (Oxford University Press 2015), at 194–229.

7 Peng, supra note 2, at 28.

8 See generally Jane Bambauer, "Is Data Speech?" (2014) 66 Stanford Law Review 57.

9 "User-Generated Content" refers to "Media content that is produced by users of that medium rather than by media professionals. Although traditional media have often included some UGC (*e.g.*, the letters page of a newspaper), the term is mainly associated with the new electronic media and embraces such phenomena as blogs, wikis, and digital video (YouTube)." Oxford Reference, "User-Generated Content" <https://www.oxfordreference.com/view/10.1093/oi/authority.20110803114939679>.

10 Anupam Chander, "Section 230 and the International Law of Facebook" (2022) 24 Yale Journal of Law & Technology 393, at 420 (analyzing the implications of big tech on global speech).

media structure of broadcaster/publisher to audience/reader. Nonetheless, the risks associated with defamation, mis-/disinformation, and other harmful or illegal behavior are becoming more and more challenging, as social media is now a critical component of most people's lives. The dynamic nature of UGC leads to the question of whether digital platforms, which act as "intermediaries" in facilitating user interaction, should be liable for UGC on their sites.

This question has been transformed into a matter of significant controversy in recent years, especially in the US, where social media was born and has been widely used in politics. The policy debate was fueled by Twitter's suspension of former US President Trump's account in response to his unsubstantiated tweet of election fraud. Social media's decision to deny Trump a platform was certainly a move applauded by Trump's political opponents but criticized by free speech advocates.[11] More recently, a Texas law prohibiting large social media companies from taking down UGC based on their political viewpoints went into effect after the 5th US Circuit Court of Appeals gave the Texas social media law a green light.[12] The legal battle, of course, is not over yet. The Supreme Court may still reject the Fifth Circuit's decision and strike down the Texas social media law. In any event, what's behind those sensational news headlines is the question of to what extent datafication-enabled content moderation on social media platforms counts as "censorship."

Placing these issues in the political economy context, what do we want social media platforms – today's global public square – to look like? Additionally, how have different approaches emerged in different countries? Should platform content moderation extend to "lawful but awful" UGC? If so, whose judgment holds on "awful content"? Elon Musk, in a statement about the acquisition of Twitter, described Twitter as "the digital town square, where matters vital to the future of humanity are

[11] Former US President Trump pressed Congress to completely repeal Section 230 of the US Communications Decency Act (CDA 230). He also instructed the FCC through an executive order – the legality of which was in question – to clarify whether certain behavior by social media platforms constitutes actions taken in good faith. See Administration of Donald J. Trump, "Executive Order 13925: Preventing Online Censorship" (May 28, 2020) <www.govinfo.gov/content/pkg/DCPD-202000404/pdf/DCPD-202000404.pdf>.

[12] See, for example, Jesus Vidales, "Texas Social Media 'Censorship' Law Goes Into Effect After Federal Court Lifts Block" (*The Texas Tribune*, September 16, 2022).

debated."[13] Such an ambition to create a speech platform that allows unfettered free speech has been criticized as "a complete fantasy."[14] Social media platforms are important forums for speech, but an unregulated forum may discourage the free exchange of speech. As discussed below, Section 230 of the US Communications Decency Act (CDA 230) serves as the best example of such a dilemma.[15]

4.2.2 Speech-Platform Liability for UGC: The Dilemma of the US CDA 230

In most jurisdictions, "traditional media," such as newspaper publishers and television stations, can be held liable for publishing or broadcasting harmful or illegal content. The emergence of UGC in the 1990s, however, disrupted the media landscape and brought about the question of whether digital services suppliers should be liable for third-party content on their services.[16] In the US, where free speech enjoys relatively stronger constitutional protections in the world, one leading case in this regard is Stratton Oakmont v. Prodigy Services,[17] in which the court ruled that Prodigy – a digital bulletin board services supplier – could be held liable for the "speech of their users."[18] In the view of the court, Prodigy had become a "publisher" because it voluntarily deleted some users' offensive messages from its bulletin board. As a result, it was liable for other users' defamatory postings on its service, which it had failed to take

[13] See, for example, Pascale Davies, "Why does Elon Musk want Twitter?" (*Euronews*, October 28, 2022).

[14] See Jean Burgess, "The "Digital Town Square?" What Does It Mean When Billionaires Own the Online Spaces Where We Gather?" (*The Conversation*, April 27, 2022).

[15] Communications Decency Act of 1996 Section 230, 47 U.S.C. Section 230 (CDA 230). Section 230(c): "Protection For 'Good Samaritan' Blocking and Screening of Offensive Material. (1) Treatment of Publisher or Speaker.—No provider or user of an interactive computer service shall be treated as the publisher or speaker of any information provided by another information content provider. (2) Civil Liability.—No provider or user of an interactive computer service shall be held liable on account of— (A) any action voluntarily taken in good faith to restrict access to or availability of material that the provider or user considers to be obscene, lewd, lascivious, filthy, excessively violent, harassing, or otherwise objectionable, whether or not such material is constitutionally protected; or (B) any action taken to enable or make available to information content providers or others the technical means to restrict access to material described in [subparagraph (A)]."

[16] Chander, supra note 10, at 406–416 (explaining how CDA 230 provides legal protection from platform liability).

[17] Stratton Oakmont v. Prodigy Servs. Co., N.Y. Sup. Ct. May 24, 1995.

[18] *Ibid.*

down.[19] In this particular case, the fact that Prodigy moderated "some" offensive or indecent content made it a "publisher," and therefore it could be held liable for "all" content, regardless of whether or not it moderated all of its content. In other words, those services that did not screen any content risked less liability than those that screened some or all content. Against this backdrop, the US Congress enacted the CDA 230 to protect "interactive computer services" (*e.g.*, digital speech platforms) from defamation lawsuits over UGC.[20]

The protection under the CDA 230 is twofold: Digital platforms cannot be held liable if they choose not to moderate UGC and, at the same time, digital platforms cannot be held liable if they choose to moderate UGC. To illustrate, the twofold protection can be summarized as follows: First, CDA 230 grants speech platforms such as Facebook (Meta) or Twitter immunity from liability that is based on their treatment, "as the publisher or speaker," of any content posted by their users. As a result, when a user's posts or tweets defame a third party, any defamation claim against the platforms would be barred by CDA 230.[21] To a great extent, such an immunity "negates" the duty of platforms to actively monitor material on their sites and allows them to ignore hate speech, misinformation, and other dangerous or harmful content. Second, CDA 230 grants speech platforms immunity from filtering UGC that it finds "objectionable" without incurring liability for doing so. In other words, speech platforms have the freedom, through their "content moderation" process, to keep the content they see fit, as well as to remove the content they consider "unlawful conduct or harassment."[22] Users generally do not have any remedies if the platforms take down the content "in good faith."[23]

CDA 230 has incited immense controversy over the past quarter century. Many scholarly writings have explained how the US courts have stretched CDA 230's plain language and granted (over)broad, if not absolute, immunity, which is not supported by the CDA's congressional

[19] *Ibid.* See also Adam Candeub, "Reading Section 230 as Written" (2021) 1 Journal of Free Speech Law 139, at 142.

[20] 47 U.S.C. Section 230(f)(2). The CDA defines "interactive computer service" as "any information service, system, or access software provider that provides or enables computer access by multiple users to a computer server."

[21] See generally Gregory M. Dickinson, "Rebooting Internet Immunity" (2021) 89 George Washington Law Review 347.

[22] See, for example, Twitter, "Terms of Service" <https://twitter.com/en/tos>.

[23] 47 U.S.C. Section 230(c)(2).

intent of 1996.[24] By pointing out that the "benefit" of CDA 230 has been extended to mobile applications through expansive judicial interpretation, commentators have criticized the US courts for failing to consider the "outer limits" of CDA 230.[25] On the politics front, not surprisingly, CDA 230 has been a hot potato within and beyond the US, and its future at the time of this writing remains in flux. The dilemma facing policymakers is evident, as documented below.

On the one hand, opponents of CDA 230 argue that the Act allows platforms to turn a blind eye to hate speech, mis-/disinformation, and harassment on their sites. In particular, those platforms that lack the incentive to combat such activities may become breeding grounds for harmful UGC and thus threaten public interests.[26] At the same time, for those platforms that actively engage in content moderation, the Act's blanket immunity means that such platforms have broad discretion in determining whether certain speech is socially acceptable. As a result, some UGC may be prejudicially censored, including some controversial political speech that is constitutionally protected from government censorship. Critics of CDA 230 have pointed out that UGC is routinely subjected to arbitrary censorship by dominant platforms. These platforms may, when they wish, suppress users' expressions or even completely oust a user[27] – literally playing the role of "judges of truth." In fact, the scale of speech restrictions by large platforms is evident. Twitter, as an example, reported that from January to June of 2021, it removed 5,913,337 posts, among which 1,606,979 posts were deemed to constitute "hateful conduct."[28] Meta, as another example, reported that in the first quarter of 2022, it took action on 15.1 million Facebook posts and 3.4 million Instagram posts considered to constitute "hate speech" – one of its many content moderation standards.[29] Specifically, Meta alone removed 205,556 "hate speech" posts per day.[30]

[24] Michael L. Rustad and Thomas H. Koenig, "Creating a Public Health Disinformation Exception to CDA Section 230" (2021) 71 Syracuse Law Review 1255, at 1295–1299 (elaborating how the US federal court decisions have stretched the scope of CDA 230).

[25] Benjamin Edelman and Abbey Stemler, "From the Digital to the Physical: Federal Limitations on Regulating Online Marketplaces" (2019) 56 Harvard Journal on Legislation 142, at 176.

[26] Dickinson, supra note 21, at 362–364.

[27] Chander, supra note 10, at 7.

[28] Twitter, "Transparency: Rules Enforcement" (2021) <https://transparency.twitter.com/en/reports/rules-enforcement.html#2021-jan-jun>.

[29] Meta, "Transparency Center: Hate Speech" (2022) <https://transparency.fb.com/policies/community-standards/hate-speech/>.

[30] *Ibid.*

On the other end, supporters of CDA 230 have labeled it "the law that built the Internet."[31] They have credited the Act for playing "an indispensable role in facilitating the growth of the world's largest online platforms."[32] In their view, without such a "catalyst," the digital industry would never have become what it is today. They also believe that the immunity has incentivized social media to moderate UCG, which has significantly contributed to the protection of the Internet from objectionable content. Without such a safe harbor, platforms would have under-moderated to avoid being punished for policing content.[33] Moreover, the costs of moderating UGC do not deter the growth of platforms because they are not required to police all content.

In any event, it is worth underscoring that CDA 230, together with other factors, makes the US a haven for social media. It is apparent that the Act has given a distinctive boost to digital platform services for UGC that impact the daily lives of most people. It goes without saying that big tech has repeatedly and vigorously defended CDA 230. Any efforts to narrow the broad immunity it provides will prompt significant opposition from those tech giants,[34] as evidenced by their recent strong resistance to the Texas social media law. The controversy surrounding CDA 230 is now reaching a fevered pitch, which raises the question of whether digital platforms can be immunized when they algorithmically "recommend" UGC. As Chapter 5 will further explore, when a platform's algorithmic system promotes specific UGC, is such an action of algorithmic amplification still protected by CDA 230? Indeed, the operation of CDA 230 has gone far beyond its legislative intent in creating such immunity.

4.2.3 Exporting Speech Regulation: Immunity Abroad?

Of course, the fire from the battle over CDA 230 is not limited to the US, as large platforms would grab any opportunity throughout the world to advance their agenda of immunity protection. It is no secret that big tech firms have attempted to influence trade negotiations. From CPTPP to USMCA to IPEF, big tech companies have been advocating for digital

31 Susan Benkelman, "The Law That Made the Internet What It Is Today" (*The Washington Post*, April 26, 2019).

32 Isaac Rounseville, "Drawing A Line: Legislative Proposals To Clarify the CDA, Reinforce Consumer Rights, and Establish a Uniform Policy For Online Marketplaces" (2020) 60 (4) Jurimetrics 263.

33 *Ibid.*

34 Edelman and Stemler, supra note 25, at 193–194.

trade rules that "overwhelmingly favor their interests."[35] To further pursue their "digital trade agenda," big tech firms have been lobbying,[36] perhaps through "behind-the-scenes access to the trade officials," to push for trade rules that protect their interests.[37] If the allegation of Warren and other US lawmakers is true, the Office of the US Trade Representative (USTR) has been granting "insider status" to Amazon and Google lobbyists throughout the stages of international trade negotiations.

The "footprint" of CDA 230 has been extended to US-led international trade agreements, and in particular, the US–Japan Digital Trade Agreement and the USMCA.[38] Moreover, CDA 230-like immunity can be found in the consolidated negotiating text of the ongoing WTO JSI on E-Commerce.[39] More specifically, for example, Article 18(3) of the US–Japan Digital Trade Agreement mimics CDA 230(c), which protects digital platforms from liability for voluntarily removing harmful or objectionable content in good faith. Additionally, similar to CDA 230, the bilateral trade deal contains exceptions for enforcing intellectual property rights, criminal law, or other lawful orders of a law enforcement authority.[40] It should be noted, however, that the US and Japan have agreed to a side letter, in which the parties recognize that there are differences between their "respective legal systems governing the liability of interactive computer services suppliers"[41] and have therefore agreed that Japan need not "change its existing legal system, including laws,

[35] Office of Senator Elizabeth Warren, "Big Tech's Big Con: Rigging Digital Trade Rules to Block Antitrust Regulation" (May 2023) <www.warren.senate.gov/imo/media/doc/USTR%20REPORT.pdf>.

[36] *Ibid.* See also Ariel Ezrachi and Maurice Stucke, *Virtual Competition: The Promise and Perils of the Algorithm-Driven Economy* (Harvard University Press 2016), at 244–246.

[37] *Ibid.*, at 5. Big tech companies push for trade rules to "protect their interests – defending their monopolistic, self-dealing, discriminatory AI algorithms, and abuse of consumer… privacy" as stated by Warren's office.

[38] The US–Japan Digital Trade Agreement establishes relatively high-standard rules in digital trade. For the treaty text and the Side Letter on Interactive Computer Services, see US–Japan Digital Trade Agreement <https://ustr.gov/countries-regions/japan-korea-apec/japan/us-japan-trade-agreement-negotiations/us-japan-digital-trade-agreement-text>.

[39] This book was written during 2021 fall to 2023 spring, during which the WTO JSI on E-Commerce was still under negotiations, and the negotiating results remain uncertain.

[40] US–Japan Digital Trade Agreement, Article 18.

[41] *Ibid.*, the Side Letter on Interactive Computer Services between Ambassador of Japan Mr. Sugiyama Shinsuke and US Ambassador Mr. Robert E. Lighthizer (October 7, 2019).

regulations, and judicial decisions, governing the liability of interactive computer services suppliers,"[42] in order to comply with Article 18 of the bilateral trade deal. As a result, the side letter has literally negated Japan's treaty obligations to amend its platform liability law.

Just months after the signing of the US–Japan Digital Trade Agreement, the USTR continuously extended CDA 230 to its neighbors through Article 19.17 of the USMCA. In particular, Article 19.17(3), which is virtually identical to Article 18(3) of the US–Japan Digital Trade Agreement, once again mirrors the language of CDA 230(c)(2)(a).[43] Considering that neither Canada nor Mexico have a comparable statute in effect that covers the same grounds or provides the same protections as those afforded under the CDA 203, USMCA Article 19.17 can be seen as a tool to broaden the landscape of the CDA – "exporting" the US policy to the North and South.[44] Questions have therefore been raised regarding whether the expansion of the CDA 203 can be seen as a form of "American imperialism."[45]

Nonetheless, it is too soon to say that Canada and Mexico are now obligated to enact a CDA 230-equivalent statute at home, and that the US has successfully transplanted its controversial social media immunity abroad.[46] As a matter of fact, the real ramifications of USMCA Article 19.17(3) might be less apparent when reading other provisions together. Footnote 7 of the Digital Trade Chapter of the USMCA clarifies that a party may comply with Article 19.17 "through its laws, regulations, or

[42] *Ibid.*

[43] USMCA, Article 19.17(3): "No Party shall impose liability on a supplier or user of an interactive computer service on account of: (a) any action voluntarily taken in good faith by the supplier or user to restrict access to or availability of material that is accessible or available through its supply or use of the interactive computer services and that the supplier or user considers to be harmful or objectionable; or (b) any action taken to enable or make available the technical means that enable an information content provider or other persons to restrict access to material that it considers to be harmful or objectionable."

[44] As elaborated by the Council on Foreign Relations in the policy brief, leading US tech companies have pushed to "export Section 230 via U.S. trade deals." Anshu Siripurapu, "Trump and Section 230: What to Know, the Council on Foreign Relations" (December 2, 2020) <www.cfr.org/in-brief/trump-and-section-230-what-know>.

[45] Chander, supra note 10, at 416.

[46] Cf., Eric Goldman, "Five Things to Know about Section 230" (2021) Center for International Governance Innovation <www.cigionline.org/articles/five-things-to-know-about-section-230/>.

application of existing legal doctrines as applied through judicial decisions." This raises the question of whether Canadian case law is sufficient for compliance with USMCA Article 19.17.[47] More importantly, it is not immediately apparent if the rulings of the Canadian courts will consistently result in broad CDA-style immunity for social media, as was the case among US judges.[48] After all, as discussed above, today's broad immunity stemming from CDA 230 is actually the product of expansive judicial interpretations of US courts. The mere fact that the US has transplanted the legislative text of the CDA 230 to the USMCA does not necessarily mean that the judicial interpretations of the US courts will guide the rulings of the Canadian courts.[49]

In conclusion, with respect to the question of whether Article 19.17 of the USMCA is a big win for big tech, the answer is: perhaps, if the seeds planted continue to increase in size and gain strength.[50] In view of this, the ongoing WTO e-commerce trade negotiations represent a key battle that could set the tone for the future of platform immunities. Currently, CDA 230-like immunity can be found in the negotiating text of the WTO JSI on E-Commerce. The US-proposed language for "interactive computer services" clearly tracks Article 18 of the US–Japan Digital Trade Agreement and Article 19.17 of the USMCA.[51] Paradoxically, the USTR continues to embrace and propagate CDA 230-like platform immunities in international trade agreements, no matter how much political controversy the Act stirs up at home.

47 USMCA, Article 19.17, Footnote 7.

48 Sonja Solomun et al., "Platform Responsibility and Regulation in Canada: Considerations on Transparency, Legislative Clarity, and Design" (2021) 34 Harvard Journal of Law & Technology 1, at 10 (explaining how Canada will comply with Article 19.17 of the USMCA).

49 Vivek Krishnamurthy et al., "CDA 230 Goes North American? Examining the Impacts of the USMCA's Intermediary Liability Provisions in Canada and the United States" (2020) The Samuelson-Glushko Canadian Internet Policy and Public Interest Clinic (examining the impact of the USMCA on the intermediary liability regimes in Canada); Amir Eftekharpour, "Demystified: USMCA"s Digital trade Provisions on ISP Liability in Canada" (arguing that ISP immunity in Canada may develop in line with current Canadian law) <www.jdsupra.com/legalnews/demystified-usmca-s-digital-trade-40676/>.

50 Note that the US has pursued similar platform immunity provisions in trade negotiations with the United Kingdom and other countries, although negotiations had not been completed at the time of this writing.

51 Inside US Trade, "WTO E-commerce Text: Section 230 Language, Exceptions to Data Rules" (February 12, 2021).

4.2.4 *Platform Content Moderation: Regulatory Landscape and Trade Governance*

4.2.4.1 UGC Moderation under the DSA: The Gold Standard?

The potential for the CDA 230 to morph into a global standard for platform governance is further diminished under the EU's accelerating effort to regulate digital platforms' content moderation.[52] Aiming to establish a benchmark for platform regulation at the global level, the "rules-based" platform governance model led by the EU is now a strong power in balancing CDA-based social media self-regulation. In a nutshell, transatlantic digital fragmentation has been bolstered by the DSA. On the other side of the Atlantic, the EU's DSA has introduced a new set of obligations for online platforms. By setting high standards for effective intervention, the DSA increases the obligations of platforms and the powers of regulators, and it also empowers users to report illegal content in an easier way and challenge platforms' content moderation decisions.[53]

In particular, depending on the function and size of a digital services supplier, the DSA provides "cumulative obligations" – the larger a supplier is, and the more "critical" the services it supplies, the more obligations apply. Specifically, the DSA distinguishes between four tiers – intermediary services, hosting services, online platforms, and VLOPs – and applies asymmetric obligations to each tier.[54] Such a classification features four risk categories, and the DSA imposes increasingly severe obligations pursuant to the principle of proportionality. Accordingly, VLOPs and very large online search engines (VLOSEs), defined by the DSA as online platforms and online search engines providing more than 45 million average monthly active users in the EU (which represents

[52] The DSA is designed to provide a single, uniform legal framework across the EU. For example, Germany's Network Enforcement Act (known as NetzDG), which requires social media companies with two million users to remove "manifestly unlawful" content within 24 hours of receiving a complaint, has been criticized for forcing platforms to censor potentially lawful speech due to the short takedown periods and the heavy penalties. See Anupam Chander and Haochen Sun, "Sovereignty 2.0" (2021) Georgetown Law Faculty Publications and Other Works (2021).

[53] EU Monitor, "Explanatory Memorandum to COM (2020)825: Single Market for Digital Services (Digital Services Act)" (2020) <www.eumonitor.eu/9353000/1/j4nvhdfdk3hydzq_j9vvik7m1c3gyxp/vlenigitokp2>.

[54] EU DisinfoLab, "User-Guide to the EU Digital Services Act" (October 2022) <www.disinfo.eu/wp-content/uploads/2022/11/20221020_DSAUserGuide_Final.pdf>, at 3.

10 percent of the 450 million users in the EU market), are subject to the most broad and stringent requirements.[55] The EU legislative documents stress that very large players are emerging as "quasi-public spaces" for the exchange of information in this digital age, which may "pose particular risks for users' rights, information flows and public participation."[56] As such, they should "take mitigating measures at the level of the overall organisation of their service" to facilitate public debate, and to influence how people obtain information online.[57]

Regarding content moderation of UGC, the DSA obliges online platforms to remove illegal content upon the receipt of an order issued by relevant authorities.[58] Online platforms are also required to put user-friendly mechanisms into place to allow any individual to notify them of any illegal content on their sites.[59] They are required to include information on "any policies, procedures, measures and tools used for the purpose of content moderation, including algorithmic decision-making and human review" in their terms and conditions.[60] Moreover, the DSA imposes transparency reporting obligations on platforms, including the publication of "easily comprehensible and detailed reports on any content moderation they engaged in during the relevant period,"[61] which includes "any use made of automatic means for the purpose of content moderation."[62] Furthermore, the DSA imposes additional obligations on VLOPs to manage risks.[63] They are required to carry out regular assessments of the systemic risks stemming from their services. When conducting risk assessments, they should take into account how their content moderation systems influence the dissemination of illegal content.[64] Further, they have an obligation to take measures to mitigate any systemic risks.[65]

[55] DSA, Article 33 (very large online platforms).

[56] European Commission, "Questions and Answers: Digital Services Act" (November 14, 2022) <https://ec.europa.eu/commission/presscorner/detail/en/QANDA_20_2348>.

[57] *Ibid.* Note that smaller social media platforms fall within the scope of "online platforms" that also have important obligations.

[58] DSA, Article 9.

[59] DSA, Article 16.

[60] DSA, Article 14.

[61] DSA, Article 15.

[62] DSA, Article 15.

[63] DSA, Section 5.

[64] DSA, Article 34.

[65] DSA, Article 35.

As a whole, the DSA represents a big move toward a rules-based cyberspace order. Contrary to the laissez-faire approach taken in the CDA 203, the DSA aims to turn the unfettered market for UGC into a more heavy-handed, regulated public square.[66] By requiring social media to carefully curb hate speech, disinformation, and other extreme and unsafe content on their sites or otherwise risk billions of dollars in fines, the DSA, to a large extent, ends the era of content moderation's self-regulation, in which speech platforms decide what content will be retained or removed based on their own unilaterally imposed policies.

4.2.4.2 Moving toward a Rules-Based Digital Order? The Elephant(s) in the Room

It should be noted that digital platforms established outside of the EU that offer their services in the EU are also subject to the obligations under the DSA. In April 2023, the EC officially designated the first batch of VLOPs and VLOSEs.[67] These big tech and other powerful firms will have to meet new EU requirements, including submitting yearly audits of systemic risks linked to their services. Needless to say, big tech firms boosted their EU lobbying in 2021–2022, during which the DSA was under discussion by the European Parliament and Council. With combined lobbyist spending of over 27 million euros in one year,[68] big tech certainly tried to influence EU policymaking on platform governance. At the end of the day, however, the EU's "unilateral global governance," as framed by Krisch,[69] "targets U.S. companies."[70] Brussels eventually put the brakes on big tech's uncontrolled power over content moderation.

66 See Olivier Sylvain, "Platform Realism, Informational Inequality, and Section 230 Reform" (2021) 131 Yale Law Journal 475, at 486–487 (pointing out that the unregulated market for interactive computer services has promoted experimentation and innovation).

67 European Commission, "DSA: Very Large Online Platforms and Search Engines" (April 25, 2023) <https://digital-strategy.ec.europa.eu/en/policies/dsa-vlops>. The EC designated the following platforms as VLOPs: Alibaba, Amazon, Apple, Booking, Facebook, Google Maps, Google Play, Google Shopping, Instagram, LinkedIn, Pinterest, Snapchat, TikTok, Twitter, Wikipedia, YouTube, and Zalando. The EC also designated Bing and Google Search as VLOSEs.

68 Corporate Europe Observatory, "Big Tech's Last Minute Attempt to Tame EU Tech Rules: Lobbying in Times of Trilogues" (April 23, 2022) <https://corporateeurope.org/en/2022/04/big-techs-last-minute-attempt-tame-eu-tech-rules>.

69 Nico Krisch, "Jurisdiction Unbound: (Extra)territorial Regulation as Global Governance" (2022) 33(2) European Journal of International Law 481, at 513.

70 Kati Suominen, "Implications of the European Union's Digital Regulations on U.S. and EU Economic and Strategic Interests" Center for Strategic & International Studies

What is most concerning to international economic legal order is the question surrounding to what extent speech platform governance formulated by the DSA will serve as a landmark that drives regulatory efforts beyond Europe. Under the trends of datafication, there is worldwide concern that states are no longer capable of regulating data.[71] The DSA is now serving to spur a rules-based Internet. Countries such as Singapore and Taiwan have attempted to follow the EU's example in regulating platforms with respect to UGC moderation.[72] The years to come will be critical to the global governance of digital platforms. Key indicators include whether more and more countries will adopt DSA-like regulations along the EU regulatory path, whether the implementation of the DSA will have the same global influence as the General Data Protection Regulation (GDPR) does, and whether the EU's accelerating "strategic autonomy" may effectively suppress the spread of the CDA 230 and eventually change the distribution of power in the social media ecosystem.

Of course, platform governance is not only about the US' CDA model and the EU's DSA model. The dispute between Twitter and the Indian government serves as a typical case pointing toward the bumpy road ahead for the global governance of speech platforms. India's Section 69 (A) of the Information Technology Act allows authorities to issue blocking orders to social media intermediaries.[73] Blocking orders can be issued for, among other reasons, the "public order" of India's society. Such discretionary power has been a major tool for the government of India to place pressure on big tech, as a social media services supplier can face criminal action and risk losing access to the Indian market for not complying with an order to take down certain content.[74] In July 2022, Twitter initiated legal action in the Indian administrative court for a

(November 2022) <https://csis-website-prod.s3.amazonaws.com/s3fs-public/2023-02/221122_EU_DigitalRegulations-3.pdf?VersionId=04r7zBzS2kHNhsISAqn4NkC6lGNgip7S>, at 30.

71 European Parliament, "Digital Sovereignty for Europe" (July 2020) <www.europarl.europa.eu/RegData/etudes/BRIE/2020/651992/EPRS_BRI(2020)651992_EN.pdf>, at 4.

72 On June 29, 2022, the National Communications Commission (NCC) of Taiwan released a draft of the Digital Intermediary Services Act, which aims to establish greater accountability for social media platforms and refers to the EU's Digital Services Act. The draft Digital Intermediary Services Act has led to polarized reactions from the public and is now on hold.

73 Section 69 of India's Information Technology Act.

74 Billy Perrigo, "India's New Internet Rules Are a Step Toward Digital Authoritarianism" (*Time*, March 12, 2021).

judicial review of such orders,[75] claiming that blocking orders from the Indian government are procedurally and substantively deficient under Section 69 (A) of the Information Technology Act. Twitter alleged that Indian officials have abused their power, failed to meet the procedural requirements, and fallen short in demonstrating how the content at issue is under the purview of Section 69 (A). Additionally, Twitter argued that in many cases, the orders were "disproportionate, overbroad and arbitrary."[76]

There are other, even larger elephants in the room. Russia recently fined Google millions of USD for not deleting banned content on YouTube,[77] not to mention China's data governance regime, which has long been the key cause of the fragmentation of global data policies.[78] There are also many smaller elephants in the room, such as Vietnam and Myanmar, which have mirrored the Chinese authoritarian model of data governance.[79] Ultimately, these competing models of platform governance will use international trade instruments, most likely through e-commerce/digital trade provisions, to influence other countries' digital policies.

4.3 Regulating VSS: Trade Aspects of Cultural Policy

4.3.1 Global Dominance of the Streaming Platforms: Cut the Cord!

Now turning to the other angle of digital media content regulation – cultural expression on VSS. There are different terms used to describe broad and unique types of streaming platforms, which are often based on their business models. For the purpose of this chapter, "video streaming services," as defined by the Body of European Regulators for Electronic Communications (BEREC)[80] and the Australian Communications and Media Authority (ACMA), refers to the "streaming of video content over

75 Karan Deep Singh and Kate Conger, "Twitter, Challenging Orders to Remove Content, Sues India's Government" (*The New York Times*, July 5, 2022).

76 *Ibid.*

77 "Russia Fines Google $370 Million for Repeated Content Violations" (*Reuters*, July 19, 2022).

78 See generally Henry Gao, "Digital or Trade? The Contrasting Approaches of China and US to Digital Trade" (2018) 21(2) Journal of International Economic Law 297.

79 See Gerard McDermott and Alice Larsson, "The Quiet Evolution of Vietnam's Digital Authoritarianism" (*The Diplomat*, November 19, 2022) (describing a new system of digital surveillance and control that has emerged in Vietnam).

80 See generally Body of European Regulators for Electronic Communications (BEREC), "Draft BEREC Report on the Internet Ecosystem" BoR (22)87 (June 9, 2022) <www.berec.europa.eu/en>, at 29, 52.

the public Internet," which provides "professionally produced content – either by the in-house film studios or through licensing deals, including on-demand services and/or linear content."[81] This content is subscription-based[82] and ad-supported.[83] Unlike traditional audiovisual services such as broadcasting or cable television stations, for which video transmission requires a television aerial, a satellite dish, a set-top box, or a coaxial cable to connect to the services, VSS, such as Netflix, Disney+, Amazon Prime, or iQIYI, are delivered over the public Internet. Simply put, VSS allow audiences to bypass traditional distribution and thus "cut the cord."[84]

Digital media content has changed the landscape of the television industry. The increasing availability of public Wi-Fi, faster broadband Internet speeds, and unlimited mobile data plans offered by telecommunications operators have bolstered the growth of VSS. Dominant VSS platforms such as Netflix are transforming the prospects of the audiovisual industry and are now commonly considered a ready substitute for traditional television.[85] By way of illustration, in the US, VSS have significantly cut into cable's market share, reducing the number of cable subscriptions from 85 percent of households in 2015 to 71 percent in 2021.[86] More and more people are turning to VSS for their television consumption, which had reached a US household penetration rate of 80 percent by March 2022.[87] The television landscape continues to transform, and this transformation has gone international.[88]

[81] ACMA, "Supporting Australian Stories on Our Screen-Options Paper" (March 2020) <www.infrastructure.gov.au/have-your-say/supporting-australian-stories-our-screens-options-paper>.

[82] VSS are typically provided on the basis of a catalogue of programs selected by the media services suppliers in exchange for payment, that is, subscription video streaming services such as Netflix, or are delivered in bundles of other services such as Amazon Prime Video. BEREC, "Report on Harmonized Definitions for Indicators Regarding Over-the-Top Services" BoR (21) 127 (30 September 2021).

[83] These include Hulu, Disney+, and iQIYI, China's second-largest video streaming platform.

[84] Cord-cutting refers to consumers cancelling their traditional cable services and switching to VSS. See generally Bastiaan Baccarne et al., "The Television Struggle: An Assessment of Over-the-Top Television Evolutions in a Cable Dominant Market" (2013) 92(4) Communications & Strategies 43.

[85] Shin-yi Peng, supra note 2, at 24–25.

[86] The Henry Fund Research, "Video Streaming Service Industry" (February 9, 2022).

[87] Insider Intelligence, "Top OTT Video Streaming Services in 2022 by Viewer Count and Growth" (March 18, 2022).

[88] See, for example, The UK's Department for Digital, Culture, Media & Sport, "Consultation Outcome Audience Protection Standards on Video-on-Demand Services" (April 28, 2022) <www.gov.uk/government/consultations/audience-protec

Cord-cutting is becoming the norm in the Asian-Pacific region. In South Korea, Netflix alone had more than 5 million subscribers by June 2022.[89] In Japan, the VSS market, primarily offered by Amazon Prime Video, Netflix, and Disney+, had a total of 44 million subscribers as of the end of August 2021.[90] In Australia, approximately 71 percent of Australian adults had at least one subscription streaming service in their household in 2020.[91]

The trend of cord-cutting brought about new regulatory challenges for national media regulators. Television has traditionally played a major role in forming public opinion, shaping cultural identities, and promoting linguistic diversity, thus contributing significantly to social inclusion. Within the domestic legal framework, the sector has been heavily regulated.[92] The justification for such heavy regulation of television content, however, has been weakened, because viewers of "traditional" television services also watch streaming content, which generally is not subject to the same regulation.[93] To illustrate, in most jurisdictions, there is a major dichotomy between (traditional) regulated television and (modern) unregulated video streaming services. In other words, although facing a looming regulatory storm, to a large extent, VSS remain totally unregulated, existing in a "regulation-free zone."[94] Because VSS are steadily becoming a substitute for traditional television, policymakers are struggling over whether and how to eliminate regulatory distinctions that have left traditional television services suppliers handicapped in the face of streaming services. Should existing media regulations be extended to manage streaming services? Here, an important consideration that further complicates this regulatory issue is the reality that for most countries – probably only except the US and China, where the dominant streaming services are run by domestic rather than foreign companies – such a regulatory dichotomy is literally about whether "foreign-owned"

tion-standards-on-video-on-demand-services/audience-protection-standards-on-video-on-demand-services#changing-landscape>.

[89] See, for example, Shirley Zhao and Lucas Shaw, "Netflix Needs New Subscribers" (*Business Standard*, January 14, 2022).

[90] See, for example, Patrick Brzeski, "Amazon Leads Netflix, Disney+ in Japan's Expanding Streaming Market" (*The Hollywood Reporter*, October 4, 2021).

[91] ACMA, supra note 81.

[92] Peng, supra note 2, at 40.

[93] CASBAA, "A Titled Playing Field: Asia-Pacific Pay TV and OTT" (2012) <www.casbaa.com/publication/a-tilted-playing-field-asia-pacific-pay-tv-and-ott/> (pointing out that viewers of cable television also watch streaming content).

[94] *Ibid.*, at 8.

VSS should be subject to the same regulations as local broadcasters and cable channels. Admittedly, there has been unequal competition between "foreign" streaming platforms and "domestic" television legacies. To translate this phenomenon into WTO language, most WTO members are the "importing countries" of VSS. However, VSS fall outside the scope of these countries' domestic media law. As a result, local broadcasters and cable channels are at a significant business disadvantage compared to foreign VSS suppliers in terms of local bureaucracy, legal compliance costs, and other content regulations. The tension is sharp.[95]

4.3.2 Leveling the Playing Field: Regulating Up or Down?

Traditional media services suppliers have been calling for a "level playing field," or fair conditions between competitors in the media industry. On the one hand, it is a commonly shared regulatory principle to "treat like services alike" and refrain from using regulations as a means of choosing technological winners. Media regulators should not discriminate against different business models or technological features. Unequal and differential regulatory treatment in favor of the streaming platforms may mean that the regulators inevitably choose winners in the media industry. The business environment is that VSS gain "unfair" advantages by bypassing existing media content regulations.[96] It can be said that the asymmetric regulation has impeded the ability of broadcasters and cable channels to compete with their online competitors. This raises the question of whether the same requirements should be imposed on all services suppliers competing in the audiovisual sector, no matter whether the services are supplied via a traditional or a platform-based method.[97]

Trade associations such as the Cable and Satellite Broadcasting Association of Asia (CASBAA) advocate that VSS should be categorized as television services and thus be subject to traditional broadcasting and/or cable rules. The association stresses that national regulators should "reduce regulatory asymmetries and foster competition" by "extending

[95] For a more detailed discussion, see Peng, supra note 2, at 40–41.

[96] Vanessa Katz, "Regulating the Sharing Economy" (2015) 30 Berkeley Technology Law Journal 1067, at 1072–1081.

[97] See generally Telecommunications Management Group, "Trends and Issues in Online Video Regulation in the Americas" (June 2021) <www.tmgtelecom.com/wp-content/uploads/2021/06/TMG-Trends-and-issues-in-online-video-regulation-in-the-Americas-June-2021.pdf>.

traditional regulation to online video services."[98] To promote the concept of a "level playing field,"[99] the British Broadcasting Corporation's (BBC) director-general has publicly stated that "TV-like" streaming services should be regulated to the same extent as the UK's traditional TV so as to promote British content and preserve cultural heritage.[100] Conversely, the VSS groups emphasize that traditional television and video streaming has "inherent technical and functional differences."[101] They argue that different viewer experiences are a key consideration in distinguishing streaming platforms from their offline analogues. Some believe that the even-handed approach is not only unnecessary, but also infeasible. Additionally, extending old regulations to new media platforms could potentially harm business innovation, which in the long run may cause the decline of "media pluralism."[102] The primary position is that regulators should not interfere with new services in order to protect "old" services.[103]

The question of whether the two types of services at issue should be required to meet the same standards involves the assessments of sector-specific policy objectives and market conditions under which legacy suppliers and digital platforms compete. In this regard, the Canadian Radio-television and Telecommunications Commission, while recognizing the need for a level playing field, ultimately decided that the two types of services at issue are "fundamentally different and warrant different regulatory treatment."[104] Similarly, the ACMA also decided not to expand legacy media regulations to online players. Alternatively, however, the government reduced several general regulatory obligations for the broadcasters so as to level the playing field.[105] In other words, instead of "regulating up," the Australian government reflected on the traditional

98 CASBAA, supra note 93, at 9.

99 Here, New Zealand represents an extreme case in that the same regulatory framework applies to both traditional television and VSS in a "technology-neutral" and "even-handed" manner. Asia Video Industry Association (AVIA), "OTT TV Policies in Asia" (2018) <https://avia.org/wp-content/uploads/2018/08/PUB-OTT-TV-Policies-in-Asia-2018.pdf>, at 19.

100 See, for example, Michael Savage, "BBC Chief Says TV Streaming Services Squeeze Out British Culture" (*The Guardian*, March 15, 2020).

101 Telecommunications Management Group, supra note 97, at 15.

102 *Ibid.*, at 17. See generally Henry Allen et al., "Media Pluralism: What Matters for Governance and Regulation?" (2017) 30(2) Journal of Media Economics 47.

103 Telecommunications Management Group, supra note 97, at 15.

104 *Ibid.*

105 *Ibid.*, at 25.

media regulations and pursued regulatory parity by "deregulating down" the requirements imposed on incumbents.

4.3.3 *Local Content Requirements on Netflix: Cultural Expression*

Nevertheless, there is a legislative trend across various jurisdictions to issue new regulations to impose local content and local investment requirements on video streaming platforms. In other words, although many countries have decided that existing media law should not be applied across the board to all, they have opted to impose local content requirements on digital platforms. In Europe, the amended Audiovisual Media Services Directive (AVMSD) requires member states to ensure that VSS maintain at least a 30 percent quota of "European works" in their catalogues, with an emphasis on "the prominence of those works."[106] In addition, the amended AVMSD permits member states to adopt measures to financially support European works, including direct investment in local content and contributions to national funds. Such financial contributions can only be based on the revenues earned in that member state and must consider other financial contributions levied by other member states.[107] Put simply, VSS, such as Netflix, Disney+, and Amazon Prime Video, must ensure that at least 30 percent of their libraries are dedicated to local content in the EU, either through production or licensing.[108] Moreover, they may be required to invest, directly or indirectly, in local content. As stressed in the background papers of the Directive amendment,[109] video streaming platforms directly compete with broadcasters but have circumvented the local content requirement. By imposing a minimum 30 percent quota on VSS, "European expression" and cultural diversity will be promoted. At the same time, by increasing the investment in original European content, local employment in the media industry will likely surge.[110]

[106] Audiovisual Media Services Directive (AVMSD 2018), Directive (EU) 2018/1808 of the European Parliament and of the Council of November 14, 2018, Article 13.1.

[107] AVMSD 2018, Articles 13.2 and 13.3.

[108] Arguably, in order to meet the quota, streaming platforms can simply reduce the size of their catalogues by limiting the content the viewers can access in Europe in order to decrease the denominator. The platforms can also add outdated local reruns by acquiring existing content from local producers.

[109] European Commission, "Shaping Europe's Digital Future: Audiovisual and Media Services" <https://digital-strategy.ec.europa.eu/en/policies/audiovisual-and-media-services>.

[110] *Ibid.* See also Piero Papp, "The Promotion of European Works: An Analysis on Quotas for European Audiovisual Works and their Effect on Culture and Industry" (2020) Stanford – Vienna Transatlantic Technology Law Forum Working Papers No. 50.

Under the mandate, some EU countries have introduced tailored legislation to implement AVMSD, while others are in the midst of transposing the AVMSD onto the domestic legal framework. For example, Spain requires VSS to reserve 30 percent of their catalogues for European works, and half of them must be spoken in the language of Spain.[111] The government of Portugal imposes an annual fee that levies 1 percent of VSS income to support Portuguese language film productions.[112] The French decree implementing the AVMSD obliges services suppliers of video streaming platforms to invest 20–25 percent of their revenue earned in France in local content. Similar requirements have been adopted in other EU member states, such as Italy and Switzerland.[113]

Outside of Europe, local content requirements for VSS have been carried out or are being considered by many countries, including Australia, Argentina, Canada, Mexico, and Taiwan, to name just a few.[114] In its policy consultation paper, the Australian media regulator pointed out that the ecosystem which supports domestic content is fading. Australian programs represent only 1.7 percent of titles for Netflix's entire catalogue. In spite of this, Australian viewers are increasingly ditching local broadcasters that rely on advertising revenue to survive. Without regulatory intervention, local broadcasters will soon become unable to produce Australian content to meet quota requirements.[115] The government is therefore aware of the urgent need to require VSS to make or source "quality Australian stories" that help Australians to "understand each other."[116]

In brief, more and more national media laws are deciding to impose local content requirements on streaming platforms, ranging from including a certain amount of local content in their catalogues, displaying a minimum percentage of content in the local language, producing a certain amount of media content locally, and making financial contributions to local content production.[117] Such a legislative trend, however,

[111] Joan Faus, "Spain to Force Streaming Platforms to Air Shows in Regional Languages" (*Reuters*, November 24, 2021).

[112] Branislav Pekic, "Portugal: SVoD Platforms to Pay 1% Annual Tax" (*Advanced Television*, August 26, 2021).

[113] John Revill, "Swiss Voters Approve "Lex Netflix" TV Streaming Funding Law" (*Reuters*, May 17, 2022).

[114] Telecommunications Management Group, supra note 97, at 29, 39.

[115] ACMA, supra note 81.

[116] *Ibid.*

[117] Telecommunications Management Group, supra note 97, at 14–20.

has been labeled a potential "trade barrier" by the US – the dominant "exporting country" of VSS – as it may impose an unnecessary compliance burden on digital platforms and limit global market access of VSS. This raises the question of whether the local content requirements placed on digital platforms violate obligations under international trade agreements, especially in the FTA context.[118]

4.3.4 *"Foreign" and "Domestic" Streaming Content: Definitions, Likeness, and Exceptions*

4.3.4.1 Performance Requirement: "Domestic" Streaming Content

First, a preliminary issue is how to define "domestic content" on video streaming platforms. How can we determine the "origin" of a streaming TV show or film? Indeed, the definition of "domestic content" becomes even more complicated when considering the winds of coproduction and outsourcing. Netflix, among other streamers, has extensively grown its coproduction partnerships in recent years.[119] The industry reality is that digital media content is comprised of sophisticated inputs from multiple sources. Should the Netflix TV show series "Emily in Paris" be considered European content due to that fact that it was filmed in Europe (*i.e.*, Paris)? Or should it be deemed non-European content because it was produced by an American company (*i.e.*, Netflix) and it starred a British and American actress (*i.e.*, Lily Collins) as the eponymous Emily? Will "cultural identity" be a factor in deciding the "nationality" of a TV show? Will it be a consideration if many French critics condemned the show for stereotyping Parisians and misrepresenting French culture? All of these questions lead us to rethink issues of cultural diversity in the digital context.[120]

In this regard, the nationality assessment under the AVMSD serves as a proper illustration. The question of whether a TV show is a "European work" under the meaning of Article 13 of the AVMSD is determined

[118] USTR, "National Trade Estimate Report on Foreign Trade Barriers" (2022), at 36–37 (Australia); 82 (Canada); 212 (France); 213 (Portugal); 214 (Spain); 323 (Korea); 352 (Mexico); 375 (Nigeria); 435 (Russia); 498 (Turkey).

[119] See generally Adelaida Afilipoaie et al., "The 'Netflix Original' and What It Means for the Production of European Television Content" (2021) 16(3) Critical Studies in Television: The International Journal of Television Studies 304.

[120] Mira Burri, "EU External Trade Policy in the Digital Age: Has Culture Been Left Behind?" (2022) Trade Law 4.0 Working Paper Series University of Lucerne, at 21.

according to the criteria provided in Article 1. To be qualified as "European works," the works must originate in EU member states or from European third-country states that are parties to the European Convention on Transfrontier Television (ECTT)[121] and must also fulfill certain conditions set out in the AVMSD.[122] Alternatively, the works must be coproduced within the framework of agreements related to the audiovisual sector concluded between the EU and third countries and must fulfill the conditions set out in those agreements.[123] Overall,[124] key considerations provided by the AVMSD include the place of residence of authors and employees of a work, the place of establishment of the producers, and the financial contributions of coproduction costs.[125] In other words, whether streaming content can be qualified as a European work must be assessed based on relevant information and evidence proving the percentage of European authors, workers, producers, and fiscal sponsors in a specific TV show.

Such an exercise, however, may constitute performance requirements for investment in services. Most FTAs lay out general rules for the treatment of investors and investments. Local content requirements – whether they involve hiring a certain proportion of local "TV people" or increasing investment in local production facilities – must be considered with respect to their potential violation of international economic law. For example, Article 14.10 of the USMCA prohibits the parties from imposing any requirement to "purchase a service from a person in its territory,"[126] or to "achieve a given level or percentage of domestic content."[127] Such a provision, on its face, serves as a protection against

[121] The European Convention on Transfrontier Television of the Council of Europe (AVMSD 2010), Directive 2010/13/EU of the European Parliament and of the Council, March 10, 2010.

[122] AVMSD 2010, Article 1 (a)(b).

[123] AVMSD 2010, Article 1 (c).

[124] AVMSD 2010, Article 1(3): "The works referred to in points (n)(i) and (ii) of paragraph 1 are works mainly made with authors and workers residing in one or more of the States referred to in those provisions provided that they comply with one of the following three conditions: (i) they are made by one or more producers established in one or more of those States; (ii) the production of the works is supervised and actually controlled by one or more producers established in one or more of those States; (iii) the contribution of co-producers of those States to the total co-production costs is preponderant and the co-production is not controlled by one or more producers established outside those States."

[125] *Ibid.*

[126] USMCA, Article 14.10 (c).

[127] USMCA, Article 14.10 (b).

local content requirements on digital platforms.[128] Based on that, the US has been "actively monitoring" whether Mexico's audiovisual reform bill, which calls for local content requirements on VSS, is consistent with the USMCA obligations.[129]

4.3.4.2 Nondiscrimination: "Like Digital Products"

Another important issue is discrimination. Let us continue the analysis in the FTA context using the USMCA as an example. Article 19.4 of the USMCA requires parties to ensure "non-discriminatory treatment of digital products" by according no "less favorable treatment" to "like digital products."[130] A USMCA party may not discriminate against digital products originating in another party, either because they were "produced in another party" or because they were "produced by a person of another party."[131] According to Article 19.1, "digital products" include a video that is "digitally encoded, produced for commercial sale or distribution, and that can be transmitted electronically."[132] It is worth mentioning that a similar provision can be found in Article 14.4 of the CPTPP, with an additional subparagraph clarifying that the provision shall not apply to broadcasting.[133] In any event, taking the example of Mexico' s audiovisual reform bill from above, a Mexican law imposing local content quotas on VSS may be considered as treating US TV shows less favorably than Mexican TV shows on digital platforms. Here, a violation could be found by comparing US and Mexican TV shows. If they are "like TV shows," the adverse treatment of the US TV shows under the Mexican measure may be considered discrimination.

At the core of the question is how to determine "likeness" when the products at issue are those directly associated with cultural expression. The tension between the liberalization of the audiovisual trade and the preservation of cultural identity is an old "trade v. culture" debate. The

[128] It should be noted that the obligation does not apply to the performance requirements a party has set out in Annexes I and II. See Section 3.4.2.

[129] USTR, supra note 118, at 352.

[130] USMCA, Article 19.4 (1).

[131] Note that a subsidy or grant provided by a party is not subject to the nondiscriminatory obligations. USMCA, Article 19.4(2). The carve-out is important because these cultural measures, by their very nature, are applied in a discriminatory fashion, that is, they are available to local but not foreign services suppliers. In practice, governmental financial support is often provided to ensure the viability of certain domestic production and distribution of audiovisual services so as to sustain the availability of local content.

[132] USMCA, Article 19.1.

[133] CPTPP, Article 14.4(4).

production and distribution of television programs typically fall under the definition of "core cultural products" within the meaning of the United Nations Educational, Scientific and Cultural Organization's (UNESCO) Cultural Diversity Convention.[134] Now, the streaming technologies put the old wine into new bottles: Can the difference in cultural perspectives be taken into account when assessing the likeness of digital media content?

The *Canada – Periodicals* dispute, in which the confrontation between trade and culture is best demonstrated, can be used as an apt source in answering this question.[135] Aiming to protect the Canadian publications industry, the Canadian Parliament amended the Excise Tax Act and imposed an advertising tax on split-run editions of foreign periodicals, targeting popular US magazines such as *Time*.[136] According to the official statement from Canada, the measures were intended to "foster conditions in which indigenous magazines can be published, distributed and sold in Canada on a commercial basis,"[137] thus, to "maintain an environment in which Canadian magazines can exist in Canada alongside imported magazines."[138] The US brought the case to the WTO, claiming that Canada's discriminatory measures violated GATT Article III on national treatment. The panel basically agreed with the US position that the "cultural products" at issue, namely the US split-run magazine and the Canadian magazine, were "like products" in terms of relevant factors, including the magazines' end uses in the Canadian market, consumers' tastes and habits, and the magazines' properties, natures, and qualities.[139] The Appellate Body took a different approach and found that the imported US split-run periodicals were "directly competitive or substitutable" with domestic Canadian non-split-run periodicals in the Canadian market.[140]

The arguments put forth in *Canada – Periodicals*, now more than two decades old, still echo today's cultural concerns. Throughout the litigation, Canada argued that the two products in dispute were not "like products" within the meaning of Article III:2 of the GATT. Canada

[134] UNESCO, "Universal Declaration on Cultural Diversity" (November 2, 2001).

[135] Panel Report, *Canada – Certain Measures Concerning Periodicals (Canada - Periodicals)*, WT/DS31/R, March 14, 1997; Appellate Body Report, WT/DS31/AB/R, June 30, 1997.

[136] Panel Report, *Canada – Periodicals*, para. 5.12–5.45.

[137] *Ibid.*, para. 3.31.

[138] *Ibid.*, para. 3.140.

[139] *Ibid.*, para. 5.22.

[140] Appellate Body Report, *Canada - Periodicals*, at 25–29.

stressed that the split-runs substantially reproduced foreign editorial material, whereas the local magazines were developed for the Canadian market.[141] Canada further pointed out that the nature of the magazines was for intellectual consumption, which differed from normal goods in terms of physical use and physical consumption.[142] It followed that the "prime characteristic" of cultural goods should be their "intellectual content" rather than the criteria for noncultural goods, such as a bicycle or canned tuna fish.[143] Nevertheless, both the panel and the Appellate Body rejected Canada's "cultural claims" because "cultural identity was not at issue in the present case."[144] The former USTR Mickey Kantor even called the Canadian "cultural identity claim" an "excuse to protect the economic viability of the Canadian (cultural) industry."[145]

The *Canada – Periodicals* dispute demonstrates the status of "culture" in the determination of "likeness." Turning back to the scenario above, if we follow WTO jurisprudence, there is little room for a trade tribunal to rule that US TV shows and Mexican TV shows on streaming platforms contain different cultural elements and are therefore "unlike digital products." Local content requirements for VSS may therefore violate the obligations of nondiscriminatory treatment of digital products under the Digital Trade/E-Commerce Chapter of the FTAs, simply because the domestic regulation treats "like TV shows" unlike.

4.3.4.3 "Digital Cultural Exemption" and Side Letter

The ultimate question is therefore whether the local content requirements, if found to be inconsistent with international trade or investment rules, can be justified under the exceptions. Looking back to the WTO negotiating history, "cultural exceptions" had been proposed during the Uruguay Round Negotiations but were eventually dropped from the

141 Panel Report, para. 5.24.

142 Panel Report, para. 3.61.

143 *Ibid.*

144 *Ibid.*, paras. 3.84, 5.45. The panel pointed out the following: "Many products, as diverse as works of art, designer clothing, phonograph records and cinematographic films contain intellectual or cultural content. Like magazines, these products were in widespread use prior to the adoption of GATT 1947. But of all these products, only cinematographic films were accorded special treatment in GATT 1947. Had the drafters of GATT 1947 sought to treat other intellectual or cultural products differently from products in general, they would have done so."

145 Joseph Devlin, "Canada and International Trade in Culture: Beyond National Interests" (2005) 14(1) Minnesota Journal of International Law 177, at 180.

negotiating texts.[146] As a result, neither GATT nor GATS explicitly provides for any "cultural exception" to WTO law.[147] Although the media landscape has gone through a digital transformation since then, little progress has been made within the WTO in this regard.[148] The question of how to adequately preserve cultural policy space for members has not been properly addressed in the WTO since the conclusion of the Uruguay Round. The debate, to a large extent, has been shifted to the arena of the FTAs. For example, the screen quota issue was at the heart of the controversy of US–South Korea FTA (KOURS) negotiations in the late 2000s, but South Korea decided not to seek a cultural exception under the KOURS.[149]

The concept of "cultural exceptions" has been at least partially realized in recent FTAs through mechanisms such as exemptions or side letters. In particular, Chapter 32 of the USMCA[150] – Exceptions and General Provisions – contains a far-reaching exemption to protect Canada's cultural industry, including the cultural content of digital platforms. To further clarify, Canada's cultural industry exemption from NAFTA has been continued in Article 32.6 of the USMCA to allow Canada to protect its "cultural industries," in particular, the production and distribution of television, video recordings, and film.[151] It should be noted, however, that additional text on retaliation in Article 32.6 has been added to allow the US and Mexico to take measures toward "equivalent commercial effect" in response to any action taken by Canada to protect its cultural industry.[152] Nevertheless, Article 32.6 of the USMCA effectively safeguards Canada's regulatory autonomy over cultural industries. Accordingly, cultural measures on VSS, including local content requirements, are subject to the "cultural carve-out."

[146] See generally Paul, supra note 4.

[147] See generally Chi Carmody, "When Cultural Identity Was Not at Issue: Thinking About Canada – Certain Measures Concerning Periodicals" (1999) 30 Law & Policy of International Business 231 (proposing a waiver to the WTO Agreement with an aim of bringing WTO practice into closer conformity with international law); Tania Voon, *Cultural Products and the World Trade Organization* (Cambridge University Press 2007).

[148] See generally Burri, supra note 120.

[149] See, for example, Park Moo-jong, "Dispute over Screen Quota" (*The Korean Times*, May 2, 2019).

[150] USMCA, Articles 32.1, 32.2.

[151] USMCA, Article 32.6 (1).

[152] USMCA, Article 32.6 (4).

A less comprehensive and somehow more straightforward approach has been taken in the CPTPP. Canada has concluded bilateral agreements with all other CPTPP parties via the exchange of side letters to "ensure Canada's ability to adopt programs and policies that support its cultural sector, including in the digital environment."[153] In the side letters, CPTPP parties agree that Canada has the discretion to define "Canadian content," to protect its online content, and to maintain full policy flexibility to protect its cultural sector.[154] Although its civil society criticized the side letters, contending they do not constitute a broad cultural exemption to ensure the production of high-quality Canadian content in the digital environment, the CPTPP side instruments leave the door open for the Canadian government to regulate VSS in line with its cultural policy. In fact, at the time of this writing, Canada's parliament had just passed the Online Streaming Act to impose local content requirements on streaming platforms.[155] By requiring foreign streaming giants like Netflix and Spotify to feature a certain amount of Canadian content, the Act aims to "ensure Canadian stories . . . are widely available on streaming platforms," and to "reinvest in future generations of artists and creators in Canada."[156]

To conclude, the "trade v. culture" history has a new chapter: the protection of local culture in global digital platforms. For decades, trade policy debates surrounding the audiovisual sector have been prominent, given that the sector is closely concerned with cultural activities. The same holds true in the twenty-first century, where certain digital media content can be seen as the manifestation of a culture. Some TV shows on streaming platforms can be described as a way to reflect the social characteristics of a country and its people, as well as a venue by which to present a country's cultural identity to the rest of the world.[157] When VSS stream such content, they convey and expand certain cultural

153 Government of Canada, "What Does the CPTPP Mean for Canadian Culture?" (2018) <www.international.gc.ca/trade-commerce/trade-agreements-accords-commerciaux/agr-acc/cptpp-ptpgp/sectors-secteurs/culture.aspx?lang=eng>.

154 See, for example, CPTPP, Singapore – Side Instruments, <www.international.gc.ca/trade-commerce/trade-agreements-accords-commerciaux/agr-acc/cptpp-ptpgp/text-texte/sl_la-singapore-singapour.aspx?lang=eng#1>.

155 Government of Canada, "Online Streaming Act receives Royal Assent" (April 27, 2023) <www.canada.ca/en/canadian-heritage/news/2023/04/online-streaming-act-receives-royal-assent.html>.

156 *Ibid.*

157 See Chris Barker, *Television, Globalization and Cultural Identities* (Open University Press 2000), at 31–32.

expressions to their audiences. Notwithstanding, the audiovisual sector is also an economically significant sector that shares commercial characteristics common to other services sectors. The argument that a certain portion of digital media content is more entertaining than cultural characters and they are therefore in no way different from any other commercial product is convincing and hard to rebut.[158] From Hollywood to Silicon Valley, international trade agreements have been struggling to play a more prominent role in mitigating the collision between commercial and cultural interests. As Burri pointed out, there are many paths open to improve the approaches to cultural diversity in the trade context.[159] Amid the hype over the Metaverse, the media landscape is now developing into a collective space created by VR technologies that allow users to interact with one another through avatars.[160] Cultural diversity in the VR space will be even more challenging and multifaceted to policymakers when it comes to avatars. The "trade v. culture" clash in international economic law will continue, and it will also become much more complex in a datafied world.

4.4 Media Platformization and Local Presence

4.4.1 Jurisdiction and Law Enforcement Problems

In any event, media platformization brings about issues surrounding jurisdiction. No matter how carefully crafted, both angles of this chapter – speech regulation on UGC and cultural policy on VSS – must face enforceable reality. Given the global access of the digital platform services, the platforms regulations discussed above – whether content moderation obligations or local content requirements – should ideally be evenly enforced, both onshore and offshore. In this regard, a survey conducted by the EU when the DSA was being introduced revealed that 83 percent of the stakeholders believed that the territorial scope of the Act should be expanded to "digital services established outside the EU when they provide services to the EU users."[161] However, technically

158 WTO, "Background Note by the Secretariat, Advertising Services" S/C/W/47 (July 9, 1998); WTO, "Joint Statement on the Negotiations on Audiovisual Service" TN/S/W/49 (June 30, 2005).

159 Burri, supra note 120, at 22.

160 See Section 6.4.1.

161 European Commission Staff Working Document, "Impact Assessment Report Annexes Accompanying the Document Proposal for a Regulation of the European Parliament

speaking, digital platforms that house their servers outside a country's territory are largely out of regulatory reach in terms of law enforcement.[162] How, then, can we govern services suppliers based in other jurisdictions?

In the age of the platform economy, if offshore services suppliers can easily escape the same level of regulation, such a law enforcement problem will create a misalignment of incentives for their media market to be served from overseas. For example, Singapore's Content Code for Over-The-Top (OTT) Services (the Content Code) applies to both local and offshore OTT TV services suppliers.[163] Even so, although "the law in the books" makes no distinction between onshore and offshore services suppliers, "the law in action" might be quite different, simply because it is much more difficult for its media regulator – the Infocomm Media Development Authority (IMDA) – to compel offshore OTT TV services suppliers to comply with the Content Code.[164] Such an uneven enforcement of law can effectively force local suppliers to relocate and hollow out the local industry.

Placing this problem in WTO language, the legal question here is how to evenly enforce domestic regulation on services suppliers of cross-border services trade (Mode 1) and commercial presence (Mode 3). In this regard, a notable example is Turkey's Regulation on the Transmission of Radio, Television, and On-Demand Services on the Internet (Turkey's Internet Regulation), which requires streaming services suppliers to comply with a comprehensive licensing scheme and to establish a commercial presence in Turkey[165] – virtually restricting digital platforms from supplying services merely on a cross-border basis without establishing a physical presence in Turkey.

In a similar vein, a relatively soft requirement has been adopted in the DSA. Article 13 of the DSA requires digital platforms that offer services in any of the EU member states but do not have an establishment therein to designate "a legal or natural person as their legal representative" within the EU. Such a legal or natural person should be mandated by the platform companies to cooperate with the relevant authorities and

and the Council on a Single Market For Digital Services (Digital Services Act) and amending Directive" 2000/31/EC, 15.12.2020, SWD(2020) 348 final PART 2/2, at 22.

162 See CASBAA, supra note 93, at 27.

163 AVIA, supra note 99, at 7.

164 *Ibid.* (Pointing out that the resulting lighter regulation on overseas competitors creates incentives for home market to be served from overseas.)

165 USTR, supra note 118, at 498.

comply with the DSA. The same Article further states that "the designated legal representative can be held liable for non-compliance with obligations" under the DSA, without prejudice to the liability and legal actions that could be initiated against the platform company.[166] It should be noted, however, that unlike the "commercial presence requirements" under Turkey's Internet Regulation above, the DSA explicitly states that the designation of a legal representative within the meaning of Article 13 shall not amount to an establishment in the EU.[167] It may be presumed from the preparatory documents of the DSA that Article 13 is a dedicated drafted provision that is designed, on the one hand, to ensure similar supervision regardless of the place of establishment of the digital platforms, and on the other hand, to comply with the EU's market access commitments undertaken in the GATS.[168]

4.4.2 Local Presence as a Condition for Digital Platform Services

From the above, and in the light of media platformization, jurisdiction and law enforcement problems, among others, can be addressed through requirements for commercial presence (as stipulated in Turkey's Internet Regulation) or legal representatives (as required by the DSA). At any rate, local presence requirements have long been identified by the US as a trade barrier for cross-border services trade.[169] The US efforts to prevent the spread of local presence requirements can be traced back to the US-led trade deals in the early 2010s.[170] A typical provision can also be found in the Annex on E-commerce of the Trade in Services Agreement (TiSA) negotiating text.[171] Such a provision has become a "template" for the services chapter in several subsequent FTAs.[172] For example, Article 10.6 of the CPTPP states the following:

166 DSA, Article 13(3).

167 DSA, Article 13(1).

168 European Commission Staff Working Document, supra note 161, at 22.

169 Communication by the United States, "Work Programme on Electronic Commerce" S/C/W/359, December 17 (2014), para. 4.1 (Information Flow and Localization Requirements).

170 See, for example, US–Japan Trade Principles for ICT Services. See also US–EU Trade Principles on Information, Communication Technology <https://ustr.gov/issue-areas/services-investment/telecom-e-commerce/information-and-communication-technology-ict>.

171 Peng, supra note 2, at 42.

172 See, for example, RECP, Article 8.11 (Local Presence); CPTPP, Article 10.6 (Local Presence).

> **Article 10.6: Local Presence**
> No Party shall require a service supplier of another Party to establish or maintain a representative office or any form of enterprise, or to be resident, in its territory *as a condition* for the cross-border supply of a service (emphasis added).[173]

Nevertheless, this obligation may be subject to a reservation in a party's schedule. For example, the nonconforming measures maintained by Australia, as set out in its Schedule of the CPTPP Annex II, reserve the country's right to adopt or maintain any local presence measures with respect to audiovisual services transmitted electronically.[174] It is surprising to note, however, that the reservation of a local presence on digital media services is, to date, rarely used in international trade agreements.

All in all, international trade rules that ban local presence requirements enable platform companies to supply services without establishing a local presence, which may have significant implications for the ability of governments to regulate and enforce platform regulations. From the perspective of law enforcement, governments have many reasons to introduce local presence requirements as a condition for foreign digital platforms to supply services on a cross-border basis, as it is virtually a prerequisite for a government to ensure that domestic regulation can be effectively applied and thus enforced. In countries where there is no requirement to maintain a local presence, digital platform operations may circumvent regulatory obligations.[175] As advocated by civil society, "without a local presence of companies, there is no entity to sue and the ability of domestic courts to enforce [local] standards ... is fundamentally challenged."[176] Said another way entirely, a platform company with a locally registered entity would render the authority's law enforcement much easier, in that the companies can be legally compelled by the local authority to engage with the administrative process, submit information,

[173] CPTPP, Article 10.6.

[174] CPTPP, Annex II (Non-Conforming Measures) – Australia-9 (Broadcasting and Audiovisual Services, Advertising Services, and Live Performance).

[175] International Trade Union Confederation, "E-Commerce, Free Trade Agreements, Digital Chapters and the Impact on Labor" (2019) < www.ituc-csi.org/IMG/pdf/digital_chapters_and_the_impact_on_labour_en.pdf >, at 24–25.

[176] Australian Fair Trade & Investment Network, "Submission to the Department of Foreign Affairs and Trade on the Plurilateral Negotiations on Trade-Related Aspects of Electronic Commerce" (February 2020) <www.dfat.gov.au/sites/default/files/digital-trade-submission-aftinet.pdf>, at 18.

and thus comply with domestic regulation.[177] In the case of digital media content regulation, a local presence requirement helps to ensure that the regulators maintain their ability to enforce UGC content moderation as appropriate. Digital speech platforms with a local presence can be sued for breaches of domestic regulations, brought to the local court, and held accountable for a legal remedy to address illegal content. Similarly, in the case of a local content requirement, local presence also means that cultural policies and court judgments against VSS can be more effectively enforced.

The challenges of holding digital platform companies accountable without a local presence are evident. In view of this, international trade rules prohibiting local presence requirements constrain a state's policy space to address free speech and cultural expression. To conclude, international trade agreements in the age of datafication now face this dilemma. At one end of the spectrum, a state's sovereignty to enforce regulations against platforms might be compromised without their local presence. At the other end of the spectrum, cross-border digital trade without a local presence in other countries may be the most efficient business model for many platforms, especially SMEs. Requiring a digital platform supplying services from offshore to have a local presence in the country may inevitably add operational costs and thus constitute a market access barrier to cross-border services trade.

4.5 Conclusion

In this chapter, we have examined the interplay between digital media content regulation and international economic law. To better explain their interactions, this chapter spotlights two policy areas – UGC moderation and VSS screen quota – as windows for exploration. When data becomes speech and expression, data governance requires perspectives that extend well beyond technological and economic factors. Both the UGC and VSS regulations analyzed in this chapter are prime examples demonstrating the need to regulate content moderation, to alter the power distribution in the Internet ecosystem, and to protect noneconomic values such as cultural diversity in global digital platforms. The

[177] Australian Council of Trade Unions (ACTU), "Australia-Singapore Digital Economy Agreement, Submission by the Australian Council of Trade Unions to the Joint Standing Committee on Treaties" (September 25, 2020) <www.actu.org.au/media/1449300/d49-actu-submission-australia-singapore-digital-economy-agreement.pdf>, at 7.

findings from this chapter extend beyond issue-specific contexts to identify the contradictions between, on the one hand, the free trade and global expansion path offered by the international trade regime and, on the other hand, the public policy objectives pursued by national media law and policy. It goes without saying that the excessive market concentration of social media platforms, acting as "gatekeepers" of the flow of digital media content, may systematically discriminate against certain "speech" in datafication-enabled content moderation or promote extremist speech through algorithmic amplification. It is equally obvious that the overwhelming global market share of the dominant streaming platforms may work against the goals of media pluralism and cultural diversity. This "competition" angle is our focus in Chapter 5.

5

Data as Capital and Algorithmic Input

Competition, Transparency, and Trade Rules

5.1 Introduction

The most important feature of platformization is scale. A platform can only provide value to users if it grows to a significant size.[1] When a digital platform reaches a certain scale, it gains access to more and more of its users' data. Of course, this feature is not even remotely novel, because larger factories have always been more efficient than smaller ones, even in the "old economy." However, datafication forces this economic logic to the extreme.[2] In this regard, companies in smaller countries are often disadvantaged vis-à-vis companies in larger countries, simply because of the constraints of smaller markets in terms of efficiencies of scale and volume of data.[3] The leading platforms – including Google, Facebook, Amazon, Baidu, and Alibaba – were launched in the US or China, where they could operate and reach the necessary scale in a large domestic market before they went global.[4]

More importantly, big tech companies have the ability to commoditize our data, which is the key ingredient of many digital services, including

The first two parts of this Chapter (5.1 and 5.2) were an abridged and revised version of Shin-yi Peng, "The Uneasy Interplay between Digital Inequality and International Economic Law" (2022) 33(1) European Journal of International Law 205–235.

[1] EMAG, "Digital Platform's Market Power" (September 30,2019) <https://ec.europa.eu/competition/information/digitisation_2018/contributions/emag.pdf>, at 2.

[2] European Commission, "Competition Policy for the Digital Era" ("EU Competition Policy") (May 20, 2019) <https://op.europa.eu/en/publication-detail/-/publication/21dc175c-7b76-11e9-9f05-01aa75ed71a1/language-en>.

[3] Communication from India and South Africa, "The E-Commerce Moratorium: Scope and Impact" ("E-Commerce Moratorium") WT/GC/W798 (March 10, 2020), para. 3.2.

[4] EMAG, supra note 1, at 3.

AI.[5] Many commentators have rightly pointed out that data is the single-largest lasting asset of these globally dominant companies.[6] Indeed, data is now becoming a form of capital.[7] The ability to collect, use, and apply data is a competitive parameter whose relevance is quickly increasing.[8] The data held by these leading platforms is particularly valuable due to the scale and scope of user data collected, which further provides these big players with strong competitive advantages, allowing them to dominate in the relevant market, create entrance barriers to potential competitors, attract more and more users, build richer and richer data sets, and reinforce their market power.[9] In short, control over data may effectively act as a market entry barrier.[10] Big platforms' control over our data strengthens their market position and makes it easier for them to enter new markets. In the case of Meta, as an example, access to data not only enables Facebook to tailor services, but also to use data to benefit other business lines, such as Messenger, WhatsApp, and Instagram.[11]

The reality of this battle is clear: Big platforms' business practices interlock a combination of forces to dominate the data market – presenting a new form of modern monopoly.[12] To some extent, the emerging phenomenon of leading platforms that appropriate and extract data for

[5] See generally Tom Taulli, *Artificial Intelligence Basics: A Non-Technical Introduction* (Apress 2019), at 36; Chris Skinner, *Digital Human: The Fourth Revolution of Humanity Includes Everyone* (UNKNO 2018), at 58–60.

[6] See, for example, Alex Moazed and Nicholas L. Johnson, *Modern Monopolies: What It Takes to Dominate the Twenty-first Century Economy* (St. Martin's Press 2016), at 99; "The Rise of Data Capital" (*MIT Technology Review Insights*, March 21, 2016) <www.technologyreview.com/2016/03/21/161487/the-rise-of-data-capital>.

[7] Richard Baldwin, *The Globotics Upheaval: Globalization, Robotics, and the Future of Work* (Oxford University Press 2019), at 216–217. As Baldwin quoted the comments of Eric Posner and Glen Weyl, "once we give our data to [the big tech] companies," they can "use it as much as they like." Such a practice is governed by the "data-as-capital" view. However, under the "data-as-labor" view, we maintain data ownership, and the big tech companies would have to pay us for the data we "create."

[8] EU Competition Policy, supra note 2; Shoshana Zuboff, *The Age of Surveillance Capitalism: The Fight for a Human Future at the New Frontier of Power* (Public Affairs 2019), at 338.

[9] Australian Competition and Consumer Commission (ACCC), "Digital Platforms Inquiry – Final Report" (July 26, 2019) <www.accc.gov.au/publications/digital-platforms-inquiry-final-report>, at 57.

[10] See generally Lina M. Khan, "Amazon's Antitrust Paradox" (2017) 126 Yale Law Journal 710, at 785.

[11] EU Competition Policy, supra note 2, at 13, 115.

[12] Moazed and Johnson, supra note 6, at 99; Francesco Ducci, *Natural Monopolies in Digital Platform Markets* (Cambridge University Press 2020), at 24.

profit can be conceptualized as "data colonialism."[13] Overwhelming "economies of scope" empower these large incumbent platforms, giving them a strong competitive advantage.[14] Platformized transactions further enable the expansion of data capitalism, which works both domestically on a home country's populations, and also on a global scale. In this twenty-first century version of colonialism, big tech companies benefit from colonization all over the world. From this aspect, the North–South divide does not seem to matter as much as it usually does.[15] The US and East Asia account for 90 percent of the market for large-scale digital platforms, whereas Africa and Latin America's combined share comprises only 1 percent of the market.[16] These uneven, if not one-way, transnational data flows indicate that "data" – the input for AI and other technologies – has largely originated abroad for the benefit of big tech's data analysis.[17] Given the inordinate concentration of digital technologies in developed economies and a few Asian countries, most developing countries are becoming "net data exporters" that consistently supply valuable data without fairly benefiting from the digital economy.[18]

Against this backdrop,[19] this chapter explores two notable features of the platform economy: First, data has become capital. At the crux of the matter are questions regarding how to "decolonize" data, how public policy should evolve to promote competition in the digital market, and how data capitalism as a whole should be confronted.[20] More importantly, what role can international law assume in promoting competition

[13] See Nick Couldry and Ulises A. Mejias, *The Costs of Connection: How Data Is Colonizing Human Life and Appropriating It for Capitalism* (Stanford University Press 2019), at 83–85, 187–196; Sarah Myers West, "Data Capitalism: Redefining the Logics of Surveillance and Privacy" (2019) 58(1) Business & Society 20, at 24.

[14] Zuboff, supra note 8, at 128–137; Jonathan Haskel and Stian Westlake, *Capitalism without Capital: The Rise of the Intangible Economy* (Princeton University Press 2018), at 118–119.

[15] See María Soledad Segura and Silvio Waisbord, "Between Data Capitalism and Data Citizenship," (2019) 20(4) Television & New Media 412, at 412–419.

[16] E-Commerce Moratorium, supra note 3, para. 3.4.

[17] "Data" is an asset for value creation, and thus, control over massive volumes of personal data is the key to market power. Common concerns therefore emerge regarding the privacy risks posed by market concentration and the abuse of market dominance. See Section 6.3.1.

[18] E-Commerce Moratorium, supra note 3, para. 3.4.

[19] Also note that global digital platforms are among the "winners" of the pandemic in past years because their dominant role has been further reinforced as a result of the boom in e-commerce attributable to the lockdown. *Ibid.*

[20] EU Competition Policy, supra note 2, at 13.

in the digital market? Second, data has become input or feeds for platforms' algorithmic recommendations, which are at the heart of the datafied economy's business models. Problems arising from this phenomenon are potential unfair competition and the lack of algorithmic transparency and accountability. Big tech's datafication-enabled advertising, or, more generally, its overall business model, calls for deep thinking about how to appropriately regulate associated datafication practices. Recognizing that our behavioral data has increasingly become a commodity, the surveillance power of the digital platforms, left without proper constraints, will deepen the negative effect of datafication. What are the necessary steps toward holding digital platforms accountable due to their crucial roles in this datafied society? Are existing regulatory tools sufficient to provide domestic regulators with the information they need to ensure the adequate transparency of algorithmic systems in order to supervise how digital platforms moderate, rank, and recommend content to their users?[21] In particular, what is the interplay between international trade agreements and national algorithmic transparency requirements? These are the key issues this chapter seeks to address.

5.2 Trade and Competition Policy for a Platform Economy

5.2.1 When Winners Act Globally and Take All

Much like the persistently unequal distributions in the broadband networks, the upper layer of the Internet architecture – the platforms – is now facing threats posed by data capitalism. The digital economy is gradually being shaped by increases in market concentration on a global scale, the proliferation of anti-competitive practices by digital platforms, and the abuse of dominant market positions by platform monopolies.[22] Taken as a whole, "winner takes all" is a predictable phenomenon of the digital economy,[23] in which big tech companies do not "compete in the

[21] See Position by Algorithm Watch, "Input to the High Commissioner Report on the Practical Application of the United Nations Guiding Principles on Business and Human Rights to the Activities of Technology Companies" (February 2022) <www.ohchr.org/sites/default/files/2022-03/AlgorithmWatch.pdf>, at 7.

[22] EU Competition Policy, supra note 2, at 98–100.

[23] Cf., Herbert Hovenkamp, "Antitrust and Platform Monopoly" (2021) 130 Yale Law Journal 1952, 1970 (arguing that only a few platforms are natural monopolies, and that the market for digital platforms is rarely winner-take-all).

market," but, rather, "compete for the market" to displace each other.[24] In this context, competition policy must be tailor-made in order to ensure its effectiveness vis-à-vis dominant digital players, thereby safeguarding competition in the markets.[25]

In fact, big tech firms have increasingly been investigated for abuse of dominance and anti-competitive behavior all over the world, which offers plenty of food for thought about data capitalism. Many are in the midst of investigations by competition authorities, some are facing the scrutiny of the administrative courts, and several cases have been concluded.[26] For example, in its Apple Dating app case,[27] the Netherlands Authority for Consumers and Markets (ACM) found that Apple abused its dominant market position by imposing unreasonable terms and conditions on the services suppliers of the dating app in the App Store. In the view of the ACM, Apple enjoys a dominant position in the relevant market of the mobile operating system for dating app providers. "Having a dominant position is not illegal in and of itself. Abusing one, however, is," explained the ACM.[28] Due to the fact that Apple restricts dating app providers' freedom of choice, including banning them from referring within their own dating apps to alternative payment systems outside the app, the ACM came to the conclusion that Apple violated the Dutch Competition Act.[29] Similarly, in the Google Shopping case,[30] the European Commission concluded that Google, by favoring its own comparison shopping service, had abused its dominant position in the relevant market for online general search services. According to the commission's decision,[31] Google breached the EU

24 OECD, "Big Data: Bringing Competition Policy to the Digital Era" DAF/COMP (2016) <https://one.oecd.org/document/DAF/COMP(2016)14/en/pdf>, at 17 (explaining the features of the digital economy).

25 *Ibid.*, at 14.

26 See Henri Piffaut, "Algorithms: The Impact on Competition" (2022) 23(1) Business Law International 5, at 18.

27 The Netherlands Authority for Consumers and Markets (ACM), "ACM Obliges Apple to Adjust Unreasonable Conditions for its App Store" (December 24, 2021) <www.acm.nl/en/publications/acm-obliges-apple-adjust-unreasonable-conditions-its-app-store>.

28 *Ibid.*

29 *Ibid.*

30 European Commission Decision, "Google Search (AdSense)" CASE AT.4041 (March 20, 2019) <https://ec.europa.eu/competition/antitrust/cases/dec_docs/40411/40411_1619_11.pdf>.

31 *Ibid.*, at 8.2. The Commission found that Google's own comparison shopping service was "prominently positioned at the top of Google's general results pages," and displayed in an eye-catching manner.

competition rules because it had "systematically given prominent placement to its own comparison shopping service."[32] Google appealed this decision, and the European General Court upheld the Commission's decision,[33] finding that Google's self-preferential practices constitute an abuse of dominance and have potential anticompetitive effects.[34]

Overall, these cases have led to emerging regulatory efforts with regard to digital platforms. In particular, these decisions underscore the difficulties in correcting *ex-post* negative effects on competition and the need to have *ex-ante* regulations in place to constrain big tech's behaviors and require platform transparency. The trend of rising inequality between those who provide the data and those who control the use of such data challenges our existing legal approaches to the problem of anticompetition. There is an urgent need to revisit the fundamental goals of competition law in the light of digital trade.[35]

5.2.2 *Emerging Competition Law for Data Markets*

5.2.2.1 Big Tech and Competition Policy

Today, competition authorities all over the world are considering the benefits associated with digital platform obligations.[36] One potential mechanism, among others, is to require leading digital platforms to share data with other services operated by their potential rivals, which may "enhance data access, resolve data bottlenecks, and contribute to a fuller realization of the innovative potential inherent in data."[37] In any event, all of the approaches require greater cross-border collaboration. Big tech companies act globally, and dominant platforms are global in scope. The impact of their market power can be more meaningfully addressed

32 European Commission, Press Release, "Antitrust: Commission Fines Google €2.42 Billion for Abusing Dominance as Search Engine by Giving Illegal Advantage to Own Comparison Shopping Service" (June 27, 2017) <https://ec.europa.eu/commission/presscorner/detail/en/IP_17_1784>.

33 Judgment of the General Court, Google and Alphabet v Commission (Google Shopping), The Court of Justice of the European Union, Case T-612/17 (November 10, 2021) <https://curia.europa.eu/juris/liste.jsf?num=T-612/17>, para.168.

34 *Ibid.*

35 Couldry and Mejias, supra note 13, at 191.

36 Ariel Ezrachi and Maurice Stucke, *Virtual Competition – The Promise and Perils of the Algorithm-Driven Economy* (Harvard University Press 2016), at 203, 205.

37 ACCC, supra note 9.

through competition rules at the international level.[38] Compared with national regulations, competition disciplines at the international level would be more effective in defining the relevant (global) market, identifying the abusive market power (globally), addressing (cross-border) collusive practices and digital cartels, and reviewing mergers of (global) platforms. After all, the leading platforms operate on a global scale, and as such, efforts at the international level would be more commensurate with the scale of impact of digital platforms.[39]

In practice, the competition assessment will necessarily depend on the extent and type of data to be shared, the precise form of the data-sharing arrangement, the degree of transparency requirements, and the definition of the relevant market.[40] However, the gap in competition policies and enforcement among jurisdictions will likely leave any competition authority ill-equipped to effectively address the anticompetitive practices of the big tech companies, simply because data flows do not stop at borders.[41] In short, more and more countries are now focusing their regulatory attention on big tech. Recent regulatory progress toward defining "dominant platforms" and establishing ground rules to promote competition reflect a growing understanding that the platform economy requires tailored intervention. The dynamics of global data flows, however, make it legally challenging to enforce data competition policies without global regulatory harmonization. The lack of consistency among national competition laws demonstrates the need for a more consistent, streamlined system among competition regimes – either through greater international collaboration or the creation of additional cross-border disciplines for competition policy.

A number of new regulations and regulatory recommendations have been floated at both the national and the regional level. Among these, the Organization for Economic Co-operation and Development (OECD) policy papers point to the high concentration of data-driven markets, express caution regarding the absorption of new entrants through acquisitions by dominant incumbents, and call for competition rules that seek

[38] UNCTAD, "Digital Economy Report" (2019) <https://unctad.org/publication/digital-economy-report-2019>, at 19.

[39] *Ibid.*, at 147–148.

[40] Arne Hintz et al., *Digital Citizenship in a Datafied Society* (Polity 2019), at 63–68; Maurice Stucke and Allen Grunes, *Big Data and Competition Policy* (Oxford University Press 2016), at 168, 202.

[41] Stucke and Grunes, *ibid.*, at 338 (arguing that the competition policy gap leaves consumers and SMEs vulnerable).

to promote the efficient use and exchange of data.[42] The European Parliament, in addition to the adoption of the two landmark pieces of legislation on digital platforms – the DSA and the Digital Markets Act (DMA) – has also passed or proposed regulations including the Data Act, the Data Governance Act, and the Artificial Intelligence Act, which seek to provide an overall framework for data governance.[43] At the same time, examples in the Asia Pacific region include Australia's News Media and Digital Platforms Mandatory Bargaining Code, which was developed by the Australian Competition and Consumer Commission (ACCC) to address "bargaining power imbalances between the digital platforms and Australian news media."[44] Moreover, the ACCC has already conducted public consultations on policies that would provide for greater regulatory oversight of digital platforms with strong market positions, such as Google and Facebook.[45]

5.2.2.2 EU as Global Norm-Setter?

While various regulatory initiatives are still subject to policy debates, and certainly there are divergent views on how competition law should be restored to account for specific concerns brought about by datafication and data capitalism, the legal approaches share common elements:

- Relevant Markets and Market Power: All of the proposals address the need to clarify what constitutes the "relevant market" of a digital platform. To summarize, identifying relevant markets inside the ecosystem of "data" can prove particularly challenging, because big tech companies always assume multiple roles.[46] Competition authorities must identify a multi-side market and consider relevant data flows in the market.[47]
- Dominant Position and Anti-Competitive Practices: A closely related issue is market power assessment in the context of data access and data

42 OECD, supra note 24, para. 87.

43 At the time of this writing, an agreement between the European Council and the European Parliament on the Artificial Intelligence Act seemed possible by mid-2023.

44 ACCC, News Media Bargaining Code (2021) <www.legislation.gov.au/Details/C2021A00021>.

45 ACCC, "Digital Platforms Inquiry" (December 10, 2018) <www.accc.gov.au/focus-areas/inquiries-ongoing/digital-platforms-inquiry/preliminary-report>.

46 UNCTAD, supra note 38, at 19, 39.

47 OECD, supra note 24, paras. 30, 34, 45. See Section 5.2.3.3 for further discussion on this point.

control, which requires, among other things, specific criteria to assess the impact of a dominant market position. It is a generally shared view among competition authorities that when data is overly concentrated in the hands of big tech companies, it may provide these firms with a substantial competitive advantage against new entrants.[48] The misuse of data to maintain market power should be considered an anticompetitive practice that requires governmental intervention.[49] Most policy papers attempt to identify the types of anticompetitive conduct that are enabled through the control of data, including collusive practices and digital cartels.[50] As emphasized in several policy papers, the incentive for digital platforms to use data to collude with each other is enormous.[51] As a result, the need for competition authorities to adapt tools to address digital cartels is overwhelmingly strong.

- Mergers and Acquisitions: Another closely linked dimension is "data-driven mergers and acquisitions."[52] As evidenced by the Facebook/WhatsApp merger,[53] it is not uncommon for digital platforms to acquire other digital companies and start-ups, which increases the risk of monopolization of data.[54] Policymakers increasingly understand the need to examine the impact of mergers on data, the overall competitive implications of mergers and acquisitions involving digital platforms, and the new threshold for merger control in competition law.[55]

Against this backdrop, the EU's DMA sets a high global benchmark for regulating digital platforms.[56] Overall, the DMA addresses digital market "imbalances" in the EU, imposes tailored asymmetric *ex-*

48 *Ibid.*, paras. 20, 64 (pointing out how market power may increase market entry costs).

49 *Ibid.*, para. 64.

50 *Ibid.*, para. 75; Stucke and Grunes, supra note 40, at 234.

51 OECD, "Algorithms and Collusion: Competition Policy in the Digital Age" (2017). <www.oecd.org/daf/competition/Algorithms-and-colllusion-competition-policy-in-the-digital-age.pdf>, at 20–21, 29; Cf., Nicolas Petit, *Big Tech & the Digital Economy: The Moligopoly Scenario* (Oxford University Press 2020), at 252–256 (arguing that consumer protection regulation is the appropriate tool to address the harms inherent to big tech companies).

52 UNCTAD, supra note 38, at 14.

53 Stucke and Grunes, supra note 40, at 74.

54 UNCTAD, *ibid.*, at 139; EU Competition Policy, supra note 2, at 110.

55 EU Competition Policy, *ibid.*, at 113.

56 Regulation (EU) 2022/1925 of the European Parliament and of the Council of 14 September 2022 on contestable and fair markets in the digital sector and amending Directives (EU) 2019/1937 and (EU) 2020/1828 (Digital Markets Act).

ante rules on "gatekeeper platforms,"[57] provides a legal mechanism based on market investigations, and establishes harmonized rules prohibiting certain unfair practices among gatekeeper platforms.[58] In particular, the DMA establishes a set of defined criteria for qualifying a large digital platform as a "gatekeeper,"[59] with the underlying principle that digital platforms with a certain degree of market power should be subject to more stringent obligations than smaller players.[60] In September 2023, the EC has designated six gatekeepers: Alphabet, Amazon, Apple, ByteDance, Meta and Microsoft.[61] Within six months of being designated gatekeepers, digital platforms are obliged to comply with a number of "special obligations." More specifically, the DMA imposes obligations and prohibitions to limit gatekeepers' abilities to process and use personal data,[62] to negotiate certain conditions with business users,[63] and to restrict end users from switching between digital applications.[64] Note that the European Commission, based on market investigations, has the discretion to "update" obligations for gatekeepers to ensure the obligations are "up to date."[65]

Such an ambitious agenda reveals the EU's aim to be a global norm-setter in digital markets.[66] Expectedly, the DMA will assert significant regulatory control over digital platforms, both within Europe and beyond. The rules will bind global platforms, rendering them *de facto* global standards – more commonly known as the "Brussels Effect." As for big tech, the stakes are particularly high, because the EU is one of the world's largest consumer markets. They must accept the

57 *Ibid.* The DMA will apply only to providers of "core platform services."

58 *Ibid.* Gatekeeper platforms carry additional responsibilities, including the requirement to comply with a defined set of obligations to avoid certain unfair practices, to ensure interoperability with its platform, and to share data that is provided or generated by business users and their customers in their use of the platform.

59 DMA, Article 3 (Designation of Gatekeepers). Infra note 105.

60 Put simply, a platform that has a significant impact on the EU market, provides a core platform service, has a strong economic position, and is active in multiple EU countries shall be designated as a gatekeeper.

61 European Commission, "Digital Markets Act: Commission Designates Six Gatekeepers" (September 6, 2023) <https://ec.europa.eu/commission/presscorner/detail/en/ip_23_4328>. Infra note 106.

62 DMA, Article 5(2).

63 DMA, Article 5(3)(4).

64 DMA, Article 5(6).

65 DMA, Article 12 (Updating obligations for gatekeepers).

66 The DMA was signed into law on September 14, 2022 and became applicable, for the most part, in May 2023.

EU's "terms of business" as the price of admission. To conclude, driven by economic and strategic rationales, the EU has been leveraging its economic muscle and vying for a leadership role in shaping the global rulebook governing digital platforms. The EU's intensified efforts to set international standards for the digital economy could be part of the solution tool kit to curb data capitalism.

5.2.3 Calling for a WTO "Data Reference Paper?"

5.2.3.1 Trade and Competition

At the multilateral level, competition was one of the so-called new issues under the WTO framework two decades ago, at which time members attempted to address how domestic and international competition policies interact with international trade.[67] To a certain extent, international economic law and competition policy are grounded in complementary principles.[68] While the former emphasizes free trade and prohibits discrimination between trading partners, the latter aims to preserve the freedom of business activities and control the anticompetitive conduct of private enterprises.[69] Much discussion has been carried out in relevant legal literature regarding the importance of competition policy to trade liberalization, which generally describes how international cartels affect international trade, how transnational abuses of a dominant position constitute trade barriers to goods or services,[70] and how anticompetitive vertical market concentrations exclude foreign suppliers from a market.[71] Indeed, the rationales underlying both trade and competition are arguably closely related. Nonetheless, to date no significant consensus on the convergence of the two areas has emerged.[72]

To illustrate, historically, the interaction between trade and competition policy has been an important element of both multilateral and

[67] WTO, Interaction between Trade and Competition Policy, <www.wto.org/english/tratop_e/comp_e/comp_e.htm> (visited May 25, 2020).

[68] Ernst-Ulrich Petersmann, "Competition-oriented Reforms of the WTO World Trade System-Proposals and Policy Options" in Roger Zach et al. (eds.), *Towards WTO Competition Rules* (Kluwer Law International 1999), at 65.

[69] International Trade Center, *Combating Anti-Competitive Practices: A Guide for Developing Economy Exporters* 10 (2012) < https://intracen.org/media/file/12106>, at 10.

[70] *Ibid.*

[71] *Ibid.*

[72] Philip Marsden, *A Competition Policy for the WTO* (Cameron May 2003), at 201–235.

regional trade negotiations.[73] The issue of competition policy, however, was dropped from the Doha Round of the WTO trade negotiations.[74] In brief, negotiating efforts to create a general agreement on competition policy under the WTO have been unsuccessful, and the Working Group on the Interaction between Trade and Competition Policy has been inactive since 2004.[75] At the same time, competition policy has been addressed in FTAs,[76] with an evident trend toward a dedicated chapter in recent years,[77] which to a certain degree implies a growing perceived need for common competition disciplines among countries.[78] Given such a trend,[79] the interface between international trade and competition policy is now primarily manifested by the incorporation of "basic competition principles" in the FTAs.[80] Most specifically use the terms "anti-competitive agreements" and "abuses of market power,"[81] while few mention "anti-competitive mergers," "merger control," and "merger review."[82] It should also be noted that approximately half of the FTAs contain competition provisions pertaining to cooperation and technical assistance.[83]

Notwithstanding those "WTO-plus" obligations at the regional level, key problems remain. "General competition policies," which prohibit or require broad categories of business behaviors defined in rather general

73 Robert D. Anderson et al., "Competition Policy, Trade and the Global Economy" World Trade Organization Working Paper (2018).

74 *Ibid.* The Working Group on Trade and Competition under the WTO has been inactive since then.

75 *Ibid.*

76 *Ibid.*, at 74.

77 See, for example, CPTPP, Chapter 16 (Competition Policy); USMCA, Chapter 21.

78 The USMCA's competition chapter, for example, adds provisions on limiting antitrust exemptions, nondiscrimination in enforcement, and comity. The chapter also includes a new article addressing procedural fairness disciplines.

79 For more discussions on general competition principles under the FTAs, see OECD, "Regional Competition Agreements: Benefits and Challenges" (November 29, 2018) <www.ftc.gov/system/files/attachments/us-submissions-oecd-2010-present-other-international-competition-fora/regional_competition_agreements_united_states.pdf>. It has been observed that the competition policy chapters of the FTAs appear to be drafted with vagueness and ambiguity. Parties to the FTAs only agreed to minimum standards for the key elements.

80 *Ibid.*

81 OECD, "Competition Provisions in Trade Agreements – Contribution from Mexico" (December 1, 2019) <www.oecd.org/daf/competition/competition-provisions-in-trade-agreements.htm>.

82 *Ibid.*

83 *Ibid.*

terms, are not sufficient to address digital cartels and data monopolization. The digital sector needs specifically tailored regulatory disciplines. How can international economic law help to ensure that additional pro-competitive regulations are put into place? The real question is this: How can we restore the relevance of international economic law in the digital economy? Could such a restoration be launched with the modernization of the WTO Telecommunications Reference Paper for the data-driven economy?

5.2.3.2 Telecom Reference Paper as a Model

While WTO members have to date failed to agree on competition rules, in the context of the post-Uruguay Round WTO negotiations on Basic Telecommunications Services, most WTO members have committed to the regulatory principles spelled out in the Telecom Reference Paper under the GATS,[84] which sets out specific obligations for competition.[85] In the absence of general competition rules under the WTO regime, the Telecom Reference Paper serves as a sector-specific competition agreement, through which anticompetitive practices can be challenged using the WTO dispute settlement system.[86]

The Telecom Reference Paper requires members to adopt and maintain competitive safeguarding rules to prevent abusive restrictions on bottleneck facilities, which may result in a *de facto* limitation on market access to basic telecommunications services.[87] It also prohibits discriminatory competition conditions within the markets and prevents anti-competitive practices among dominant suppliers.[88] Key provisions include the following:

- Relevant Market and Dominant Supplier: The Telecom Reference Paper defines "major supplier" as a supplier that has the ability to

[84] Telecom Reference Paper. See Section 1.4.2.

[85] David Luff, "Telecommunications and Audiovisual Services: Considerations for a Convergence Policy at the World Trade Organization Level" (2004) 38(6) Journal of World Trade 1059; Lee Tuthill, "The GATS and New Rules for Regulators" (1997) 21 Telecommunications Policy 783.

[86] Mitsuo Matsushita et al., "Competition Policy and Trade" in Mitsuo Matsushita et al. (eds.) *The World Trade Organization: Law, Practice, and Policy* (Oxford University Press 2015), at 739; Mitsuo Matsushita, "Trade and Competition Policy" in Daniel Bethlehem et al. (eds.), *The Oxford Handbook of International Trade Law* (Oxford University Press 2009), at 658.

[87] Telecom Reference Paper, Section 1.

[88] *Ibid.*

materially affect the terms of participation surrounding price and supply in the relevant market for basic telecommunications services as a result of: (a) control over essential facilities; or (b) use of its position in the market.[89]

- Anticompetitive Practices: The Telecom Reference Paper imposes obligations on WTO members to maintain measures for the purpose of preventing suppliers – which alone or together are major suppliers – from engaging in or continuing anticompetitive practices.[90]
- Interconnection Arrangement and Transparency: There is a clear stipulation that interconnection with a major supplier should be provided under nondiscriminatory terms, conditions, and rates, and should be of a quality no less favorable than that provided for its own like services or its subsidiaries.[91]

In brief, the Telecom Reference Paper requires WTO members to ensure that dominant companies do not abuse their market position. As discussed in Chapter 1 of this book, the case of *Mexico – Telecom* represents a concrete application of competition policy within the framework of the Telecom Reference Paper.[92] In this case, the US claimed that the interconnection rates negotiated by Telmex, the incumbent supplier in Mexico, were not cost-oriented. The panel found that Mexico had failed to fulfill its commitments under Section 2.2(b) of the Telecom Reference Paper, in that it did not ensure a major local supplier to provide interconnection at cost-oriented rates to other members' suppliers for the cross-border supply of telecommunications services.[93] The panel also found that Mexico had not met its GATS commitments under Section 1 of the Telecom Reference Paper to maintain "appropriate measures" to prevent anticompetitive practices.[94]

By pointing to the model in the Telecom Reference Paper, this book raises the following questions: To what extent is a set of sector-specific competition disciplines for the data industry possible? Further, what should comprise the "Data Reference Paper?" Turning back to the

[89] *Ibid.*

[90] *Ibid.*

[91] Telecom Reference Paper, Section 2. There is also a requirement that interconnection should be provided in a timely fashion, with terms, conditions, and cost-oriented rates that are transparent and reasonable. A major supplier should make publicly available either its interconnection agreements or an interconnection offer.

[92] Matsushita et al., supra note 86, at 793.

[93] Penal Report, *Mexico – Telecom*, para. 7.216.

[94] *Ibid.*, para. 7.264.

common elements of the regulatory recommendations by the OECD, the EU, and the Australian competition authority, the proposed Data Reference Paper should be a binding set of commitments, perhaps the lowest common denominator, which would serve to guide WTO members to better regulate data, to discipline dominant players, and to thereby help smaller tech companies enter these markets. Much like the regulatory disciplines for the telecommunications market, the concept of "essential facilities" might be applied to big tech companies to prevent the abuse of market dominance by platforms. Similarly, based on the model of the Telecom Reference Paper, a Data Reference Paper would impose obligations on WTO members to maintain measures for the purpose of preventing dominant services suppliers from engaging in or continuing anticompetitive practices. Appropriate mechanisms to prevent collusive practices and review mergers should also be put into place. In addition, a similar focus on pro-competitive effects could include the principles of nondiscrimination and transparency, which would prohibit big platforms from engaging in self-preferential practices that favor their own services.[95]

By imposing cross-border disciplines for competition policy and thus curbing the power of big digital platforms, the proposed Data Reference Paper may well be an effective instrument to address data colonization, which, as discussed in Chapter 3, is an unforeseen phenomenon that interacts with GATS digital trade market access. Moreover, if a set of international competition rules that frame competition concerns in a policy context can be established, there would be less need for *ex-post* enforcement of competition law by competition authorities in developing countries and LDCs, which have relatively limited resources to tackle issues pertaining to digital cartels and data monopolization.[96] To conclude, the increasing inequality in datafication, and in particular the dissymmetric power between those who are the sources of the data and those who accumulate the data, calls for a set of WTO data-specific competition rules to appropriately address market power in the data sector. There is a renewed need for a WTO Reference Paper 2.0, which migrates the competition disciplines from the context of the telecommunications industry to that of the data industry.

[95] See the Google Shopping case, supra note 30.

[96] OECD, supra note 24, at 22.

5.2.3.3 The Inherent Complexity: Sufficient Momentum Needed

Will the need for international competition disciplines for the data sector find an outlet along the path of international economic law, as it did in the telecommunications sector two decades ago? Serious challenges lie ahead. The idea of creating a WTO "Data Reference Paper" may prove difficult in gaining sufficient negotiating momentum to bring it to fruition, primarily because of two structural problems. The first main obstacle is the highly complex, legally technical nature of regulating the digital market. To the extent that the regulatory principles spelled out in the Telecom Reference Paper can inform the development of the data regulatory framework, some adaptations are needed due to the specific characteristics of the data market. As pointed out by the Ofcom, the UK's communications regulator, the regulatory principles of telecommunications services cannot simply be "read-across" and "applied as they exist" to digital services.[97] There are significant similarities between the telecommunications and digital markets. Nevertheless, substantial differences remain.

More specifically, in terms of assessing the "relevant market," far more factors must be taken into consideration when defining the relevant market for digital platforms. All of the "big tech" firms are characterized as multi-sided, which renders the scope of the relevant market even more difficult to define. What constitutes the relevant market of a digital platform inside the big data ecosystem, when various players are involved and have assumed multiple roles? For example, Apple – as a digital platform through the Apple Store and iTunes – also plays an important role in cloud computing services using the iCloud. At the same time, Apple closely interacts with other key social media businesses, including Facebook and LinkedIn. Should each side of the above be defined as a separate market?[98] The multi-sided platform structure poses new difficulties for competition regulations.

Moreover, in terms of assessing abuses of market power, determining "market power" is less straightforward in digital markets. In the case of telecommunications services, dominant market position and significant

[97] See Ofcom, "European Commission Consultation on the Digital Strategy: A Framework of Analysis for an Online Regulatory Regime: Reflections from Ofcom" (September 17, 2020) <www.ofcom.org.uk/__data/assets/pdf_file/0011/203024/european-commission-digital-strategy-170920.pdf>, at 11.

[98] UNCTAD, Digital Economy Report, supra note 38, at 19.

power are closely related to natural monopolies in physical infrastructure, that is, network facilities. Digital services, however, are not necessarily natural monopolies, because their market powers are primarily derived from their access to large datasets created from their users.[99] In practice, market shares in telecommunications markets (*i.e.*, the 25 percent threshold) typically provide useful indications of market importance.[100] In most jurisdictions, a telecom operator is presumed to have significant market power when it holds more than a 25 percent share of a market in a particular geographical area.[101] On the other hand, the possession of data can be used as a barrier to entry, thus becoming the primary source of market power in digital services. The relationship between "market share" and "control over data," however, would prove difficult for competition authorities to investigate.[102] In this regard, the "qualitative criteria" set out by the DMA have been criticized as "arbitrary thresholds"[103] that lack "methodological considerations."[104] It is particularly problematic that the designation of gatekeepers is based on the presumption that the "qualitative criteria"[105] will be met by a firm if it meets the "quantitative criteria."[106] In summary, traditional measuring

[99] Ducci, supra note 12, at 36–43.

[100] Charles H. Kennedy, *An Introduction to U.S. Telecommunications Law* (Artech House 2001), at 231. It should be clarified that market share is not the sole determinative factor in finding significant market power in the telecommunications market.

[101] *Ibid.*

[102] OECD, supra note 24, at 20.

[103] Philip Hanspach and Magdalena Viktoria Kuyterink, "You Can (Try to) Keep the Economists Out of the DMA but You Cannot Keep Out the Economics" (*CPI Competition Policy International*, December 22, 2022).

[104] Christophe Carugati, "The Difficulty of Designating Gatekeepers under the EU Digital Markets Act" (*Bruegel Blog*, February 20, 2023).

[105] DMA Article 3 (Designation of gatekeepers): "1. An undertaking shall be designated as a gatekeeper if: (a) it has a significant impact on the internal market; (b) it provides a core platform service which is an important gateway for business users to reach end users; and (c) it enjoys an entrenched and durable position, in its operations, or it is foreseeable that it will enjoy such a position in the near future."

[106] DMA Article 3 (Designation of gatekeepers): "2. An undertaking shall be presumed to satisfy the respective requirements in paragraph 1: (a) as regards paragraph 1, point (a), where it achieves an annual Union turnover equal to or above EUR 7.5 billion in each of the last three financial years, or where its average market capitalization or its equivalent fair market value amounted to at least EUR 75 billion in the last financial year, and it provides the same core platform service in at least three Member States; (b) as regards paragraph 1, point (b), where it provides a core platform service that in the last financial year has at least 45 million monthly active end users established or located in the Union and at least 10,000 yearly active business users established in the Union, identified and calculated in accordance with the methodology and indicators set out in the Annex; (c)

tools, such as market shares, must be adapted in a digital platform context. All of this highly technical complexity will lead to endless technical discussions and will become an obstacle toward the goal of creating a set of international competition principles for digital services.

Another equally or even more important consideration that may impede the creation of such international disciplines is the inherent complexity of the political economy surrounding digital capitalism. Looking back at its history, the telecommunications industry began to rapidly develop in the late 1990s. As a result, the political momentum toward telecommunications liberalization rendered market access and regulatory discipline under WTO negotiations possible. In other words, adoption of the Telecom Reference Paper was seen by "key" delegations – notably, the US, the EU, Canada, Australia, and Japan – as necessary,[107] given the risk that competition in foreign countries' infrastructure markets may be restricted by incumbent operators' abuses of market power. To illustrate, the telecommunications market, especially decades ago, has exhibited specific features that enable incumbents to maintain a certain degree of market power over the competition.[108] Major incumbent suppliers have strong incentives and ample opportunities to delay the provision of interconnection to new entrants, and such delays can significantly inhibit competition.[109] The incumbents could also, for example, impose anticompetitive interconnection conditions on their competitors.[110] National measures might be needed to prevent incumbent operators from using their market power to distort competition. From the perspective of international trade, market access commitments alone cannot guarantee that a market will become truly liberalized. To be able to effectively compete, telecommunications companies of developed countries must be ensured a level playing field in foreign markets.

as regards paragraph 1, point (c), where the thresholds in point (b) of this paragraph were met in each of the last three financial years."

107 Damien Geradin and Michel Kerf, "Levelling the Playing Field: Is the WTO Adequately Equipped to Prevent Anti-Competitive Practices in Telecommunication?" in Damien Geradin and David Luff (eds), *The WTO and Global Convergence in Telecommunications and Audio-Visual Services* (Cambridge University Press 2004), at 135.

108 *Ibid.*

109 *Ibid.*

110 Shin-yi Peng, "Trade in Telecommunications Services: Doha and Beyond" (2007) 41(2) Journal of World Trade 293, at 318.

However, such political economy momentum, which led to the conclusion of the Telecom Reference Paper, cannot be found in the context of digital services. Unlike the negotiation background of the telecommunications services industry, the economic interests (as well as the regulatory approaches) of the data services industry are quite divergent among key players. Generally speaking, US digital platforms have been persistently dominant in the world, including the European market. At the same time, China – by establishing its own self-sufficient platform economy through Chinese digital giants Baidu, Alibaba, and Tencent[111] – has largely escaped US domination. Nonetheless, three different models for data governance are emerging: The US generally favors an *ex-post* approach, which broadly seeks punitive action for past infractions. Such an innovation-friendly approach is primarily driven by the concept of self-regulation.[112] The EU model, as discussed above, is holding the normative high ground. The *ex-ante* regulations would result in sweeping supervisory actions that impact Silicon Valley's future. China's main concern, however, is to ensure its political stability and security. It is conceivable that China will continue to rely on domestic protectionist regulations to restrict cross-border data flows.[113] When these three models interface in an international organization, it is less likely to result in a compromise given the associated concerns.[114]

5.2.3.4 Digital Trade and Competition Disciplines

How can international economic law contribute to overcoming these impediments? The first direction is the soft law mechanism, which leaves sufficient space for national regulators. Here again, the FTAs provide some inspiration. Although to date none of the Digital Trade/E-Commerce Chapters of the FTAs have incorporated competition rules for the data market, the lesson we have learned from their general

[111] Henry Gao, "Digital or Trade? The Contrasting Approaches of China and U.S. to Digital Trade" (2018) 21(2) Journal of International Economic Law 297, at 308.

[112] *Ibid.*, at 316. See generally Julien E. Cohen, *Between Truth and Power: The Legal Constructions of the Informational Capitalism* (Oxford University Press 2019), at 214–217 (pointing out that the positions of the BRICS – Brazil, Russia, India, China, and South Africa – group are also significant in making the conflicts more complex).

[113] Gao, supra note 111, at 319.

[114] Mira Burri, "Towards a New Treaty on Digital Trade," (2021) 55(1) Journal of World Trade 77, at 99.

approaches pertains to the soft legal nature of key provisions.[115] The USMCA parties, for example, merely "recognize the importance" and "endeavor to" comply with certain rules under the Digital Trade Chapter.[116] It might therefore be criticized as a weak instrument. Nevertheless, it can always be argued that without such vague provisions, the Digital Trade Chapter would never have been finalized by the parties. In future trade negotiations on data governance, the "softness" of a treaty requires that substantive rules remain somewhat general. For example, it might be necessary to leave key concepts such as "anticompetitive practices" undefined to allow for policy alternatives. The lack of specificity in the treaty language would allow parties to cater to differences in local needs and maximize the likelihood that the rules will be effectively implemented by regulators. Given the variations that exist in the digital markets of different countries, the strategic use of hard and soft law is of practical significance in introducing a set of data rules into the WTO regime.

The second approach concerns flexible negotiating modality, which helps to reach a critical mass of trade negotiation results. Against this contentious political and economic backdrop, the probability of reaching a consensus under the "single-undertaking" system seems slight.[117] Balancing the interests of 164 WTO members across diverse issues surrounding data governance has made it difficult, if not impossible, to conclude negotiations that "bind all WTO Members equally." In this regard, negotiating on the basis of a critical mass approach, which involves arrangements between a number of parties that do not represent the entire membership but account for a very high proportion of international trade in data services, seems to be a more realistic direction. In this context, despite strong opposition from several members,[118] the

[115] See, for example, USMCA, Article 19.15 (Cybersecurity); Article 19.18 (Open Government Data).

[116] See, for example, USMCA, Article 19.5 (Domestic Electronic Transactions Framework); Article 19.8 (Personal Information Protection); Article 19.9 (Paperless Trading); Article 19.14 (Cooperation).

[117] Alberta Fabbricotti, "Multilateralizing Regionalism and the Future Architecture of International Trade Law as a System of Law: The Paradox of Multilateralizing Regionalism through Flexibility" (2009) 103 Proceedings of the American Society of International Law 119, at 120. The "single undertaking" concept essentially means that all of the instruments which make up the complex body of WTO law are equally binding upon all members, regardless of their stage of economic and social development.

[118] Inside US Trade, India, "South Africa: Plurilaterals Legally Inconsistent with WTO Rules" (February 22, 2021). India and South Africa have maintained that ongoing

ongoing JSI on E-commerce offers a pathway for the WTO to remain responsive and relevant in the digital economy.[119]

5.3 Trade Rules and Algorithmic Transparency

5.3.1 Algorithms and Platform Competition

A closely related but distinct aspect is algorithmic transparency, which can serve as a regulatory starting point for global platform governance. In this data-driven world, one important legal tool to promote platform competition is to ensure that algorithms are fair and transparent.[120] As illustrated above, platform capitalism would not ever have existed without big data analytics algorithms. In summary, the market dominance of big tech can be simplified in the following pattern. By taking advantage of their vast user base, big tech companies provide datafication-enabled advertising services to businesses, which in turn bring big tech advertising revenues. Big tech companies then invest more in their data analytics tools to enhance the accuracy of target advertising, which allows big tech to attract more users and collect more data. The more data that is collected, the more the algorithms can learn.[121] Under this pattern, with more and more data amassed, big tech companies are able to attract even more advertisers. The cycle continues.

To put it another way, each time we Google a product and then click on the sponsored ads, Yahoo not only loses a search query to Google, but also loses our behavioral data, which represents an opportunity for its algorithms to learn, as well as potential advertising revenues. This results in a gap between Google and Yahoo in their ability to train their AI, to personalize search results, and to enhance the accuracy of targeted advertising. The more people Google, the wider such gaps grow.[122]

negotiations on the plurilateral e-commerce agreements are "legally inconsistent" with WTO rules and principles. Cf., Inside U.S. Trade, "U.S., EU, Others Defend Plurilaterals after Criticism from India" (March 3, 2021).

119 Cf., Jane Kelsey, "The Illegitimacy of Joint Statement Initiatives and Their Systemic Implications for the WTO" (2022) 25 Journal of International Economic Law 2.

120 For the purpose of coherence, this chapter focuses on issues pertaining to the algorithmic transparency of private digital platform companies. Administration of AI in the public sector thus falls outside the scope of this book.

121 Stucke and Grunes, supra note 40, at 38; Marco Iansiti and Karim R. Lakhani, *Competing in the Age of AI: How Machine Intelligence Changes the Rules of Business* (Harvard Business Review Press 2020), at 96–97.

122 Stucke and Grunes, *Ibid.*, at 202.

In this context, concerns have been raised in relation to the abusive use of algorithms. After all, it may amount to the unfair treatment of competitors if algorithms are programed – wittingly or unwittingly – to prioritize a platform's own services over those of competitors.

Accordingly, increasing consideration is being given to why an algorithm of a search engine makes certain recommendations, as well as how a consumer can achieve different search results or access different ranking systems. In addition, turning back to the social media moderation practices discussed in Chapter 4, AI plays a material role in content moderation, including some context-specific content such as hate speech. When our behavioral data becomes algorithmic input, it is important to empower consumers to understand how a social media algorithm makes content moderation decisions, whether it is appropriate to use that content-moderating algorithm, and how consumers can receive objective algorithmic decisions.

More and more governments and civil societies are addressing commensurate algorithmic practices and calling for algorithmic transparency. They express caution over the unfair outcomes due to the lack of algorithmic transparency and advocate for algorithmic accountability, primarily to require platforms to disclose how their algorithms generate certain outputs.[123] In this regard, disclosing the algorithms or the source code that drives a platform's system may reveal whether the platform values one type of content over another. Alternatively, a lower degree of transparency that informs users of the main parameters that determine ranking, using plain language, may also be useful for the public in understanding how search engines work. Conversely, as discussed in greater detail below, some experts have pointed out that such transparency requirements may prove neither meaningful nor feasible due to the protection of trade secrets and the nature of machine learning.[124] The design of algorithmic systems is the product of substantial investment and may easily be duplicated by competitors if disclosed.

At this moment, regulators all over the world are contemplating various forms of regulation that will improve platform accountability, AI ethics, and algorithmic transparency and explainability for automated

[123] See Heike Felzmann et al., "Towards Transparency by Design for Artificial Intelligence" (2020) 26 Science and Engineering Ethics 3333.

[124] See generally, Dan L. Burk, "Algorithmic Legal Metrics" (2021) 96 Notre Dame Law Review 1147.

decision-making.[125] Algorithms can be governed by various regulatory choices, including who and what will be regulated, to whom information will be disclosed, and how disclosure will occur.[126] In the context of international economic law, the interplay between AI regulation and international trade agreements centers on questions relating to how to ensure that algorithmic accountability is appropriately distributed, as well as how to safeguard public access and oversight over algorithms. More profoundly, how can we balance competing interests in particular trade secrets and prevent AI regulations from being overly trade restrictive?

5.3.2 Platform Transparency Requirements

To answer the above questions, five "representative" digital/data regulations – including the DSA, the DMA, the GDPR, the Montréal Declaration for a Responsible Development of Artificial Intelligence (Montréal AI Declaration),[127] and the US bill on the Algorithmic Justice and Online Platform Transparency Act (Algorithmic Justice Act)[128] – are selected for an in-depth investigation. Transparency requirements in the five digital/data regulations, including both hard law and soft law, are reviewed to reveal the variables and their relationships. To clarify, this approach provides examples and is not meant to be comprehensive, as there are plenty of AI-related regulations or draft bills floating around,[129] but it aims to serve as an illustration to better

125 Stucke and Grunes, supra note 40, at 1.

126 Shin-yi Peng et al., "Artificial Intelligence and International Economic Law: A Research and Policy Agenda" in Shin-yi Peng et al. (eds), *Artificial Intelligence and International Economic Law: Disruption, Regulation, and Reconfiguration* (Cambridge University Press 2021), at 10.

127 Université de Montréal, The Montréal Declaration for a Responsible Development of Artificial Intelligence (2018). The Declaration is a set of nonbinding ethical guidelines that provide the basis for future national regulation.

128 The Algorithmic Justice and Online Platform Transparency Act, S.1896, 117th US Congress (2021–2022) <www.congress.gov/bill/117th-congress/senate-bill/1896>. The Act, introduced by US Senator Edward Markey, aims to bring digital platforms into the regulatory framework, especially when using algorithms to moderate and recommend content. At the time of this writing, there were other key bills in the US House and Senate. Given the growing number of pending proposals, the selection of the Algorithmic Justice Act is not intended to predict that it will come to pass but, rather, to represent potential regulatory trends in the US.

129 In particular, the EU Artificial Intelligence Act. Proposal for a Regulation of The European Parliament and of the Council Laying Down Harmonized Rules on

understand the key dimensions of platform transparency requirements in a comparative context.

5.3.2.1 Who: The Scope of the Regulatory Targets

As noted in Chapter 4, obligations under the DSA are cumulative depending on the function and size of a services supplier. The larger a services supplier is, and the more extensive the services it provides, the greater the number of obligations that apply. In terms of transparency, the DSA imposes a baseline transparency requirement, which applies to all intermediary services suppliers, and it then adds obligations for hosting services and online platforms, and then once again adds a further set of transparency obligations for VLOPs. In other words, VLOPS must comply with all of the transparency requirements imposed by the DSA, including transparency reporting,[130] transparency of recommender systems, transparency of online advertising,[131] and data sharing with authorities and researchers.[132]

Similarly, as stressed in the DMA's preamble, in most cases, gatekeepers provide online advertising services to business users in a nontransparent manner, which results in higher costs for online advertising services. To address this problem, it is important to ensure that the platform environment, and in particular, the conditions that apply to advertising services and rankings, is generally fair, transparent, and contestable. Therefore, the transparency obligations primarily fall to the gatekeepers.[133]

Unlike the asymmetric regulatory models of the DSA and the DMA, the scope of the regulatory targets of the GDPR, the Algorithmic Justice Act, and the Montréal AI Declaration is broader and more general. This is because concerns surrounding the lack of platform transparency extend to all kinds of platforms, regardless of their size.[134] In this regard, under the GDPR, provisions on platform transparency and accountability apply to all data controllers and processors, as defined in

Artificial Intelligence (Artificial Intelligence Act) and amending Certain Union Legislative Acts, COM/2021/206 final.

130 This obligation applies to all intermediary services.

131 These obligations apply to hosting and online services.

132 This application applies to VLOPs only.

133 Preamble to the DMA, paras. 45, 52, 58, and 72.

134 Google's submission, "Digital Services Act package: Open Public Consultation" (2020) <https://blog.google/documents/89/Googles_submission_on_the_Digital_Services_Act_package_1.pdf/>.

Article 4.[135] Likewise, the principles in the Montréal AI Declaration are general and abstract and aim to apply to the digital and artificial intelligence field in a broad sense.[136] As broad as it may sound, however, the nonbinding nature of the declaration means that implementation is on a voluntary basis. Finally, the Algorithmic Justice Act imposes transparency obligations on an "online platform," which is defined as "any public-facing website, online service, online application, or mobile application which is operated for commercial purposes and provides a community forum for user generated content"[137] – a rather broad net.

5.3.2.2 What and to Whom: The Degree of Transparency

The five regulations vary in terms of what type of information should be transparent, ranging from algorithm-based advertising, algorithmic content moderation, algorithmic reporting, factors and parameters shaping algorithmic decisions, auditable records of the algorithmic process, and source code. Indeed, the degree of disclosure is controversial, and the policy options involve trade-offs. Unfettered government access to source code and algorithms may help to ensure that algorithms are fair but may also lead to unnecessary intrusion into privacy and trade secrets.[138] Taken to the extreme, platforms may be required to disclose source code.[139] However, would it be more proportionate to require them to make their algorithms transparent? Or is it more reasonable for platforms to merely publish the general factors and logic involved in algorithmic decisions? These questions must be analyzed in conjunction with the question of who receives transparency. As discussed below, the question of "disclosure to whom" dictates "what to disclose."

▪ **Authorities and Experts** As shown in Figure 5.1, platforms' disclosure obligations to regulatory bodies generally rank high on the scale

135 GDPR, Article 4(7), 4(8).

136 Preamble to the Montréal AI Declaration.

137 Algorithmic Justice Act, Section 3(9).

138 See generally Neha Mishra, "International Trade Law Meets Data Ethics: A Brave New World" (2020) 53(2) New York University Journal of International Law and Politics 305.

139 See Section 5.3.3 of this book for further discussions. Note that algorithms and course code are different but related. Source code expresses algorithms. Algorithms are ideas – a process for solving a problem – while source code expresses and executes algorithms. Experts refer to algorithms as "conceptual" and to source code as "the manifestation of the concept in a particular programming language." For the difference between algorithm and code, see "Software Engineering" <https://softwareengineering.stackexchange.com>.

Legal Instruments / Variables	DSA	DMA	GDPR	Montréal AI Declaration	Algorithmic Justice Act
Disclosure Obligations to Authorities and Experts	H	H	H	H	M
Disclosure Obligations to Interested Parties	L	L	M	H	N
Disclosure Obligations to the Public	M	L	L	M	M
Explanation Obligations	H	H	H	L	L

Figure 5.1 Transparency requirements in context
Notes:
-Degree of Disclosure Obligations (Rows 1–3)
H: high (all data including algorithms and source code)
M: medium (algorithm parameters, algorithm auditing)
L: low (transparency reports, standard contracts)
N: none (no explicit rules)
-Degree of Explainability (Row 4)
H: high (inspections and interviews)
M: medium (machine-readable formats)
L: low (meaningful and comprehensible descriptions)
N: none (no explicit rules)

when measuring transparency. To illustrate, transparency can be restricted to governmental authorities. The rationale is that authorities need to use these records to verify compliance with regulatory requirements. On this matter, the GDPR focuses on supervisory authorities' investigative powers to obtain access to any premises of the data controller and the processor, including "any data processing equipment and means."[140] The Montréal AI Declaration, although nonbinding in nature, stresses the need for the code for algorithms to be accessible to relevant public authorities for verification and control purposes.[141] The Algorithmic Justice Act also calls for platforms to maintain records of algorithmic processes, and to make available to the supervisory agency

[140] GDPR, Article 58.
[141] Montréal AI Declaration, Principle 5(3).

complete records upon request.[142] After all, the algorithm itself may only be part of the story. Algorithmic decision-making cannot be accurately audited by reviewing the algorithms alone. It is important to ensure that the data on which an algorithm is trained is equally accessible.

In practice, however, the disclosed information, whether algorithms or source code, may not be understood by regulators, let alone the general public. Government agencies in most circumstances do not have the technical expertise to keep pace with and thus oversee the industry's sophisticated algorithms, which represents an impediment that would negate many benefits of disclosure.[143] Disclosure requirements may therefore need to involve specialized experts in carrying out necessary analyses.[144] In other words, authorities most likely rely on experts who are in a position to make assessments of the disclosed technical details. In this regard, the DSA explicitly stipulates that auditors and experts appointed by the EC during administrative inspections may require VLOPs to provide necessary information, including their information technology systems and algorithms.[145] Similarly, the DMA states that the Commission may require access to any data and algorithms of undertakings and information in order to carry out its duties.[146] Persons working under the supervision of the authorities, including auditors and experts appointed pursuant to the DMA, shall not disclose information acquired during inspections.[147] Limiting transparency to regulators and researchers, but not to the general public, appears to be an important mechanism by which to protect potentially sensitive information and data that would not be considered releasable to the public.

▪ **Interested Parties** Variations can be found in platforms' disclosure obligations to interested parties. In Figure 5.1, the degree of the obligations ranks low in the DSA and the DMA, medium in the GDPR, high in the Montréal AI Declaration, and is nonexistent in the Algorithmic Justice Act. To illustrate, both the DSA and the DMA have transparency provisions that would be available to interested parties, but the obligations are limited to relatively general information, without associated

[142] Algorithmic Justice Act, Section 4.
[143] Ezrachi and Stucke, supra note 36, at 231.
[144] Burk, supra note 124, at 1187.
[145] DSA, Article 69(5).
[146] DMA, Articles 21 and 36.
[147] *Ibid.*

technical details. For example, regarding content moderation, a platform should inform the recipient at the time of the removal of the decision through "a clear and specific statement of reasons" when it removes specific content.[148] Likewise, regarding advertising and ranking, a gatekeeper shall provide each advertiser to which it supplies advertising services with information regarding prices, fees, and remunerations. The gatekeeper shall also provide advertisers and publishers with access to "the performance measuring tools of the gatekeeper and the data necessary for advertisers and publishers to carry out their own independent verification of the advertisements inventory, including aggregated and non-aggregated data."[149]

On the contrary, the Montréal AI Declaration empowers "stakeholders and those affected by the situation" the same opportunity to access "the code for algorithms" for verification and control purposes.[150] The GDPR, in this regard, requires the data controller to provide individuals with the information necessary to ensure fair and transparent data processing. Where automated decision-making is involved, the disclosure obligations include the provision of "meaningful information about the logic involved" and "the envisaged consequences of such processing" to individuals.[151] A great deal of literature has explored what constitutes "meaningful information."[152] In any event, it can be presumed by reading in context that the information required under Articles 13 and 14 of the GDPR, although it need not be source code or complex algorithms, must be more than a general overview of the decision-making system – sufficiently concrete for the data subject to understand the reasons for a specific decision.[153] It therefore ranks medium in terms of the degree of transparency.

▪ **The Public** Finally, in connection with disclosure obligations to the public, among the five selected regulations, three of them rank medium, while two rank low. As revealed in Figure 5.1, the transparency requirements toward the public under the DSA, the Montréal AI Declaration, and the Algorithmic Justice Act extend to the level of algorithms'

[148] DSA, Article 17.
[149] DMA, Articles 5 and 6(8).
[150] Montréal AI Declaration, Principle 5(3), 5(4).
[151] GDPR, Article 14(2)(g).
[152] See, for example, Andrew D Selbst and Julia Powles, "Meaningful Information and the Right to Explanation" (2017) 7(4) International Data Privacy Law 233.
[153] *Ibid.*, at 236.

parameters and auditing, whereas those in the DMA and the GDPR remain at the level of general transparency reporting and standard contracts. More specifically, under the DSA, VLOPs are required to publish transparency reports at least every two months, and to release, in their terms and conditions, "the main parameters used in their recommender systems, as well as any options for the recipients of the service to modify or influence those main parameters."[154] The "main parameters" include but are not limited to "the criteria which are most significant in determining the information suggested to the recipient of the service" and "the reasons for the relative importance of those parameters."[155] In a similar manner, the Montréal AI Declaration calls for public transparency of "the social parameters of the artificial intelligence systems,"[156] while the Algorithmic Justice Act advocates that the online platform should disclose, among other matters, "the method by which the type of algorithmic process prioritizes, assigns weight to, or ranks different categories of personal information to withhold, amplify, recommend, or promote content to a user."[157]

In terms of a textual comparison, public transparency obligations under the DMA and the GDPR are less specific and are therefore weaker. Under the DMA, gatekeepers are required to publish and update non-confidential summary of transparency reports, as well as make publicly available and update an overview of the audited descriptions.[158] The obligation is even less clear in the GDPR, under which the EC has the power to "lay down standard contractual clauses" for data processing. In addition, associations representing platforms may prepare codes of conduct addressing "fair and transparent processing."[159] On the whole, the degree of transparency to the broad public is relatively low in these two instruments.

5.3.2.3 How: The Degree of Explainability

Some skeptics emphasize that algorithmic transparency requirements may lend themselves to legal problems, because the algorithms themselves cannot explain "how they have arrived at a particular output."[160]

154 DSA, Article 27(1).
155 DSA, Article 27(2).
156 Montréal AI Declaration, Principle 5(6), 5(8).
157 Algorithmic Justice Act, Section 4(a)(1).
158 DMA, Articles 11, 15.
159 GDPR, Articles 28(7), 40(2).
160 Selbst and Powles, supra note 152, at 234.

For example, releasing algorithms does not necessarily explain how they work and may not provide much meaningful information about, for example, the content moderation or ranking systems. Any degree of meaningful algorithmic transparency must therefore be accompanied by the requirement of explainability, that is, providing insights into the functioning of the algorithms "in a format that makes sense to the reader."[161]

The question is how. First of all, accurately explaining the functioning of algorithmic systems – particularly those developed using AI – is not always technically feasible. Algorithmic decision-making may involve complex and dynamic processes, as well as multiple profiling elements and data sources.[162] It may be commercially impossible to carry out an effective review.[163] Moreover, disclosure of incomprehensible technical details, even when available in machine-readable format, does not necessarily empower either the regulators or the interested parties to understand how they actually work.[164] Accordingly, as a subset of transparency requirements, the degree of explainability strongly correlates with to "whom to explain." As for the regulators, the power to acquire insights into how and why the algorithms work in certain ways by conducting inspections and carrying out input and output auditing is useful for supervisory purposes. Conversely, as for the general public, digital platforms' descriptions of algorithms' objectives, processes, and functioning, in plain language that is intelligible to lay people, represent meaningful information responsive to the right to know.[165]

Both the DSA and the DMA require different levels of explainability depending on "whom to explain to" and "why explain." The two instruments impose upon platforms the obligation to publish annual transparency reports "in clear, easily comprehensible language" and "in a machine-readable format."[166] Moreover, the EC has the power to conduct all necessary inspections at the premises of the VLOPs/gatekeepers, including requiring the services suppliers to provide access to and explanations of their "organization, functioning, IT system, algorithms,

[161] DOT Europe Position Paper, "Algorithmic Decision Making Transparency As Explainability" (2022) <https://doteurope.eu/wp-content/uploads/2022/01/DOT-Europe-PP-on-Algorithmic-Transparency.pdf>.

[162] *Ibid.*, at 1.

[163] Burk, supra note 144, at 1182.

[164] *Ibid.*, at 1187.

[165] *Ibid.*, at 1188.

[166] See, for example, DSA, Article 15.

data-handling and business practices," and allowing regulators to "address questions to their key personnel," and "record or document the explanations given."[167] The EC can also require access to any data and algorithms and request explanations of them.[168] Furthermore, the EC is mandated to carry out interviews and take statements during the investigation and is entitled to "record such interviews by any technical means."[169] As shown in Figure 5.1, the VLOPs/gatekeepers' cumulative obligations for explanations rank high in the given context. In contrast, requirements that algorithmic decision-making is explainable are relatively light in the Montréal AI Declaration and the Algorithmic Justice Act, which basically obligate services suppliers to provide a description of how the algorithmic process operates,[170] or to justify AI-based decisions in plain language that is understood by individuals whose quality of life and reputation are affected by the consequences of the algorithmic process.[171]

In this regard, it is worth noting that the text of the GDPR has provoked debate over whether it imposes upon data controllers an obligation of explainability when algorithmic decision-making is involved. Article 22 states that individuals "have the right not to be subject to a decision based solely on automated processing, including profiling" if such a decision has "legal effects or similarly significant effects" on concerned individuals. The same article requires a services supplier to "implement suitable measures" to safeguard individuals' "rights and freedoms and legitimate interests."[172] This requirement has been a source of controversy over whether algorithmics should be explainable. Note that suitable safeguards, according to Article 22, must include "at least the right to obtain human intervention on the part of the controller, to express his or her point of view and to contest the decision." The term "at least" indicates that this is not an exhaustive list of rights. Namely, it is an open list of suitable safeguards, and a services supplier is expected to do more than the basic requirements. Additionally, Recital 71 has added that the suitable safeguards are to include a right to an explanation of an automated decision. This textual interpretation thus creates a *sui generis* due process for algorithmic

[167] DSA, Article 69(5); DMA, Article 23(2)(d).
[168] DSA, Article 72(1); DMA, Article 21.
[169] See, for example, DMA, Article 22.
[170] Algorithmic Justice Act, Section 4(a)(2)(A)(iii).
[171] Montréal AI Declaration, Principle 5(2).
[172] GDPR, Article 22.

practices – a right to be heard, to be given an explanation, and to challenge an automated decision.[173]

In any event, just as the DSA and the DMA empower authorities to demand a high level of explainability for supervisory purposes, Article 58 of the GDPR states that authorities' investigative powers include access to any premise of the services supplier, any data processing equipment and means, as well as the ability to order the services supplier to "provide any information it requires for the performance of its tasks" – an outright obligation of explainability.[174] For this reason, the GDPR ranks high in terms of explainability, as shown in Figure 5.1, which denotes the cumulative degree of a given regulation.[175]

5.3.2.4 Variables and Comparison

To summarize, the five regulations selected implement various transparency measures, depending on the regulatory objectives and their context. Generally speaking, of the four dimensions assessed in Figure 5.1, the transparency obligation to authorities and experts appears in all five regulations and is the most significant requirement in terms of what must be disclosed. It is worth noting that the most evident variations are seen in transparency obligations to the interested parties and to the public. Moreover, the degree of technical detail required for explanation also varies greatly, from detailed auditable trails of algorithmic processing to general, plain-text descriptions. However, consistency has been found in the DSA, the DMA, and the GDPR, as they contain identical provisions requiring a high degree of explanation. To conclude, this case study demonstrates that the emerging regulations bring about greater transparency and oversight of the algorithms. The legal-technical details, however, differ in important ways. Although all of the five instruments place pressure on digital platforms to be more transparent, what kind of information should be provided and how it should be provided are dependent upon context, as well as to whom the disclosure is made.

Figure 5.1 measures the key elements of platform transparency and explainability reflected in the selected regulations, which form the basis of

[173] See generally European Parliament, "The Impact of the General Data Protection Regulation (GDPR) on Artificial Intelligence" (2020) <www.europarl.europa.eu/stoa/en/document/EPRS_STU(2020)641530 > .

[174] GDPR, Article 58(1)(a), (1)(e), (1)(f).

[175] See generally Laura Edelson, "Platform Transparency Legislation: The Whos, Whats and Hows" (Lawfare, April 29, 2022).

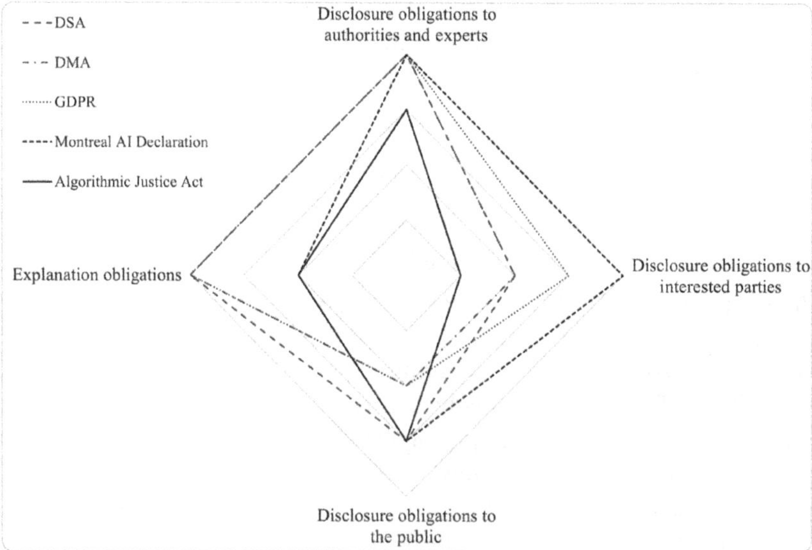

Figure 5.2 Regulatory fragmentation of transparency requirements
Notes:
–Central axis: none
–Second central axis: low
–Inner axis: medium
–Outer axis: high

the mapping exercise in Figure 5.2. Before this mapping exercise, one caveat is in order. Issues arise when comparing values across these axes, because each has a unique measuring scale. Note especially that the variables on the explanation obligations (row 4) represent different measuring scales. In other words, variables on the axis of explanation obligations are independent. With all of this in mind, Figure 5.2 shows the four variables mapped onto axes. The central axis is defined as "none," the second central axis as "low," the inner axis as "medium," and the outer axis as "high." As such, the areas of the polygons represent the overall degree of transparency and explainability requirements. Evidently, the five polygons overlap in some areas but are completely independent in other areas. Additionally, the shapes of individual polygons vary greatly. This case study thus concludes that the fragmentation of platform governance within and across jurisdictions is growing. Section 5.4 will continue to address how international trade agreements can help curb such fragmentation. However, let us first dive into the relevant provisions on nondisclosure of source code and algorithms in the FTAs. What are the relevant provisions in international trade agreements, and how, if at all, do they affect a state's ability to regulate platform?

5.3.3 *Trade Rules on Source Code Disclosure*

5.3.3.1 Source Code Nondisclosure Provisions under the FTAs

A growing number of FTAs contain provisions to restrict access to source code. Article 14.17 of the CPTPP, for example, prohibits "the transfer of, or access to, source code" as a condition of the "import, distribution, sale or use" of software.[176] Essentially, source code nondisclosure provisions aim to prevent states from requiring technology transfer in exchange for international trade. In the context of digital platforms, services suppliers generally have invested resources in the development of source code. If they are required to disclose the source code as a condition of market access, they risk exposing their technologies to competitors and losing their competitive advantage. Source code nondisclosure provisions therefore safeguard software owners' rights over their intellectual property against mandatory disclosure.[177]

Traditionally, trade secret law has been the most widely used legal mechanism to protect software source code. Nonetheless, the specific expression of innovative software ideas can also be protected through other intellectual property rights, such as copyrights and patents. In this regard, the WTO Agreement on Trade-Related Aspects of Intellectual Property Rights (TRIPS) has for some time been the most relevant legal tool in terms of source code protection under the realm of international economic law.[178] Source code nondisclosure protections under the FTAs, however, go beyond the TRIPS by directly barring governments from demanding the disclosure of source code as a prerequisite for market

[176] See, for example, CPTPP, Article 14.17; USMCA, Article 19.16; Australia-Singapore Digital Economy Agreement, Article 28; The US–Japan Digital Trade Agreement, Article 17; The EU–Japan Economic Partnership Agreement, Article 8.73; The EU–UK Trade and Cooperation Agreement, Article 207.

[177] See generally Magdalena Słok-Wódkowska and Joanna Mazur, "Secrecy by Default: How Regional Trade Agreements Reshape Protection of Source Code" (2022) 25(1) Journal of International Economic Law 91. See also the UK Parliament, "Digital Trade and Data" First Report (June 23, 2021) <https://committees.parliament.uk/publications/6451/documents/70389/default/>, paras. 73–76.

[178] TRIPS, Articles 27 and 39.

access, subject to exceptions. Arguably, the trend to include the ban on the mandatory disclosure of source code provisions in the FTAs stems from the emerging need for greater source code protections, and in particular, in response to some state actions, such as China's policy of forcing foreign firms to disclose their source code and/or "other parts of their intellectual property" as a condition for doing business in China.[179]

In addition to source code, several FTAs extend the general prohibition on disclosure requirements to algorithms. For example, Article 19.16 (Source Code) of the USMCA bans mandatory transfers and access to both the source code and the algorithm expressed in it, stating the following:

> 1. No Party shall require the transfer of, or access to, a source code of software owned by a person of another Party, *or to an algorithm expressed in that source code*, as a condition for the *import, distribution, sale or use* of that software, or of products containing that software, in its territory (emphasis added).
> 2. This Article does not preclude a regulatory body or judicial authority of a Party from requiring a person of another Party to preserve and make available the source code of software, or an algorithm expressed in that source code, to *the regulatory body for a specific investigation, inspection, examination, enforcement action, or judicial proceeding*, subject to safeguards against unauthorized disclosure[180] (emphasis added).

Here, an algorithm is broadly defined in these agreements as "a defined sequence of steps, taken to solve a problem or obtain a result."[181] At the time of this writing, similar text could be found in Section C.3 (1) – Source Code of the WTO JSI on E-commerce.[182] The inclusion of algorithms substantially broadens the scope of the source code nondisclosure provisions. By preventing the mandatory disclosure of

[179] See Cosmina Dorobantu et al., "Source Code Disclosure: A Primer for Trade Negotiators" in Ingo Borchert and Alan Winters (eds), *Addressing Impediments to Digital Trade* (CEPR Press 2021), at 105–140.

[180] USMCA, Article 19.16.

[181] USMCA, Article 19.1. See also supra note 139 for the distinction between source code and algorithms.

[182] WTO Electronic Commerce Negotiations – Consolidated Negotiating Text, INF/ECOM/62/Rev.1 (December 2020).

algorithms in addition to that of source code as a condition for market access, the USMCA-type of source code nondisclosure provision makes it clear that it also prohibits requirements to disclose algorithms. Unless justified by exceptions, a USMCA party seeking access to the algorithms used by digital platforms as a condition for digital trade market access would be inconsistent with Article 19.16 of the USMCA.

The expanded scope of the prohibition on disclosure requirements thus raises concerns about its impact on the ability of governments to regulate the use of algorithms at the domestic level. Civil societies such as the Australian Council of Trade Unions stressed that preventing relevant authorities from accessing source code and algorithms altogether would unduly restrict governments from supervising platforms' compliance with domestic regulations and ensuring algorithmic accountability.[183] They believed that keeping source code and algorithms secret also makes it difficult for the public to understand how the algorithms make decisions, and whether there is bias or discrimination within the process.[184] Indeed, compared to FTA provisions that only preclude the accessibility of source code, FTA provisions that additionally preclude the mandatory accessibility of algorithms place further restrictions on the power of authorities to protect consumers.[185] It is notable that the key source codes and algorithms that drive datafication are primarily owned by the digital platforms, and in particular the big tech companies. Some critics have therefore asserted that the consequences of restrictions to algorithm access would jeopardize the ability of governments to "develop regulatory measures that could ensure transparency of algorithmic governance tools."[186] In their view, the expanded scope of source code nondisclosure provisions in international economic law conceivably protects private capital – the source code and algorithms owned by the digital platforms – at the expense of governments' full regulatory autonomy to supervise legal compliance.[187]

[183] Australian Council of Trade Unions, "Australia-Singapore Digital Economy Agreement: Submission by the Australian Council of Trade Unions to the Joint Standing Committee on Treaties" ACTU D. No 49/2020 (25 September 2020), at 11.

[184] *Ibid.*

[185] Dorobant et al., supra note 179, at 114.

[186] Słok-Wódkowska and Mazur, supra note 177, at 93.

[187] *Ibid.* See also Jane Kelsey, "Digital Trade Rules and Big Tech: Surrendering Public Good to Private Power" (2020) Public Services International, at 16. See also the UK Parliament, supra note 177, para. 78.

5.3.3.2 The Supervision of Algorithms

To the contrary, some believe that the USMCA-type source code nondisclosure provisions, given their broad scope to cover "vital digital assets," can better help to enhance business trust and protect foreign firms from unauthorized disclosure.[188] In the view of Mitchell and Mishra, a diligent balance has been achieved in USMCA Article 19.16 by restricting governments from forcing the disclosure of both source code and algorithms on the one end, and ensuring that governments can place demands on foreign firms to disclose their source code and algorithms for accountability and regulatory purposes, on the other end.[189] Specifically, attention should be given to the second paragraph of USMCA Article 19.16, which explicitly states that the provision does not preclude a regulatory body or judicial authority from requiring access to source codes or algorithms "for a specific investigation, inspection, examination, enforcement action, or judicial proceeding."

In fact, such a similarly worded regulatory/judicial preclusion can be found in the source code nondisclosure provisions of several international trade agreements, such as the US–Japan Digital Trade Agreement, the Australia-Singapore Digital Economy Agreement (DEA), and the Korea-Singapore Digital Partnership Agreement (KSDPA).[190] Moreover, as a subset of regulatory/judicial preclusion, the EU-Japan Economic Partnership Agreement and EU-New Zealand FTA, for example, also allow a court, an administrative tribunal, or a competition authority to require access to source code owned by foreign firms to remedy a violation of competition law.[191] Altogether, source code nondisclosure provisions do not seem to compromise the regulatory autonomy on digital platforms, because governments still retain the power to investigate and audit automated content-moderating systems, biased and discriminatory algorithms, and algorithmic recommendation and ranking processes.

It should also be emphasized that the source code nondisclosure provisions in the FTAs target the market access of software businesses,

[188] Andrew D. Mitchell & Neha Mishra, "Regulating Cross-Border Data Flows in a Data-Driven World: How WTO Law Can Contribute" (2019) 22(3) Journal of International Economic Law 389, 413.

[189] *Ibid.*, at 414.

[190] See, for example, Australia-Singapore Digital Economy Agreement, Article 28. See also Korea-Singapore Digital Partnership Agreement, Article 14.19.

[191] The EU–Japan Economic Partnership Agreement, Article 8.73. See also the EU–New Zealand FTA, Article 12.11.

namely, "import, distribution, sale or use of software," for supplying international trade. Essentially, these provisions are centered on "market access" and are not designed to constrain governments from requiring information to investigate compliance. It can be argued that a country's right to regulate digital platforms would not be adversely affected by these provisions as long as the regulatory actions do not block the market access of foreign services. Turning back to the first row of Figure 5.1, platforms' disclosure obligations to the regulatory body generally rank high on the scale when measuring transparency. For instance, Article 69 of the DSA mandates that regulators conduct inspections, including requiring access to the algorithms of the very large online search engines. In a similar vein, Articles 21 and 23 of the DMA empower regulators to require access to all necessary information for the inspection, including any data and algorithms. One could contend that such inspection power under the DSA and the DMA does not necessarily constitute a condition for market access and therefore is consistent with the FTAs' source code nondisclosure provisions.

Nonetheless, as discussed in Section 3.5, there are situations in which the boundary between market access prerequisites and non-market access regulations is blurred. To some extent, any transparency requirement, no matter how "pure" its design for regulatory purposes, would potentially affect the "distribution, sale, or use" of software in the given market. Therefore, it is disputable how far the FTAs' nondisclosure provisions can go in this regard. In any event, assuming that any regulatory action had been broadly construed as a market access prerequisite, the government would have to rely on the carve-out and exceptions to justify the mandatory disclosure of the source code and algorithms.

First turning to the carve-outs for critical infrastructure services: Some source code nondisclosure provisions allow for the forced disclosure of information relating to critical infrastructure.[192] The term "critical infrastructure," however, was left undefined in the Digital Trade/E-Commerce Chapter. Accordingly, what the concept of "critical infrastructure" might cover would be interpreted pursuant to the previous discussion in Chapter 2.

[192] Article 14.17(2) of the CPTPP states: "For the purposes of this Article, software subject to paragraph 1 is limited to mass-market software or products containing such software and does not include software used for critical infrastructure."

Second, the general exceptions and the security exceptions are available in all of these provisions.[193] In my view, even if measures that are necessary to enhance platform accountability and maintain digital legal order were found to fall within the scope of market access-related restrictions, they could be justifiable under exceptions, and in particular, the public morals general exceptions. As previously discussed in Chapters 1 and 2, the country implementing the disputed transparency requirements would have to prove that the measure at issue satisfies the necessity test and the Chapeau test under the public morals exceptions. It is worth reiterating that according to WTO jurisprudence, a country has the regulatory autonomy to choose its level of protection in relation to the objective being pursued, which is, in this context, fair and transparent algorithmic decision-making in a datafied business environment. Any less trade-restrictive alternatives proposed by the governments of foreign platforms must qualify as reasonably available alternatives under the necessity test.

At the end of the day, the ambit within which source codes and algorithms can be kept secret under international economic law relies on the exceptions, entailing a delicate balance between the competing interests involving platforms' trade secrets, digital innovation, algorithmic accountability, and other legitimate public objectives. With that in mind, this book argues that international regulatory coherence and cooperation surrounding platform regulations should be an important direction for global governance in a platform economy. Good regulatory practices (GRP) with *ex-ante* regulatory impact assessment (RIA), when appropriately implemented, can help identify and address unnecessary trade restrictions, forestall potential trade disputes at earlier stages, and reduce the likelihood of lengthy and costly dispute settlement procedures. Section 5.4 will continue to discuss the opportunities and challenges of such an approach to global platform governance.

5.4 Good Regulatory Practices for Platform Governance

5.4.1 Potential Fragmentation and Overreaching

Drawing from the analysis above, the fragmentation of platform regulation – whether it relates to content moderation, competition policy, or

[193] See, for example, CPTPP, Article 14.2; Australia-Singapore Digital Economy Agreement, Article 28 and FN 17.

algorithmic transparency – is growing. The proliferation of platform regulations and algorithmic disciplines means that services suppliers are confronting more and more difficulties when attempting to comply with diverse national "behind-the-border measures." The lack of regulatory coherence among states may create costly and burdensome tasks for services suppliers, because when operating at international scale, they must meet different degrees of obligation and satisfy divergent legal standards. Such regulatory fragmentation may direct resources away from more effective business management. This is particularly true for non-big tech, small and medium-size enterprises (SMEs) that lack the resources to manage unique legal requirements in different locations. Taking transparency obligations as an example, as shown in Figure 5.2, complexity surrounding various legal approaches may become a barrier to digital trade, especially for SMEs when those rules apply to them. Truly, as Trachtman pointed out, platform regulations of different states have varying concerns and varying exceptions, and thus may prove contradictory in a complex fashion.[194] The emerging fragmentation and possible contradiction of data governance call for cross-border regulatory coherence and cooperation mechanisms to harmonize the divergent regulatory approaches stemming from disparate public policy objectives and digital trade interests.

At the same time, and relatedly, there are more and more examples of potential regulatory overreaching governmental intervention, which render global platform governance even more difficult. Going beyond the selected five regulations in Figure 5.2, several national and local regulations on algorithmic transparency have raised concerns about policymakers' emerging overreaching practices in this innovation sector. Taking China's "Qinglang – 2022 Algorithm Comprehensive Governance Special Action" as an example, which aims to keep digital platforms on tight leashes, under this special action, Chinese tech giants – including Alibaba, Tencent and TikTok (ByteDance) – have submitted algorithms used in their services to China's Internet watchdog.[195] Indeed, digital platform regulations reflect different priorities in different countries, which further complicates the question of how to manage fragmentation in global platform governance.

[194] Joel P. Trachtman, "Platforms and Global Governance: Globalization on Steroids" (2023) 26(1) Journal of International Economic Law 78, at 83.

[195] "China Regulator Says Alibaba, Tencent Have Submitted App Algorithm Details" (*Reuters*, August 15 2002).

At the crux of the matter is the desire to promote the development of a more harmonized regime that encourages innovation while protecting other public objectives. Conceptually, as denoted by the Manila Principles, platform regulations should comply with the tests of necessity and proportionality to ensure that platform obligations are linked to a specific public objective, the degree of obligations are proportionate to that objective, and regulators' powers extend only to the necessary information.[196] This raises the question of whether international economic law can serve as an effective tool to promote regulatory coherence and prevent regulatory overreach. As the global economy goes digital, how can we apply GRP to the domestic regulation given the complex issues involved in a datafied world? Can the regulatory disciplines in the GATS or the FTAs help reduce the likelihood of disguised or unnecessarily restrictive impediments to the platform economy and ease potential regulatory fragmentation and overreaching?

5.4.2 *Good Governance Obligations*

There has been substantial progress in the development of regulatory discipline through international trade instruments at both the multilateral and regional levels. The ambition of the international GRP agenda is aimed at fostering regulatory coherence by offering a systemic response to the inherent potential problems of regulation that may impose costs but add little overall benefits.[197] At the multilateral level, the WTO JSI on Domestic Regulation of Services (the "DR JSI," or "DR Reference Paper") was concluded in December 2021.[198] The participating members, which

196 Developed by NGOs, the Manila Principles are a set of standards for takedown that aim to guide governments to protect free expression. "Manila Principles on Intermediary Liability" <https://manilaprinciples.org/index.html>.

197 Martin Lodge and Kai Wegrich, *Managing Regulation: Regulatory Analysis Politics and Policy* (Palgrave Macmillan 2012), at 211. In the WTO context, Article VI:1 of the GATS, which contains procedural requirements to ensure that all measures of general application affecting trade in services are to be administered in a "reasonable, objective and impartial manner," can be seen as an obligation that imposes a fundamental standard for due process. In the FTA context, the regulatory chapters set forth specific obligations with respect to GRP, including procedural transparency and engagement with interested persons. See for example, USMCA, Article 28.4 (Internal Coordination); Article. 28.6 (Early Planning); Article 28.8 (Use of Plain Language); Article 28.13 (Retrospective Review). See also CPTPP, Article 25.8 (Engagement with Interested Persons).

198 WTO, "Declaration on the Conclusion of Negotiations on Services Domestic Regulation" WT/L/1129 (December 2, 2021).

represent more than 90 percent of the services trade, have agreed on a set of GRP, which will be implemented by incorporating the DR Reference Paper into their GATS Schedules of Commitments. While the DR JSI was negotiated plurilaterally, the outcome will be implemented on a most-favored-nation basis. In other words, the benefits will apply to all WTO members, not just the participants.[199] The DR JSI contains three core principles:[200]

- Regulatory transparency: measures aimed at promoting prompt publication and availability of information and stakeholder engagement in regulatory processes;
- Regulatory predictability: measures aimed at ensuring a reasonable time frame and procedural due process;
- Regulatory quality: measures aimed at disseminating GRP to facilitate the services trade, including ensuring that regulators develop technical standards through open processes and reach their decisions in a manner independent of services suppliers.

In the context of digital platform regulation, these regulatory disciplines establish legally binding guidelines, within which participating countries have the flexibility to regulate the platforms and pursue their policy objectives. Participating countries retain the right to impose digital/data regulations including algorithmic transparency, which arguably is a "technical standard" within the meaning of Article VI:4 of the GATS, on services suppliers.[201] However, it must be done in accordance with the regulatory disciplines laid out in the DR Reference Paper – that is, to improve the good governance landscape through regulatory transparency, predictability, and nondiscrimination.[202]

At the regional level, the development of GRP under the FTAs can be seen as a response to the issues of regulatory fragmentation and over-reaching. Within the last decade or so, good governance obligations have

[199] WTO, "Joint Initiative on Services Domestic Regulation Reference Paper on Services Domestic Regulation" INF/SDR/2 (November 26, 2021).

[200] *Ibid.*

[201] Informal Note by the Chairman, "Disciplines on Domestic Regulation Pursuant to GATS Article VI:4" Room Document (April 18, 2006), para. II:5. "Technical standards" are "measures that lay down the characteristics of a service or the manner in which it is supplied." Technical standards also include the procedures relating to the enforcement of such standards.

[202] Panagiotis Delimatsis, "Concluding the WTO Services Negotiations on Domestic Regulation – Hopes and Fears" (2010) 9(4) World Trade Review 643, at 659.

been progressively negotiated, and in some cases, incorporated into bilateral and regional trade agreements.[203] The reality that market access alone cannot sufficiently safeguard services suppliers to operate effectively in foreign markets has led international trade negotiations to address the issue of GRP.[204] Notable developments in this regard can be found in the more recent FTAs that include a comprehensive set of good governance obligations in a separate chapter. Parties to these FTAs agreed to adopt "GATS plus" regulatory obligations, which are largely equivalent to the DR Reference Paper or even extend beyond it with more advanced disciplines. More recent examples include Chapter 22 (Good Regulatory Practices and Regulatory Cooperation) of the EU–New Zealand FTA, concluded in 2022, and Chapter 26 (Good Regulatory Practice) of the UK–Australia FTA, concluded in 2021. These new regulatory disciplines are set to stipulate minimum standards that must be observed by the FTA parties when adopting and applying domestic regulations, which, if implemented effectively, might in turn offer promising venues for overcoming regulatory fragmentation and potential overreaching. The assumption is that domestic administrative practices in different jurisdictions would become more compatible and reasonable if countries observe, throughout the regulatory cycle, a set of "minimum common quality standards."[205]

Taking CPTPP and USMCA as representative instruments, the Regulatory Coherence Chapter under the CPTPP and the Good Regulatory Practices Chapter under the USMCA set forth specific obligations with respect to GRP, such as promoting information quality, procedural transparency, clear and plain regulatory language, early planning and retrospective review of regulations, central and internal coordination, and engagement with interested persons.[206] In particular, parties have committed to "minimize unnecessary regulatory differences and to

[203] Rodrigo Polanco, "The Trans-Pacific Partnership Agreement and Regulatory Coherence" in Tania Voon (ed), *Trade Liberalization and International Cooperation: A Legal Analysis of the Trans-Pacific Partnership Agreement* (Edward Elgar 2013) 231, at 232–238.

[204] Laura Baiker et al., "Services Domestic Regulation: Locking in Good Regulatory Practices" WTO Working Paper ERSD-2021-14 (September 17, 2021) <www.wto.org/english/res_e/reser_e/ersd202114_e.pdf>, at 7.

[205] Gabriel Gari, "Recent Preferential Trade Agreements' Disciplines for Tackling Regulatory Divergence in Services: How Far beyond GATS?" (2020) 19(1) World Trade Review 1, at 12.

[206] See supra note 197.

facilitate trade or investment,"[207] without compromising each state's regulatory autonomy to pursue its public policy objectives. Possible mechanisms for promoting regulatory coherence include exchanging technical information and data and exploring common approaches to tackling the risks posed by the use of emerging technologies.[208] In addition, under both the CPTPP and the USMCA, the core of GRP is the need to conduct an impact assessment when developing regulations. More specifically, the second paragraph of Article 28.11 of the USMCA delineates the procedures and considerations under which an RIA should be conducted, which highlights the procedures of the regulatory assessment as follows:

> (a) the need for a proposed regulation, including a description of the nature and significance of the problem the regulation is intended to address;
> (b) feasible and appropriate regulatory and non-regulatory alternatives that would address the need identified in subparagraph (a), including the alternative of not regulating;
> (c) benefits and costs of the selected and other feasible alternatives, including the relevant impacts ... as well as risks and distributional effects over time, recognizing that some costs and benefits are difficult to quantify or monetize; and
> (d) the grounds for concluding that the selected alternative is preferable.[209]

Amid the Biden administration's agenda to increase economic cooperation through the IPEF, it is not surprising to see that GRP is one of the key initiatives under the framework. The USTR has declared that it will seek to "advance the benefits of good regulatory practices in supporting good governance"[210] and "build on the outcome reached in the WTO Joint Initiative on Services Domestic Regulation, as appropriate."[211] In fact, when the USTR of the Obama administration led the TPP negotiations, the USTR repeatedly stressed the importance of the inclusion of a chapter on regulatory coherence in the TPP, as it reflects the growing

[207] USMCA, Article 28.17.
[208] *Ibid.*
[209] USMCA, Article 28.11 (Regulatory Impact Assessment), paragraph 2.
[210] USTR, "Ministerial Text for Trade Pillar of the Indo-Pacific Economic Framework for Prosperity" (September 23, 2022).
[211] *Ibid.*

relevance of regulatory issues to international trade and investment.[212] In light of the fact that the legal and regulatory environment in TPP parties is diverse, the USTR had advocated for the incorporation of regulatory coherence into the TPP to eliminate the problem of "overlapping and inconsistent regulatory requirements or regulations being developed unfairly and without a sound basis."[213] Now, six years after the US withdrew from the CPTPP, the IPEF seems to have the potential to reassert US economic engagement to counter China's growing influence and promote US regulatory approaches and standards in the region.

The crux of the matter, however, is to what extent good governance obligations in international trade agreements can tackle regulatory fragmentation and combat unreasonable administrative practices. Will these regulatory principles and methodological tools bring about greater policy coherence in the governance of the digital economy? When domestic regulators are faced with questions of how to regulate digital platforms, in what way can these GRP converge the fragmented legal approaches to issues such as content moderation, cultural diversity, platform competition, and algorithmic transparency? For the reasons explained below, this book contends that far more political will is needed to ensure that the GRPs/RIAs do the trick.

5.4.3 *Marching toward Policy Coherence in Platform Governance?*

5.4.3.1 The Breadth and Strength of GRP/RIA

First of all, although relatively ambitious GRP provisions can be found in some FTAs,[214] other FTAs contain only symbolic GRP provisions. For example, the chapter on the "General Provisions and Exceptions" of the RCEP establishes obligations on minimum standards of regulatory transparency and due process in the administrative proceedings. However, the RCEP is silent on many higher standards of GRPs to prevent undue delay in authorization or arbitrary administration. In particular, the absence of RIA in the RCEP implies fewer safeguards to ensure regulatory quality

212 USTR, "Summary of the Trans-Pacific Partnership Agreement" (October 4, 2015) <https://ustr.gov/about-us/policy-offices/press-office/press-releases/2015/october/summary-trans-pacific-partnership>.

213 *Ibid.*

214 Outstanding examples include the EU-Canada Comprehensive Economic and Trade Agreement (CETA), CPTPP, USMCA, Australia–UK FTA, EU-New Zealand Free Trade Agreement, etc.

than if such provisions were included, leaving the RCEP behind in the developments of GRPs compared to other recently negotiated FTAs.[215] Arguably, divergences in the regulatory frameworks of Asian countries, especially China, have made it challenging to conclude "harder GRP obligations."

Second, even for those countries that are parties to FTAs with more ambitious GRPs, one fundamental question surrounding the possible contributions of the GRPs to the quality of platform regulation is the breadth of their application. Normatively speaking, the applicable coverage of the GRPs is rather uncertain. Here, a typical example is Article 25.1 of the CPTPP, which stipulates that the "covered regulatory measure" under its Regulatory Coherence Chapter refers to "the regulatory measure determined by each Party."[216] According to Article 25.3, each party shall determine and make publicly available the scope of its covered regulatory measures. Article 25.3 further requires that "in determining the scope of covered regulatory measures, each Party should aim to achieve significant coverage."[217] In other words, although the definition of "regulatory measure" is rather broad, referring to "any measure of general application . . . adopted by regulatory agencies with which compliance is mandatory,"[218] the exact scope of the "covered regulatory measures" is flexible. Each party has the discretion to decide to what extent its domestic regulation should be subject to GRPs. Empirically speaking, some notifications from the CPTPP parties in this regard are encouraging. In particular, developed countries such as Japan and Australia have adopted "covered regulatory measures" that are general and extensive.[219] However, considering that the application of the GRPs generally requires administrative resources to complete, it is likely that some governments may tend to establish a minimum threshold in terms of the obligation to perform GRPs.[220] After all, GRPs not only require

[215] APEC, "Study on APEC's Non-binding Principles for Domestic Regulation of the Services Sector" (2021) <www.apec.org/Publications/2020/01/Study-on-APECs-Non-binding-Principles-for-Domestic-Regulation-of-the-Services-Sector>, at 23.

[216] CPTPP, Article 25.1.

[217] CPTPP, Article 25.3.

[218] CPTPP, Article 25.1.

[219] Ministry of Foreign Affairs of Japan, "Related Information on CPTPP Chapter 25 (Regulatory Coherence)" <www.mofa.go.jp/ecm/ep/page24e_000257.html>; Australian Government, "Chapter Summary: Regulatory Coherence" <www.dfat.gov.au/sites/default/files/regulatory-coherence.pdf>.

[220] This discussion draws upon materials in Shin-yi Peng, "Lessons from the TPP Regulatory Coherence Chapter: The Laws Governing Unsolicited Commercial

changes in the institutional setting, but also demand adjustments in the behavior and mindset of civil servants.[221] Therefore, platform regulations are not necessarily subject to GRPs/RIAs.

Third, even assuming that a country has made legally binding commitments to GRPs in FTAs, the real impact may not be significant due to the narrow range of domestic regulatory instruments that are subject to GRPs. For example, Article 28.1 of the USMCA explicitly limits the scope of "regulation" under the Good Regulatory Practices Chapter to the "measure of general application adopted, issued, or maintained by a regulatory authority with which compliance is mandatory."[222] The definition of "regulatory authority" under the chapter, however, is limited to "an administrative authority or agency at the Party's central level of government that develops, proposes or adopts a regulation."[223] The definition explicitly excludes "legislatures or courts."[224] In other words, the GRPs/RIAs only apply to "few" but not "all" regulatory instruments that impact platform activities. In terms of platform regulation, the fact that the GRPs only apply to the executive branch of governments but not to legislatures or parliaments means that the RIAs, in some countries, are at most carried out by agency-made digital rules.

Finally, assuming *arguendo* that a platform regulation falls within the range of regulatory instruments subject to GRPs, the strength of the application of RIAs might be weakened by divergent methodologies. As previously indicated, RIA has been defined as a systemic approach to critically identifying and assessing the regulatory effects – including the existing regulations and proposed nonregulatory alternatives.[225] In the context of digital platform regulations, policymakers should identify problems arising from platform monopolies and data capitalism, determine the need for intervention, propose alternative regulatory options ranging from competition law to algorithmic transparency, and then assess and decide upon the preferred policy option. Throughout the process, the assessment – whether it is qualitative or quantitative – can be

Electronic Messages as a Case Study" in Shin-yi Peng et al. (eds), *Governing Science and Technology under the International Economic Order: Regulatory Divergence and Convergence in the Age of Mega-regionals* (Edward Elgar 2018) 64, at 70–80.

221 *Ibid.*, at 71.

222 USMCA, Article 28.1 (Definitions).

223 *Ibid.*

224 OECD, "Regulatory Impact Assessment, OECD Best Practice Principles for Regulatory Policy" (2020), at 19–20.

225 OECD, "Regulatory Impact Analysis: A Tool for Policy Coherence" (2009), at 185.

accomplished by employing various techniques. According to the OECD, the adoption of RIA is now becoming widespread, but it operates differently within and across countries.[226] Methodologically speaking, various RIA procedures can be designed and used. As a result, policymakers' understanding of the procedure of RIA varies greatly. In practice, RIA has been uniquely practiced by different countries or even different governmental bodies.[227]

This raises the question of how the good governance obligations under the FTAs help ensure that policymakers "choose the best regulatory option" when designing and implementing platform regulations, and how the GRPs/RIAs help converge the fragmented legal approaches to the platform economy. At their heart, GRPs under the FTAs were intentionally framed in flexible terms to reserve room for an individual FTA party to decide how extensively it will commit. It is clear that the RIA provisions under the FTAs do not provide much guidance as to how to operate the process. To place these questions into a more concrete setting, both the DSA and the DMA "passed" the RIA test conducted by the EC before implementation. The European Commission's Impact Assessment Report of the DSA (the RIA Report) is over 200 pages long, containing a detailed analysis of what the problem drivers are, why the EU should act, what the policy options are, what the impacts of these options are, how the options compare, and which option is preferred.[228] The RIA Report concludes that the DSA is in full compliance with the EU's international obligations in the WTO and FTAs.[229] The RIA Report underscores that the DSA is in line with the nondiscrimination provisions of the GATS, as it establishes objective criteria, including the definition of VLOPs, regardless of the origin of the services supplier.[230] Moreover, the RIA Report states that the asymmetric regulation, which imposes additional transparency requirements on the VLOPs, does not jeopardize the protection of trade secrets of digital platforms because the DSA entails

[226] *Ibid.*, at 8.

[227] *Ibid.*, at 19–20.

[228] European Commission, "Impact Assessment Accompanying the document Proposal For a Regulation of the European Parliament and of the Council on a Single Market For Digital Services (Digital Services Act) and amending Directive 2000/31/EC" SWD(2020) 348 final (December 15, 2020).

[229] *Ibid.*, para. 8.

[230] *Ibid.*, para. 213.

a secrecy obligation on the authorities and experts with regard to trade secrets.[231]

Would the same conclusion of the RIA Report be drawn if a different RIA methodology is introduced? Probably not. As explained by Alemanno, a cost–benefit analysis in many cases can be "extra-territorially blind."[232] Both the costs of regulatory fragmentation and the benefits of regulatory coherence might be underestimated. Measurements in the RIA procedure can also be problematic when quantification is not possible, and in that case, the RIA might become a "rubber stamp" to endorse administrative decisions without carefully scrutinizing them,[233] effectively serving as a mere justification for policymakers' choices. At the end of the day, the cost–benefit analysis is more about local value preferences. When local preferences and policy priorities are involved, the process has a more subjective character.[234] As Gari observes, this world might be increasingly globalized and interconnected, but deep differences among countries remain in terms of regulatory needs.[235]

5.4.3.2 Political Support Needed for Future Governance

All in all, in light of the above, the trend of developing GRP obligations under the international trade agreements has the potential to serve as an important tool to address regulatory fragmentation, but much will depend on the political will of the governments involved. Given that the "obligations" of regulatory coherence are predominately phrased in a soft and loose way, the effectiveness of the GRPs, especially the successful incorporation of RIAs into regulatory policy, is dependent upon strong administrative determination. To put it another way, regulatory

[231] *Ibid.*, para. 259.

[232] Alberto Alemanno, "Is There a Role for Cost–Benefit Analysis Beyond the Nation-State? Lessons from International Regulatory Co-operation" in Michael A. Livermore & Richard L. Revesz (eds), *The Globalization of Cost–Benefit Analysis in Environmental Policy* (Oxford University Press 2013), at 104.

[233] OECD, "Policy Brief: Improving the Quality of Regulations" (2009), at 3; Stuart Shapiro, "The Triumph of Regulatory Politics: Benefit–Cost Analysis and Political Salience" (2012) 6 Regulation & Governance 189.

[234] Shin-yi Peng, "Levelling the Playing Field between Sharing Platforms and Industry Incumbents: Good Regulatory Practices?" in Anupam Chander and Haochen Sun (eds), *Data Sovereignty: From the Digital Silk Road to the Return of the State* (Oxford University Press 2023), chapter 7.

[235] Gari, supra note 205, at 29.

divergence can also be seen as an outcome of democratic legitimacy.[236] The potential impact of the good governance obligations under the WTO or FTAs in tackling regulatory fragmentation is therefore constrained.[237] Pushing the goals of GRPs/RIAs too far may generate concerns related to an undue degree of intrusion upon a country's right to regulate.[238] For this reason, the breadth and strength of the GRPs/RIAs fundamentally rest on political support for good-faith implementation. However, despite the above considerations, there are reasons for being optimistic about better governance through international trade agreements.

First, in terms of the applicable coverage of the GRPs, there seems to be a growing political willingness to endorse the relevant initiatives. At the WTO, additional members have joined the DR JSI to "make their regulatory environment more conducive to business," and to "lower trade costs for services suppliers seeking to access foreign markets."[239] At the regional level, more and more new-generation FTAs contain the GRP obligations. Although they are primarily drafted in flexible language, they nevertheless provide a baseline for parties to undertake regulatory reform. Over time, such soft obligations may help the parties to align with trends leaning toward more transparent and predictable regulatory frameworks – which are vital to services trade across borders.[240] Platform suppliers, especially SMEs, will eventually benefit from improved regulatory quality and facilitation.

Second, in terms of a greater political willingness to implement GRPs, one promising direction is to establish a central oversight body to perform checks of draft RIA reports.[241] Historically, it has not been unusual for regulators to conduct an "incomplete" assessment of the economic costs and benefits of regulatory alternatives.[242] Policymakers may fail to generate a comprehensive evaluation of the possible impacts of regulation, resulting in "stove-piped" internal decisions that lead to conflicting regulatory approaches in the administrative system.[243]

236 Anne Meuwese, "Constitutional Aspects of Regulatory Coherence in TTIP: An EU Perspective" (2015) 78 Law & Contemporary Problems 153.
237 Gari, supra note 205, at 28.
238 *Ibid.*, at 29.
239 WTO, "Georgia, Timor-Leste and United Arab Emirates Join Initiative on Services Domestic Regulation" (June 13, 2022).
240 Baiker et al., supra note 204, at 33, 40.
241 OECD, supra note 224, at 17–20.
242 *Ibid.*, at 17.
243 *Ibid.*, at 19.

However, according to OECD studies, more and more jurisdictions, including both OECD and non-OECD countries, have dedicated a single governmental body to be responsible for reviewing regulatory quality in the national administration from a "whole-of-government" perspective.[244] Alternatively, an increasing number of countries are establishing a specific parliamentary committee with responsibilities for monitoring the quality of the RIA system as a whole.[245] As previously discussed, in the context of platform regulation, the primary institutional challenge in the introduction of RIAs is to coordinate diverse considerations – for example, competition policy, consumer protection, freedom of speech, trade secrets, industrial innovation, and other public objectives – in an integrated manner. The fact that many countries are now creating a centralized coordinating body within their jurisdictions as a quality assurance mechanism is a sign of governments' willingness to embed GRPs and RIA scrutiny in their policymaking systems.

Finally, in terms of the methodology of RIAs, some innovative approaches have been introduced into the realm of platform regulation, which represent a significant step in promoting coherence in digital policy. For example, the "Digital Checklists" contained in the EU's "Better Regulation toolbox" are specifically designed to identify the digital issues and impacts surrounding new policies. Any proposed regulation with digital dimensions should go through the Toolbox when defining the problem, assessing impacts, developing policy options, and choosing digital policy solutions.[246] Similar approaches have been adopted in the UK's RIA guidance, which effectively integrates competition policy with RIAs by requiring the assessment to "incorporate an explicit consideration of the competition impacts of regulatory proposals."[247] More importantly, there is a general tendency to not only embrace domestic market dynamics, but to also address international aspects such as market openness.[248] The increasing degree of attention accorded data-driven factors in the RIA context indicates a

[244] *Ibid.*

[245] *Ibid.*, at 33.

[246] European Commission, "Better Regulation: Guidelines and Toolbox" (November 3, 2021) <https://ec.europa.eu/info/law/law-making-process/planning-and-proposing-law/better-regulation-why-and-how/better-regulation-guidelines-and-toolbox_en>.

[247] UK's Department for Business, Energy & Industrial Strategy, "Better Regulation Framework" (2020) <www.gov.uk/government/publications/better-regulation-framework>, at 14.

[248] OECD, supra note 224, at 20.

promising venue to advance the more coherent governance of platform activities.[249]

5.5 Conclusion

We have investigated the driving forces of platformization. When data becomes capital and the algorithmic input of the digital platforms, the interplay between national regulation and international economic law is complex and multilayered. The specific aspects considered in Chapters 3–5 help formulate views and outlooks regarding the role of international economic law in the politics of datafication. The discussions in Part II also lead us to reflect on what international trade agreements have done and can do in global platform governance. Let us now shift gears to the broad digital ecosystem and continue to explore the phenomenon of datafication from a cross-layer perspective: data flows. Chapter 6 will bring a sharper focus to privacy and cybersecurity.

[249] *Ibid.*, at 31.

PART III

Datafication and Data Flows

6

Data Flows as Digital Trade

Privacy and Cybersecurity Governance in a Datafied World

6.1 Introduction

At a time when the global economy has become more digital and more datafied, data flows are becoming increasingly integral in all sectors. As illustrated in previous chapters, data flows, which are at the heart of the datafied economy, include complex types of information – from social media, video streaming, and health and financial data to other business services. Indeed, data flows literally constitute our social relations.[1] The so-called data explosion is real, and it is here. According to AmCham, more than 4 billion people spent a total of 3.7 trillion hours on social media in 2021.[2] In 2022 alone, 74 zettabytes of data were generated.[3] Labeled "the lifeblood of the modern economy," much of today's international trade in services would not exist without cross-border data flows – the movement of data between computer servers across national borders.[4]

Parts of this chapter are based on the author's previous work: Shin-yi Peng, "Public-Private Interactions in Privacy Governance" (Concept Paper) (2022) 11(6) MDPI-Laws Special Issue: International Law as a Driver of Internet Governance, at 80; Shin-yi Peng, "Private Cybersecurity Standards? Cyberspace Governance, Multistakeholderism, and the (Ir)relevance of the TBT Regime" (2018) 51(2) Cornell International Law Journal 445.

1 Salomé Viljoen, "An Argument for Positive Political Theories of Data Governance" (2022) 6 Georgetown Law Technology Review 464, at 466.

2 Daniel S. Hamilton and Joseph P. Quinlan, "The Transatlantic Economy 2021: Annual Survey of Jobs, Trade and Investment between the United States and Europe" (2021).

3 World Trade Forum, "How Industrial Data Can Help Unleash Productivity, Innovation and Sustainability" (May 13, 2022) <www.weforum.org/agenda/2022/05/industrial-data-can-unlock-our-sustainable-future-heres-how/>.

4 OECD, "Fostering Cross-Border Data Flows with Trust" OECD Digital Economy Papers No. 343 (December 2022); The U.S. Congressional Research Service (CRS), "Data Flows, Online Privacy, and Trade Policy" (March 26, 2020).

It would be a misunderstanding if one were to think that cross-border data flows are less significant to the manufacturing sector. Data flows are now an integral part of almost all new technologies, including the IoT, AI, 3D printing, and cloud computing, etc.[5] More and more businesses depend on data flows for interconnected machinery and big data analytics. In particular, smart manufacturing – the application of digital technologies to manufacturing processes, from supply chain management to after-sales support – relies on cross-border machine-to-machine data flows.[6] Data-enabled goods and services require data and their flows across borders to support commercial activities, which generally include all of the stages of design, production, delivery, sales, and maintenance.[7] As a result, digital technologies are now connecting billions of people to one another, and they are also connecting those people to billions of devices. Furthermore, they are connecting all of those billions of devices.

In short, in terms of commercial aspects, cross-border data flows are central to the digital economy. Many sectors, including smart manufacturing, are highly reliant on digital trade and data flows. Cross-border data flows accelerate data-driven innovation and facilitate international trade in goods and services. More specifically, they enable smart manufacturing and global value chains and support cross-border services and platform activities.[8] At the same time, in terms of social aspects, the ubiquitous exchange of data across borders enables modern-day social interactions. Today's internationally connected social network is underpinned by the movement of data across borders.

Data flows connect the entire Internet ecosystem. As illustrated in Figure 0.1 of the Introduction of this book, horizontally, data flows across different servers, while vertically, data flows across different layers,

[5] See, for example, Zurich Insurance, "Cross-border Data Flows: Designing a Global Architecture for Growth and Innovation" (2022) <www.zurich.com/en/knowledge/topics/digital-data-and-cyber/cross-border-data-flows-designing-global-architecture-for-growth-and-innovation>.

[6] Frontier Economics, "The Value of Cross-Border Data Flows to Europe: Risks and Opportunities" (June 2021) <https://digital-europe-website-v1.s3.fr-par.scw.cloud/uploads/2021/06/Frontier-DIGITALEUROPE_The-value-of-cross-border-data-flows-to-Europe_Risks-and-opportunities.pdf>, at 15.

[7] OECD, supra note 4, at 10–12.

[8] CRS, supra note 4. As illustrated in Section 1.4.4, the concept of "digital trade" is understood in a broad sense. The EU defines it as "commerce enabled by electronic means – by telecommunications and/or ICT services – and covers trade in both goods and services." EU, "Digital Trade" (2023) < https://policy.trade.ec.europa.eu/help-exporters-and-importers/accessing-markets/goods-and-services/digital-trade_en >.

including the network infrastructure and digital platforms. This final chapter, therefore, is somewhat of a cross-cutting, catch-all chapter that addresses the key challenges to cross-border data flows. In the wake of the datafied economy, should data be able to flow across borders by default? How can we safeguard privacy and security while reaping the economic and societal benefits of cross-border data flows? How can international trade agreements promote the movement of data while allowing states to ensure desired protections over data that crosses national borders? More importantly, how can we facilitate national regulatory approaches that work together on a global scale? These are the primary questions this chapter attempts to address.

6.2 Data Flow Restrictions as Trade Barriers

6.2.1 Cross-Border Data Flow Restrictions

In most situations, the "raw data" we generate in our daily lives crosses a number of national borders. As illustrated in Chapter 5, businesses process and compile individual profiles for many reasons, including targeted marketing. Data can also be sold or exchanged between businesses for such purposes. All of these scenarios bring significant challenges to data privacy and security, especially when personal data is transferred to other countries.[9] Disputes arise when personal data is safeguarded domestically but is less protected in another country. Conversely, it also poses a potential trade conflict when the flow of personal data is relatively free at home but is subject to strict restrictions abroad. Such international confrontations are now being amplified by new technologies such as the IoT and AI, simply because of the increasing reliance on cross-border data flows.

Much literature has documented national regulations that constrain the free flow of data across borders. According to studies conducted by the Information Technology & Innovation Foundation (ITIF), the number of countries that have adopted data localization measures has doubled in recent years, and the total number of data localization regulations around the world reached 144 in 2021.[10] In addition to

[9] OECD, supra note 4, at 10–12.

[10] A substantial body of literature exists on how states regulate cross-border data flows. See, for example, Nigel Cory and Luke Dascoli, "How Barriers to Cross-Border Data Flows Are Spreading Globally, What They Cost, and How to Address Them" Information Technology & Innovation Foundation (ITIF) (July 19, 2021) <https://itif.org/publica

explicit data localization measures that require data to be physically stored in the country where it originates, more and more *de facto* localization measures impose stringent and sometimes arbitrary data transfer requirements. As a result, businesses "choose" to store data locally to avoid complicated and costly pre-approval procedures for data transfers.[11] Taking a broader view, increasingly, states are deciding to regulate every stage of the data flow cycle in order to protect citizens' data privacy and security. Understanding what types of data are subject to which data regulations in the domestic context is complex enough. This problem can be made much more complex when data is transferred to other countries. Governments have been placing conditions on the movement of data across borders to ensure that data protections follow the individual; namely, when data is transferred outside a specific jurisdiction, the protections over it remain equivalent.[12] Consequently, data is subject to different rules depending on where it originated, where it is located, and the type of information it contains.

For businesses, overlapping or sometimes conflicting requirements create operational uncertainty surrounding which regulations apply to which data. This, in turn, can increase compliance costs.[13] Indeed, digital fragmentation is gearing up. When data crosses jurisdictions, regulatory harmonization becomes extremely challenging considering how individuals from different cultural and social backgrounds define the boundaries of their personal space, how people accustomed to different national conditions perceive appropriate limits on governmental surveillance, and what factors must be weighed and balanced when regulating cross-border data flows. In the context of international trade, businesses confront hurdles when attempting to comply with often conflicting requirements of diverse national regulations. Divergent national approaches raise costs and thereby direct resources away from more efficient operations, a phenomenon which eventually increases the price of goods and services offered to consumers. Notably, compliance costs stemming from conflicting rules may exceed what many SMEs can afford. In this regard, a fragmented data regulatory landscape creates

tions/2021/07/19/how-barriers-cross-border-data-flows-are-spreading-globally-what-they-cost/>, at 3.

[11] *Ibid.*, at 3–4.

[12] OECD, supra note 4, at 14.

[13] *Ibid.*, at 15.

the risk of squeezing out SMEs. At the end of the day, big tech can afford big legal departments and absorb the pain better than SMEs.

Whatever the different rationales behind the restrictions on cross-border data flows, these measures have affected global digital trade. Undeniably, free transborder data flows would enable services suppliers to build their commercial networks and data centers based on their business models, thereby increasing business efficiency.[14] Data localization requirements, when strictly enforced, would force companies to "build expensive and unnecessarily redundant data centers in every market they seek to serve."[15] Moreover, data centers are capital-intensive, which may bring substantial economic and social benefits for the host state, including job opportunities, increased taxes, and technological know-how. This may also bring about the cluster effect – the overall growth of the data-driven economy of a nation. To conclude, a more liberalized, less fragmented, and more harmonized international framework for data flows would bridge the differences among jurisdictions, diffuse the threat of legal uncertainty, reduce business costs, increase compliance, and therefore provide benefits to both industry and consumers – not to mention the potential for global economic growth if the origin and destination countries of data flows are mutually bound by common, agreed-upon standards. Accordingly, reaching an international consensus regarding how to balance free data flows and national policy objectives, especially data privacy and security, is key to advancing the digital economy.

6.2.2 *A Balkanized International Marketplace?*

That said, the road moving toward regulatory interoperability,[16] which may bridge regulatory disparities and thus facilitate transborder data flows, is far from well paved. At the regional level, states' international commitments are "soft" in the sense that most of them are subject to

[14] Joshua P. Meltzer, "The Internet, Cross-Border Data Flows and International Trade" (2015) 2(1) Asia & Pacific Policy Studies 90, at 91–92.

[15] USTR, "Chapter Summary of Electronic Commerce"<https://ustr.gov/sites/default/files/TPP-Chapter-Summary-Electronic-Commerce.pdf>, at 2.

[16] For a working definition of the term "privacy interoperability," see OECD, "Going Digital Guide to Data Governance Policy Making" (2022) <www.oecd.org/science/going-digital-guide-to-data-governance-policy-making-40d53904-en.htm>, at 45, in which "interoperability" is defined as the ability to "bridge any differences in approaches and systems of privacy and personal data protection to facilitate transborder flows of personal data."

broad exceptions.[17] To be more concrete, although new generation FTAs more directly address data flows, they typically include general obligations to the free flow of data across borders, in conjunction with a commitment to maintain legal frameworks for personal data protection. In addition, they normally impose obligations to prohibit data localization, again, with accompanying exceptions. Taking the E-Commerce Chapter of the CPTPP as an example, Article 14.13 is the key provision that directly confronts data localization measures,[18] while Articles 14.8 and 14.11 lay down disciplines addressing personal data protection and cross-border data flows. Articles 14.11 (data flow) and 14.13 (data location) nevertheless recognize that the parties may impose regulatory requirements on "the transfer of information by electronic means,"[19] as well as requirements pertaining to "the use of computing facilities."[20]

More specifically, CPTPP allows parties to maintain data localization measures to achieve a legitimate public policy objective, as long as the measure "does not impose restrictions on the use or location of computing facilities greater than are required to achieve the objective."[21] Note that, unlike GATT/GATS general exceptions, the exceptions to the free flow of data in the CPTPP contain an open-ended list of public policy objectives and require a trade tribunal's determination regarding whether an objective is legitimate.[22] Considering the political and economic sensitivity surrounding cross-border data flows, leaving the key element vague may make sense in terms of reserving parties' regulatory space. The question of how far such broad exceptions can go, however, will be interpreted by CPTPP tribunals when a real dispute occurs, triggering a high level of legal uncertainty about trade rules.[23]

[17] See generally Mark Wu, "Digital Trade-Related Provisions in Regional Trade Agreements: Existing Models and Lessons for the Multilateral Trade System" RTA Exchange, ICTSD and IDB (November 2017). See also Section 2.3.4.

[18] CPTPP, Article 14.13 (Location of Computing Facilities). See Section 2.3.3 for more discussion.

[19] CPTPP, Article 14.11 (Cross-Border Transfer of Information by Electronic Means).

[20] CPTPP, Article 14.13.

[21] *Ibid.*

[22] Note that with respect to data localization, the USMCA counterpart is stronger than the CPTPP, as the former is a straightforward ban, whereas the latter is linked to a loose exception. In this regard, the Coalition for App Fairness urged the Biden administration not to "make the same USMCA mistakes in the IPEF." Inside U.S. Trade, "New Tech Coalition Warns against USMCA Mistakes in IPEF Digital Rules" (May 18, 2023).

[23] This discussion draws upon materials in Shin-yi Peng and Han-Wei Liu, "The Legality of Data Residency Requirements: How Can the Trans-Pacific Partnership Help?" (2017) 51 (2) Journal of World Trade 183.

At the multilateral level, at the time of this writing, the WTO JSI on E-commerce had launched discussions on this most intense issue – data flows, with primary attention accorded to data localization measures.[24] In view of the "fundamental differences" among the major players – namely, the US, the EU, and China, all of whom are participants in the JSI e-commerce negotiations – it would be unrealistic to anticipate any high-standard agreement with deeper commitments. A less ambitious agreement incorporating the "common elements" of the three approaches, however, would only have a symbolic or nominal impact on cross-border data flows. After all, the fragmentation of national regulations and supervisions has transformed cyberspace into what the USTR coined "a balkanized international marketplace."[25] International arrangements that form like-minded states into coalitions may serve as an avenue through which to address such fragmentation, and in practice, several PTAs appear to be showing signs of convergence toward more similar data flow principles that employ identical or similar treaty language.[26] Nevertheless, substantial divides among the big players remain.[27]

In this context, transatlantic digital fragmentation has been the focal point of global data governance for years. In the Schrems I decision, which invalidated the US–EU Safe Harbor,[28] "adequate level of protection" was interpreted by the ECJ to require the third country to ensure "a level of protection of fundamental rights and freedoms" that is "essentially equivalent" to the EU data protection law.[29] Years later, in the

[24] Inside U.S. Trade, "WTO E-Commerce Leads 'Accelerating' Discussions on Data Flows, Privacy" (October 14, 2022).

[25] USTR, "What's Happening in the TPP on Twenty-first-Century Issues" <https://ustr.gov/about-us/policy-offices/press-office/blog/2013/march/tpp-21st-century-issues>.

[26] As explained by Mira Burri, there appear to be "path dependencies in the global digital trade rule-making." Mira Burri, "Trade Law 4.0: Are We There Yet? (2023) 26(1) Journal of International Economic Law 90.

[27] See, for example, USTR, "2023 National Trade Estimate Report on Foreign Trade Barriers" <https://ustr.gov/about-us/policy-offices/press-office/press-releases/2023/march/ustr-releases-2023-national-trade-estimate-report-foreign-trade-barriers>, at 88 (pointing out that China's restrictions on cross-border data flows and the data localization requirements have severely restricted cross-border data flows and impaired US services suppliers' market access opportunities in China).

[28] Maximillian Schrems v. Data Protection Commissioner (Schrems I) C-362/14 (2015) <https://eur-lex.europa.eu/legal-content/EN/TXT/PDF/?uri=CELEX:62014CJ0362_SUM&from=en>.

[29] *Ibid.*, paras. 6–7.

Schrems II decision, which invalidated the US–EU Privacy Shield,[30] the ECJ found that US surveillance laws do not afford EU data subjects adequate levels of protection equivalent to the EU's GDPR. Thus, transatlantic data flows became unlawful unless firms use standard contractual clauses or binding corporate rules.[31] The ECJ's invalidation of the two US–EU data transfer accords, that is, Safe Harbor in 2015 and the Privacy Shield Framework in July 2020, has threatened bilateral transatlantic trade and created legal uncertainty for businesses, which are primarily SMEs.[32] More than two years after Schrems II, the Trans-Atlantic Data Privacy (TADP) Framework represents a new effort between the two sides to facilitate transatlantic data flows and digital trade.[33] As phrased by Burri, the mutual recognition framework between the US and the EU, although the "second-best" of solutions, nevertheless fosters international cooperation on data flow policies.[34] In any event, the US and the EU are making progress in becoming more closely aligned, despite their obvious differences in terms of data protection. It remains to be seen to what extent the TADP can "strengthen the privacy and civil liberties protections," and, more importantly, whether there will be a Schrems III, IV, V, and so on.

Against this backdrop, this chapter attempts to examine the issues surrounding cross-border data flows from two angles: physical–digital convergence, and public–private convergence. In light of the physical–digital convergence, "industry 4.0" further integrates physical and digital activities. Privacy and cybersecurity paradigms are in flux, a fact which calls for innovative approaches. At the same time, in light of the public–private convergence, the increasing function of soft private law instruments in data governance underscores the need to reconfigure the roles of the public and private sectors in this datafied world. The following sections respectively tackle these two angles.

[30] Data Protection Comm'r v. Facebook Ire. Ltd. & Schrems (Schrems II) C-311/18 (2020) <https://eur-lex.europa.eu/legal-content/EN/TXT/PDF/?uri=CELEX:62018CJ0311&from=E%20N>.

[31] *Ibid.*, paras. 184, 191, 192.

[32] CRS, supra note 4.

[33] On March 25, 2022, the US and the EU jointly announced an "agreement in principle" to the new Trans-Atlantic Data Privacy Framework (TADP). On December 13, 2022, the EU launched the process toward the adoption of an adequacy decision for the TADP.

[34] Mira Burri, "Interfacing Privacy and Trade" (2021) 53 Case Western Reserve Journal of International Law 35, at 87.

6.3 Privacy Governance in a Datafied World

6.3.1 Physical–Digital Convergence: Ubiquitous Data Collection

6.3.1.1 Privacy Paradigm in Flux

For decades, privacy self-management based on informed consent, commonly known as notice-and-consent or "notice-and-choice," has been the key component of any privacy regulatory regime. As reflected in the privacy protection frameworks of the OECD, the EU, and the Asia-Pacific Economic Cooperation (APEC), concepts such as "purpose specification" and "use limitation," together with individuals' positive consent to personal data collection practices, legitimize almost all forms of the collection and use of personal data.[35]

Along the path of technological developments and market changes, this consent-centric regime is facing increasing challenges, primarily surrounding its feasibility. Among all of the critiques,[36] the central question is how to ensure that consent is meaningfully granted in a manner that serves the objective of giving people purposeful control over their data.[37] Commentators contend that the notice-and-consent mechanism may function well in situations where consumers always devote sufficient time and attention to their privacy choices, and where service providers completely adhere to their privacy terms.[38] In the real world, however, both the "notice" and the "consent" components are problematic in today's complex information society, where data collection from cameras, microphones, sensors, and new facial recognition technologies is too ubiquitous to be sufficiently described under meaningful "notice." Living in this datafied world, it is simply unrealistic to issue a notice and obtain consent from every individual whose images are captured by facial recognition cameras installed on sidewalks or in supermarkets. The

[35] See generally Daniel J. Solove, "Privacy Self-Management and the Consent Dilemma" (2013) 126 Harvard Law Review 1879.

[36] See, for example, Joel R. Reidenberg et al., "Trustworthy Privacy Indicators: Grades, Labels, Certifications, and Dashboards" (2019) 96 Washington University Law Review 1409, at 1414; United States President's Council of Advisors on Science and Technology (PCAST), "Big Data and Privacy: A Technological Perspective" ("the PCAST Report) (May2014) <https://obamawhitehouse.archives.gov/sites/default/files/microsites/ostp/PCAST/pcast_big_data_and_privacy_-_may_2014.pdf>; Cf., Mike Hintze, "In Defense of the Long Privacy Statement" (2017) 76 Maryland Law Review 1044.

[37] Hintze, *Ibid.*, at 1045.

[38] John A. Rothchild, "Against Notice and Choice: The Manifest Failure of the Proceduralist Paradigm to Protect Privacy Online or Anywhere Else" (2018) 66 Cleveland State Law Review 559, at 647.

reality is that more and more personal data is passively obtained,[39] and more and more of our movements are being sensed and datafied in ways that we are not aware of. For example, retail stores are increasingly using facial recognition systems in their stores for security and operational purposes. With facial recognition technology installed, retailers are able to bar people with criminal records from entering, recognize shoppers upon entry into the store, provide personalized information and services, monitor staff members who take too many breaks, and, more importantly, collect information for future targeted marketing.[40] To be sure, an increasing proportion of personal data is now being passively collected through constant surveillance and tracking.[41] In daily lives, our faces are often being scanned absent the provision of proper "notice." When data collection occurs passively through surveillance technologies, how can individuals be meaningfully informed and thus consent to it?

At the same time, the "consent" component is equally if not more troubling in our daily lives. It has been empirically proven that privacy policies are "notoriously" long.[42] Twitter's privacy policy, as an illustration, is literally nineteen pages in length.[43] There are endless examples of privacy statements that are impossible, or at least impractical, for consumers to read and comprehend their legal implications. In most cases, consumer consent is arguably illusory, with consumers allocating only a few seconds of very limited attention to quickly scan the "offer" and then "accept" it without an adequate understanding of the transaction.[44]

6.3.1.2 Informed Consent and Big Data Analytics

Big data analytics is now a popular tool through which businesses analyze high-volume and high-variety information assets from both physical and digital spaces. To realize the benefits of big data analytics, businesses must "collect as much data as possible ... from as many sources as

[39] McKay Cunningham, "Next Generation Privacy: The Internet of Things, Data Exhaust, and Reforming Regulation by Risk of Harm" (2014) 2(2) Groningen Journal of International Law 115, at 134.

[40] See, for example, Sergio Mannino, "How Facial Recognition Will Change Retail" (*Forbes*, May 8, 2020).

[41] Shoshana Zuboff, *The Age of Surveillance Capitalism: The Fight for A Human Future at the New Frontier of Power* (2019), at 136, 139.

[42] Reidenberg et al., supra note 36, at 1412.

[43] Twitter Privacy Policy <https://cdn.cms-twdigitalassets.com/content/dam/legal-twitter/site-assets/privacy-aug-19th-2021/Twitter_Privacy_Policy_EN.pdf>.

[44] Cunningham, supra note 39.

possible,"[45] simply because the more sophisticated and larger in scale the data set is, the more successful the big data analytics. In addition, businesses need to "store" the data so they can process and utilize it at a later stage. Throughout the entire big data analytics process, individuals' data privacy and security risk being misappropriated or breached if they are not well managed.

As discussed, the "notice" and "consent" components operate awkwardly in a datafied world. It must be stressed that big data analytics has intensified the dysfunction of the privacy informed-consent regime. The ubiquitous nature of data collection and the explosive volume and variety of data processed today render the "notice and consent" framework, which has been an important pillar of privacy regulation, more and more problematic in practice. Mundie observes that "[t]here is simply so much data being collected, in so many ways, that it is practically impossible to give people a meaningful way to keep track of all the information about them."[46] Even well-informed individuals who practice due diligence may not be able to meaningfully control their data usage. Privacy policies are growing longer and becoming more "all-encompassing" in response to the potential of big data analytics. Service providers tend to craft privacy statements that will cover every possible future use and reserve the maximum space for data aggregation. Written privacy policies, which contain information regarding how service providers will collect and share data with each other, are too vague to represent meaningful notice.[47] It goes without saying that blanket consent, which allows for an unlimited array of data aggregation, is socially undesirable.[48] How can we meaningfully consent to the use of raw data if the fruit of the analysis remains a mystery? In short, big data analytics has become such a common practice that it renders the informed-consent system

[45] Institute for Human Rights and Business (IHRB), "Data Brokers and Human Rights: Big Data, Big Business" (November 2016) <www.ihrb.org/focus-areas/information-communication-technology/data-brokers-big-data-big-business>.

[46] Craig Mundie, "Privacy Pragmatism: Focus on Data Use, Not Data Collection" (2014) 93 (2) Foreign Affairs 28.

[47] See, for example, WhatsApp Privacy Policy, which states "As part of the Facebook Companies, WhatsApp receives information from, and shares information with, the other Facebook Companies. We may use the information we receive from them, and they may use the information we share with them, to help operate, provide, improve, understand, customize, support, and market our Services and their offerings" <www.whatsapp.com/legal/privacy-policy/?lang=en>.

[48] Solove, supra note 35, at 1881.

unworkable. It does not make legal sense to expect that a consumer can honestly and capably evaluate each privacy policy.

It should also be noted that the aggregation of personal data over a period of time by different service providers has brought privacy risks to a new level. Privacy harms might result from cumulative and holistic data usage. To illustrate, an individual consents to Service Provider A's use of his/her nonsensitive data at one point in time, and reveals other equally nonsensitive data to Service Provider B and Service Provider C at later points in time. Service Provider A, which has access to multiple sources of this individual's partial personal information, may be able to effectively piece together data (from Service Provider B and Service Provider C) and thereby analyze and profile sensitive information about this individual. Considering such an aggregation effect, managing personal data in every isolated transaction with separated service providers is no longer an effective way to prevent privacy harms, which may be the result of cumulative and holistic data usage.[49]

Altogether, new technological capabilities are accelerating the problems associated with privacy self-management as defined by Solove.[50] Datafication makes it possible for businesses to use data in ways that may have been technologically infeasible at the time of data collection and thus are beyond the original scope of informed consent. IoT devices, as an outstanding example, are becoming important components of the datafication process due to their ability to connect people at all times, continuously collecting and transmitting data. Sensors throughout a "smart house" track individual residents' behaviors and adjust the house conditions autonomously, including energy use and home security. Sensors in our cars gather real-time data on where the vehicle travels. Additionally, sensors at libraries "talk to" the books we borrow through the radio-frequency identification (RFID) affixed to the books. All of these sensors – at home, in our cars, and in public places – capture terabytes of data. The inevitable situation is that more and more everyday objects are connected to a network, and all of these devices constantly generate data and send it across borders. The expansion of new digital applications makes it even more unlikely that consumers will be able to precisely follow how their personal data is generated, for what purpose,

[49] *Ibid.*

[50] *Ibid.* See also Ari E. Waldman, *Privacy as Trust: Information Privacy for an Information Age* (Cambridge University Press 2018), at 83–85 (arguing that privacy policies are inadequate, confusing, and ineffective).

and by whom, as well as how much of their data is captured, sold, and ultimately used. A valid consent, however, must be "both specific and informed," providing the individual with precise details about the specific use.[51] Considering "the high threshold for a valid consent,"[52] the informed consent mechanism is gradually losing its function in today's technological and market environments.

On the other hand, privacy self-management based on informed consent may also constitute unnecessary barriers to the potential use of big data that could promote public interests and social values.[53] In the big data ecosystem, it is difficult for service providers, when providing services, to predict how the collected data might be aggregated in the future. As for the innovation sectors, a privacy regime that requires informed consent before data collection reflects an outdated technological landscape. Innovations in data aggregation and analysis are rapidly being introduced – a fact which may not be apparent when the data is collected.[54] Commentators therefore argue that the timing of consent should be more heavily focused on downstream uses rather than on the time of data collection.[55] Admittedly, the benefits of innovative and unexpectedly powerful uses of data enabled by big data analytics, to a certain extent, are defeated by the informed consent system. Bearing in mind that big data analytics has the potential to drive social benefits, from public infrastructure to medical innovations, the consent requirement at the time of data collection might serve as a *de facto* prohibition on potential big data applications.

6.3.2 Public–Private Convergence: Privacy Regulatory Models

6.3.2.1 Possible Roles of Private Actors

If the traditional "informed-consent" based, government-dominated approach has "lost much of its effectiveness"[56] and thus is ill-suited to the big data ecosystem, what should be the future direction of policy? Can private governance fill the gap created by state regulation? What

[51] The UK Information Commissioner's Office (ICO), "A Guide to International Transfer" <https://ico.org.uk/media/for-organisations/guide-to-the-general-data-protection-regulation-gdpr/international-transfers-1-0.pdf>, at 11.

[52] *Ibid.*, at 12.

[53] Solove, supra note 35, at 1889.

[54] *Ibid.*, at 1895.

[55] *Ibid.*

[56] Melanie Hicken, "Big Data Knows You're Broke" (*CNN Money*, April 29, 2014).

about a hybrid governing framework in which the public and private sectors work together to reshape the landscape of the data protection regime? As a matter of fact, privacy certifications operated by the private sector have been developed to vouch for a service provider's compliance with certain privacy standards.[57] Over the past two decades, although notable attempts at privacy certification have not been popularly adopted on a global scale, certification has been gradually incorporated into the privacy practices of many transnational corporations.[58]

More importantly, innovative approaches have been proposed to enhance the role of private actors in privacy governance. Some policymakers became aware that the fundamental problem of the informed consent system is that it places the heavy burden of privacy protection on consumers.[59] To address the "non-level playing field in the implicit privacy negotiation between provider and user,"[60] substitutes for informed consent have been proposed to ensure that individuals have meaningful choices in managing their personal data. One direction is to empower individuals to "negotiate" with service providers with the assistance of a mutually accepted intermediary.[61] We need to create a new mechanism under which individuals can "delegate" their privacy preferences to a private actor they trust, such as an app store, industry organization, or private association.[62] Such a private actor would negotiate with other providers of similar services on behalf of consumers for a preferred level of privacy protection. In other words, individuals would delegate, on a commercial or noncommercial basis, the management of their personal data to a third party, which would then carefully read the service provider's privacy "offer," ensure that the privacy statement is sufficiently clear, negotiate the terms, formulate a meaningful consent to "accept" the transaction, and investigate the service provider's privacy practices. Ideally, such a third-party service would create a "privacy watchdog" marketplace for privacy negotiation and management.[63] Some policymakers are of the view that under the intermediation of the

[57] Reidenberg et al., supra note 36, at 1413.

[58] *Ibid.*, at 1412. This raises the question of whether such attempts have effectively complemented state regulations. The case studies of APEC and the GDPR in the Section 6.3.2.3 will discuss the role of third-party privacy certification in existing legal frameworks.

[59] The PCAST Report, supra note 36, at 38.

[60] *Ibid.*

[61] *Ibid.*

[62] See generally Mundie, supra note 46.

[63] *Ibid.*

third parties, which represent critical masses of consumers, problems with the informed consent system can largely be solved. In such a marketplace, the third party would negotiate on behalf of its clients with service providers, including big tech, to adjust their offerings. Individuals could withdraw and delegate the work to different private actors in the market.[64]

In addition, from the angle of industry-specific techniques, privacy protection in this big data era requires a third party to carry out de-identification and re-identification tests. To illustrate, de-identification is an increasingly central technique that is being used in big data applications.[65] Netflix, as an example, has 125 million streaming subscribers worldwide. This large user base allows Netflix to gather a tremendous amount of data, analyze consumer behaviors, and then make business decisions accordingly. If Netflix saw that 75 percent of subscribers watched all available seasons of a TV show, there should be a good chance that subscribers will continue to watch the newest season. Amazon, as another example, collects data on how often customers shop on its website, how much they paid for a particular product, where these items were shipped, and how customers paid for the purchases. The variety, volume, and velocity of all of this information enable big data analytics.[66] At the crux of the matter is how this data is aggregated, as well as to what extent the data is de-anonymized. Equally importantly, how likely is it that the de-anonymized data will be re-identified? In real-world practices, as the amount and sources of data grow, the likelihood that individuals will be re-identified increases. Nonsensitive data might be re-associated into sensitive data or become identifiable information. Nonetheless, privacy regulations are generally considered technology neutral legislation, in that the law itself does not specify de-identification procedures and techniques. For example, the Recital of GDPR stipulates that "in order to determine whether a natural person is identifiable," consideration should be given to "all the means reasonably likely to be

[64] The PCAST Report, supra note 36, at 38.

[65] See, for example, US Department of Health and Human Services, "Guidance Regarding Methods for De-identification of Protected Health Information in Accordance with the Health Insurance Portability and Accountability Act (HIPAA) Privacy Rule" (2010)<www.hhs.gov/hipaa/for-professionals/privacy/special-topics/de-identification/index.html>.

[66] Institute for Human Rights and Business (IHRB), "Data Brokers and Human Rights: Big Data, Big Business" (November 2016) <www.ihrb.org/focus-areas/information-communication-technology/data-brokers-big-data-big-business>, at 8.

used."[67] In this regard, "all objective factors" should be taken into account to evaluate whether certain means are likely to be used to identify individuals, including "the amount of time required for identification, the available technology at the time of processing, and future technological developments."[68] Therefore, how to de-identify a particular segment of data in a particular context and better manage the risk of anonymized data being used to re-identify a natural person require sectoral technical standards.[69] Private actors, such as a certification body or industry association with the necessary technical expertise, can carry out de-identification assessments, apply state-of-the-art technology to maintain anonymization, and reduce the risk of re-identification.

6.3.2.2 Typologies: Public–Private Interactions

Private actors play an increasingly important role in global governance, in conjunction with state regulations. Private and public authority dynamics emerge in complex ways, and various efforts have been devoted to classifying them into types: namely, complement type and competition type.[70] As for privacy governance, it is important to identify how public authority and the private sector can simultaneously shape global privacy norms, as well as what type of public–private partnership (PPP) model is best suited for data governance given the technological uncertainty.

The analytical framework proposed by Cashore et al. emphasizes that the middle ground between complement and competition should be identified to capture complex PPP. They point out that the conceptualization of public and private authority as either complementary or competitive might be an oversimplified approach. They suggest that we should move beyond the complement/competition dichotomy and map "a fuller suite of mechanisms through which public and private governance interact."[71] Cashore et al. created more detailed subtypes of public–

[67] GDPR, Recital 26 (Not Applicable to Anonymous Data) <https://gdpr-info.eu/recitals/no-26/>.

[68] *Ibid.*

[69] Irene Kamara, "Co-Regulation in EU Personal Data Protection: The Case of Technical Standards and the Privacy by Design Standardization Mandate" (2017) 8(1) European Journal of Law and Technology 1, at 10.

[70] See, for example, Margot E. Kaminski, "Binary Governance: Lessons from the GDPR's Approach to Algorithmic Accountability" (2019) 92 Southern California Law Review 1529, at 1557.

[71] See Benjamin Cashore et al., "Private Authority and Public Policy Interactions in Global Context: Governance Spheres for Problem Solving" (2021) 15 Regulation & Governance 1166.

private interaction.[72] In their view, "collaboration" and "coordination" are the primary forms of interaction within complementary-type PPP. Collaboration is an active partnership that is built upon effective communications. This type of PPP works better if both parties are on equal footing, namely, there is no clear hierarchy between them. Conceptually different from collaboration, coordination refers to the "delegation" of political authority to private actors, which in most cases involves hierarchy.[73] In their analytical framework, the main subtype within the competition-type PPP is "substitution," which generally describes the substitution effects of private governance.[74] In other words, private actors intend to displace state regulation by industry self-regulation, such as a Code of Conduct (CoC).

With respect to privacy governance, the public and private sectors can either "coordinate" or "collaborate" on governance, both of which fall in the center of the public versus private continuum. On one end of the continuum is top-down, government-dominated, command-and-control state regulation, and on the other end is bottom-up, voluntary-based self-regulation. Coordinative and collaborative governance, each with a different proportion of private governance, are hybrid approaches that rely on both governmental enforcement power and private participation. Depending on the degree of state involvement, the public and private sectors coordinate or collaborate in privacy governance. Under the form of coordinative governance, the government delegates oversight to private actors;[75] Under the form of collaborative governance,[76] the state works hand in hand with the private sector, remains involved as a dynamic facilitator to "nudge" private sector participation, and uses a traditional enforcement mechanism such as a penalty only when necessary to complement the governing framework. Under both forms of coordination and collaboration, traditional command-and-control regulation remains the backup authority in driving the governance

[72] *Ibid.* First, under the category of complement, Cashore et al. further divide the group into "collaboration," "coordination," and "isomorphism." Second, under the category of competition, they further distinguish the types into "substitution" and "cooptation." Third, they introduce a third main conceptualization: "coexistence," which contains two subtypes: "layered institutions" and "chaos."

[73] *Ibid.*, at 1172.

[74] *Ibid.*

[75] *Ibid.*, at 1563, 1596.

[76] Kaminski, supra note 70, at 1561–1563.

structure.[77] Finally, under the form of "substitutive" governance, private efforts such as industry self-regulation may in some situations "preempt" state regulations.[78] Private governance can also assume a "competitive role" in which it competes directly with and even attempts to replace government standards.[79] Substitution may lead to "chaos" – with overlapping or contradicting governance goals and strategies.[80]

6.3.2.3 APEC/CBPR: From Self-Regulation to "Collaboration"?

How is PPP being implemented in the privacy protection frameworks? Let us use cases from the APEC's Cross Border Privacy Rules (CBPR) and the EU's GDPR as models for exploration. The APEC CBPR system is a self-regulatory initiative designed to facilitate cross-border data flows while protecting consumer data privacy. To be brief, CBPR is a certification system of privacy protection that service providers can participate in to demonstrate compliance with privacy "principles" reflected in the APEC Privacy Framework ("Privacy Framework").[81] The Privacy Framework, as the title indicates, establishes the minimum standards for privacy protection. Led by the US as preferable to the EU's approach to data protection, it's not surprising that the CBPR system is now recognized in the USMCA as "a valid mechanism to facilitate cross-border information transfers while protecting personal information."[82] There are currently nine participating countries in the CBPR, each of which is at a different stage of implementing the CBPR System.[83]

Essentially, the CBPR is a voluntary scheme that requires acceptance at the state level, followed by certification of the service providers seeking to be part of the system.[84] Indeed, the key component of the CBPR is that third parties are to inspect and certify the privacy practices of service providers against the Privacy Framework, and to manage privacy-related

[77] *Ibid.*, at 1562–1564.
[78] Cashore et al., supra note 71, at 1172.
[79] *Ibid.*
[80] *Ibid.*
[81] APEC, "Privacy Framework" (2017) <www.apec.org/publications/2017/08/apec-privacy-framework-(2015) >; APEC "Cross-Border Privacy Rules System" (2020) <www.apec.org/publications/2020/02/apec-cross-border-privacy-rules-system-fostering-accountability-agent-participation>.
[82] USMCA, Article 19.8.
[83] Australia, Canada, Chinese Taipei, Japan, the Republic of Korea, Mexico, the Philippines, Singapore, and the United States.
[84] APEC, "What is the Cross-Border Privacy Rules System?" <www.cbprs.org/>.

dispute resolution for certified service providers. A service provider applying to join CBPR must establish its privacy statement and practices to be consistent with either the basic standards in the Privacy Framework or domestic regulation. Following the assessment, service providers certified by an APEC-recognized Accountability Agent may display a seal or a trust mark or otherwise claim to qualify under the CBPR System.[85] To maintain the system in operation, the APEC economies should select and endorse the "accountability agents" who certify the privacy practices of service providers that wish to join the scheme. Currently, there are nine APEC-recognized accountability agents.[86] In practice, accountability agents, such as Schellman & Company in the US, typically provide certification services in accordance with APEC privacy standards. Schellman & Company, as an example, performs testing to evidence the certification's minimum requirements. The testing procedures include inquiries with relevant personnel of service providers wishing to join the CBPR, observation of the relevant process, and inspection of relevant records.[87] In addition, certified service providers are monitored throughout the certification period, including periodic reviews of the service provider's privacy policies, to ensure compliance with the Privacy Framework. Annual re-certification is required to update the CBPR Questionnaire. Certification will be suspended if the certified service provider is found to have violated the CBPR requirements, and if such a breach has not been resolved within certain time frames.[88]

In terms of PPP, several aspects deserve further exploration. First, in terms of the nature of the accountability agents, CBPR features a hybrid form of public and private organizations. While the five US-based accountability agents have private characteristics, other Asia-based agents are either government agencies or government-affiliated organizations: the Internet & Security Agency (KISA) is South Korea's Ministry of Science and ICT's suborganization;[89] the Japan Institute for Promotion of Digital Economy and Community (JIPDEC) is a public-interest corporation in Japan, which has long been in close cooperation with Japan's

[85] CBPR, "Interested in Becoming APEC CBPR Certified?" <http://cbprs.org/business/>.

[86] *Ibid.*, including TrustArc (US), Schellman (US), BBB National Program (US), HITRUST (US), NCC Group (US), JIPDEC (Japan), IMDA (Singapore), KISA (Korea), and III (Taiwan).

[87] Schellman & Company, "APEC Cross Border Privacy Rules (CBPR) Certification Process and Minimum Requirements" <www.schellman.com/apec/cbpr-process>.

[88] *Ibid.*

[89] The Internet & Security Agency (KISA) <www.kisa.or.kr/eng/main.jsp>.

Ministry of Economy, Trade and Industry;[90] and Singapore's ICT regulator, the Infocomm Media Development Authority (IMDA), is a statutory board under the Singapore Ministry of Communications and Information. While appointing an assessment body such as the BSI Group to determine whether a service provider's data protection practices conform to the CBPR requirements, the IMDA remains the Accountability Body under the Privacy Framework.[91] The Institute for Information Industry (III) in Taiwan is a nongovernmental organization that has long acted as an ICT "think tank" for the government.[92] Evidently, the degree of state involvement is more than nominal.

Another angle worth noting with regard to public–private interactions under the CBPR regime is the role of governmental enforcement authorities. By its very nature, the CBPR is an instrument of self-regulation. The main deficiency that hampers its overall effectiveness is the lack of sufficient governmental guidance and supervision. Nevertheless, there are some encouraging stories demonstrating that national regulators may sometimes act as "privacy cops" to sustain the integrity of the CBPR system. One striking example is the US Fair Trade Commission (FTC), which in 2014 fined TRUSTe (now TrustArc) for failing to timely re-certify participating companies on an annual basis, which violates its own certification policy.[93] In addition, the FTC in 2016 alleged that Vipvape had engaged in deception in its privacy statement. Vipvape had falsely advertised that it was a certified participant in the CBPR scheme, which it was not. The bilateral settlement between the FTC and Vipvape bans Vipvape from misleading the public about its certification status under the Privacy Framework. According to the FTC, "the governmental oversight and enforceability of the CBPR are mandated by the terms of the system itself."[94]

[90] The Japan Institute for Promotion of Digital Economy and Community (JIPDEC) <https://english.jipdec.or.jp/>.

[91] The Infocomm Media Development Authority (IMDA). The certification application fee is payable to the IMDA. <www.imda.gov.sg/regulations-and-licensing-listing/ict-standards-and-quality-of-service/IT-Standards-and-Frameworks/Compliance-and-Certification>.

[92] The Institute for Information Industry (III) < www.tpipas.org.tw/>.

[93] To date, the FTC has brought four actions to enforce companies' promises under APEC CBPR. See FTC, "Report to Congress on Privacy and Security" (September 13, 2021) <www.ftc.gov/system/files/documents/reports/ftc-report-congress-privacy-security/report_to_congress_on_privacy_and_data_security_2021.pdf>.

[94] "FTC Settles with Vipvape on CBPR Privacy Policy Deception" (*Data Protection Law & Policy*, June 2016).

Nevertheless, public enforcement under the CBPR remains limited. The low degree of state involvement has resulted in a lack of accountability. For consumers, there is no strong incentive to seek out those service providers that are CBPR certified. In turn, there are weak incentives for service providers to invest in and obtain CBPR certification. To conclude, the CBPR system falls between "collaborative governance" and "self-regulation" along the public versus private spectrum. Moving toward an accountable, collaborative form of governance, the future success of the CBPR depends on whether systemic and aggregate accountability over public–private interactions can be established.[95] Such accountability calls for a higher degree of state involvement and, in particular, requires national regulators to act as "privacy cops."

6.3.2.4 EU/GDPR: From State Regulation to "Coordination"?

The GDPR, on the other hand, is fundamentally a "hard law" by nature, backed by enforcement penalties.[96] Nonetheless, the regime seems to leave room for PPPs, namely, allowing private actors to complete the details of how to comply with the legal requirements through the CoC or certification mechanisms. Both the CoC and certification require an independent, third-party body to assess conformity with the normative documents, and they also require the assessor to be accredited. In addition, both the approved CoC and certification are recognized by the GDPR as factors when national regulators assess penalties for non-compliance.[97] Furthermore, both the CoC and certification, if coupled together with binding enforceable commitments to apply appropriate safeguards, can be used by controllers and processors in third countries as a legitimate basis for cross-border transfers of data.[98]

With respect to the CoC, associations or "other bodies representing categories of controllers or processors" are encouraged to draw up sector-

[95] Kaminski, supra note 70, at 1568–1580; Ira S. Rubinstein, "The Future of Self-Regulation Is Co-Regulation" in Evan Selinger et al. (eds) *The Cambridge Handbook of Consumer Privacy* (Cambridge University Press 2018), at 503.

[96] Kaminski, *ibid.*, at 1611.

[97] See generally Eric Lachaud, "What GDPR Tells about Certification" (2020) 38 Computer Law and Security Review 1, at 3–5; Clare Sullivan, "EU GDPR or APEC CBPR? A Comparative Analysis of the Approach of the EU and APEC to Cross Border Data Transfers and Protection of Personal Data in the IoT Era" (2019) 35(4) Computer Law & Security Review 380.

[98] *Ibid.*

specific CoC to "facilitate the effective application" of the GDPR.[99] The CoC may cover many aspects of the GDPR, such as "the pseudonymization of personal data" and "the transfer of personal data to third countries."[100] Wherever feasible, associations should consult stakeholders when preparing the CoC.[101] The monitoring of compliance with the CoC may be carried out by a body – including a private body – that is accredited by the national regulator.[102] Each regulator should "draft and publish the criteria for accreditation of a body for monitoring codes of conduct."[103] An accredited CoC monitoring body should "take appropriate action," for example, to suspend the controller or processor "in cases of infringement of the code by a controller or processor." A monitoring body should also report such actions to the regulator.[104] It should be noted that such an "action" from the accredited CoC monitoring body does not take the place of possible actions that can otherwise be activated by the authorities for noncompliance. Finally, in terms of service providers, "adherence to approved codes of conduct" is an element available to data controllers to demonstrate compliance with the GDPR obligations,[105] and it is also a factor when the regulator determines whether to impose an administrative fine, as well as the amount of the fine.[106]

With respect to certification,[107] the GDPR expressly recognizes data protection seals and/or marks as mechanisms for demonstrating compliance and enhancing transparency.[108] Certifications may be issued by either the European Data Protection Board, a national regulator, or a private third party that is an accredited certification body.[109] The certification bodies should conduct a "proper assessment leading to the

[99] GDPR, Recital 98.
[100] GDPR, Article 40.
[101] GDPR, Recital 99.
[102] GDPR, Article 41.
[103] GDPR, Article 57.
[104] GDPR, Article 41.
[105] GDPR, Article 24.
[106] GDPR, Article 83.
[107] Note that the European data processing board approved the very first European Data Protection Seal- Europrivacy. The Europrivacy certification can help data controllers and data processors certify privacy practices that demonstrate compliance with the GDPR. European Commission, "Shaping Europe's Digital Future" (October 17, 2022) <https://digital-strategy.ec.europa.eu/en/news/europrivacy-first-certification-mechanism-ensure-compliance-gdpr>.
[108] GDPR, Recital 100.
[109] GDPR, Article 42.

certification," or the withdrawal of certification in the case of noncompliance.[110] The certification body should also inform the regulator and provide reasons for granting or withdrawing certification. More importantly, a certification does not "reduce the responsibility of the controller or the processor for compliance with this Regulation."[111] National regulators possess the investigative power to "order the certification body not to issue certification" when the requirements for the certification are not met. National regulators also retain the power to withdraw a certification, or to order the certification body to withdraw a certification "if the requirements for the certification are no longer met."[112] Finally, like the CoC, adherence to approved certification mechanisms is a key factor to consider when regulators impose administrative fines on certified service providers for noncompliance.[113]

At the crux of the matter is whether the GDPR relies on PPP in governing data. Can the CoC and certification systems work better under coordinative-type PPP? To what extent do EU member states delegate authority to private actors in terms of governance? Obviously, there is a hierarchical relationship between public and private actors in the GDPR framework. National regulators are entitled to approve or disapprove the certification requirements. Arguably, the accredited private bodies' certifying power is conditional,[114] as the certification can be withdrawn at any time by the regulator if the conditions of issuance are no longer met. Overall, the CoC and certification mechanisms under the GDPR remain in a top-down, command-and-control arrangement. Moreover, the GDPR has serious "teeth" with regard to an accredited private body's obligations. Infringements on the obligations of the CoC's monitoring body or the certification body will be subject to administrative fines of up to 10,000,000 EUR, or up to 2 percent of the "total worldwide annual turnover of the preceding financial year," whichever is higher.[115] This results in weak incentives for private actors to actively participate in the governing scheme. Additionally, the role of a certification body is further weakened by the GDPR certification's lack of presumption of conformity. GDPR certifications are not considered to offer a "presumption of

[110] GDPR, Article 43.
[111] GDPR, Article 42.
[112] GDPR, Article 58.
[113] GDPR, Article 83.
[114] Lachaud, supra note 97.
[115] GDPR, Article 83.

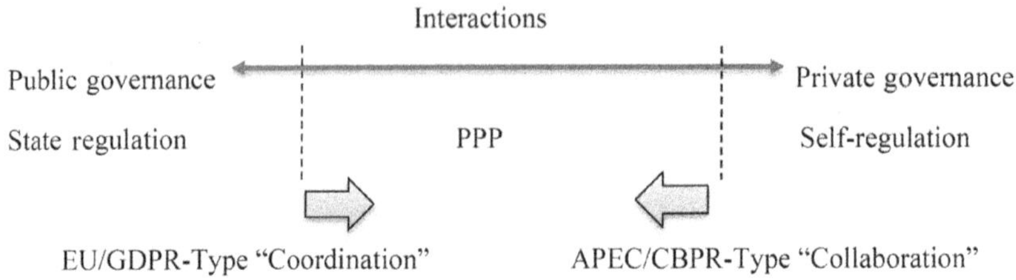

Figure 6.1 Public–private interaction in privacy governance

conformity" with the obligations under the GDPR.[116] In other words, the assessment by the certification body that a process is in line with the certification criteria merely grants a "stamp of approval" for the accountability of the certified service provider. The presence of such accountability, however, does not "reverse the burden of proof," and it does not indicate "presumed compliance" with the GDPR.[117] As such, GDPR certification does not entail *prima facie* full compliance with the GDPR. It does not act as a safe harbor from GDPR enforcement, nor does it provide the benefit of reduced regulatory scrutiny.[118] To conclude, the CoC and the certification systems rely too heavily on public governance and invoke private governance at a minimal level. The GDPR-type public–private "coordination" risks are too command-and-control oriented.[119]

The analysis above demonstrates the fluid interactions across public and private governance realms. As shown in Figure 6.1, self-regulation and state regulation are opposing ends of a regulatory continuum, with CBPR-type "collaboration" (moving from self-regulation to collaborative governance) and GDPR-type "coordination" (moving from state regulation to coordinative governance) falling somewhere in the middle. Turning to the question of how private actors can play more important roles when privacy paradigms are in flux, after assessing whether PPP is now being implemented in privacy protection, this section concludes that

[116] See Irene Kamara, "Misaligned Union Laws? A Comparative Analysis of Certification in the Cybersecurity Act and the General Data Protection Regulation" in Dara Hallinan et al. (eds), *Data Protection and Artificial Intelligence* (Hart Publishing 2021), at 83.

[117] Cf., Lachaud, supra note 97, at 7.

[118] See also Machiko Kanetake and André Nollkaemper, "The Application of Informal International Instruments Before Domestic Courts" (2014) 46 George Washington International Law Review 765.

[119] Kaminski, supra note 70, at 1599–1601.

there is an evident gap between private actors' potential governing functions and their current roles in privacy protection regimes. Looking to the future, technological developments and market changes call for further public–private convergence in privacy governance, allowing both the public authority and the private sector to simultaneously reshape global privacy norms.

6.4 Cybersecurity Governance in a Datafied World

6.4.1 Physical–Digital Convergence: Security in the Industry 4.0 Landscape

In a similar vein, physical–digital convergence posts unprecedented governance challenges to data security, which has been described by Weber as follows: "everything will inevitably be compromised at some point."[120] The core concept of Industry 4.0 is the connection of machinery to the Internet,[121] which encompasses many types of disruptive technologies.[122] The IoT applications, which feature the aggregation of many machine-to-machine connections, literally represent the penetration of the Internet into our everyday lives. It is now a regular occurrence in our daily experiences that IoT technologies tie together billions of devices, ranging from smartwatches, wearable sensors, and refrigerators to factories, cars, and drones.[123]

Industry 4.0 digitizes and integrates physical and digital activities. When everything can be connected to the Internet, everything can potentially be hacked. Consequently, the explosion of "smart" objects is causing unique security risks, which calls for a new security paradigm. It should be underscored that digital attacks on connected devices threaten both the physical and the digital world. For example, a connected car can be seen as a component of the entire IoT system. Depending on the level of automation, a connected car can interact with

120 Rolf H. Weber and Evelyne Studer, "Cybersecurity in the Internet of Things: Legal Aspects" (2016) 32 Computer Law & Security Review 715.

121 The Fourth Industrial Revolution refers to "the use of advanced digital technologies in industrial production and service delivery processes to enable new and more efficient processes for the production of goods and services combining traditional and digital technologies." See, for example, European Parliament, "Industry 4.0" (2016) <www.europarl.europa.eu/RegData/etudes/STUD/2016/570007/IPOL_STU(2016)570007_EN.pdf>, at 20, 22, 83.

122 *Ibid.*, at 22.

123 Hamilton and Quinlan, supra note 2.

its users, other cars, the surrounding transportation infrastructure, and all other IoT devices. When a connected car communicates with other cars or infrastructure, risks arise from both physical and virtual sources. Hackers can control and damage the car itself, the Internet services supporting it, and the external systems that are digitally linked with the car. In short, security concerns surrounding connected devices are complex and relate to both mechanical safety and cybersecurity.[124] From an industrial perspective, such a physical–digital integration changes security practices, the most notable of which is the concept of "security by design," which generally indicates that "security should be built into a product by design" and "integrated at every stage of the product's development."[125] In doing so, security concerns can be addressed throughout "the entire product life cycle" – from its design to its disposal.[126] For example, connected car manufacturers are required to comply with the principle of security-by-design throughout the full life cycle of the cars so as to enhance the safety of the "cyber-physical vehicle system."[127]

Looking to the future, the emerging "digital twin" has enhanced smart manufacturing to another level, relying on "a virtual model designed to accurately reflect a physical object."[128] Updated from real-time data, digital twin technology allows for the remote monitoring of facilities

[124] Shin-yi Peng, "Autonomous Vehicle Standards under the Technical Barriers to Trade Agreement" in Shin-yi Peng et al. (eds), *Artificial Intelligence and International Economic Law: Disruption, Regulation, and Reconfiguration* (Cambridge University Press 2021), at 125–126.

[125] See, for example, European Commission, "Security by Design: Definition of the Principle" <https://joinup.ec.europa.eu/collection/common-assessment-method-standards-and-specifications-camss/solution/elap/security-design>.

[126] Similarly, "Privacy by Design" means building privacy into the design, operation, and management of a given system, business process, or design specification. See Privacy Europe, "GDPR: Privacy by Design" <https://gdpr-info.eu/issues/privacy-by-design/>; Privacy measures are "embedded into the design and architecture of ICT systems and business practices." The World Bank, "Foundational Principles of Privacy by Design" <https://id4d.worldbank.org/guide/privacy-security>. The result is that privacy becomes "an essential component of the core functionality being delivered." Privacy is thus integral to the system; European Union Agency for Cybersecurity, "Privacy and Data Protection by Design" <www.enisa.europa.eu/publications/privacy-and-data-protection-by-design>.

[127] Singapore Standard Council, "Technical Reference for Autonomous Vehicles" TR68. Part II: Safety. Part III (Cybersecurity Principles and Assessment Framework).

[128] See Gartner Glossary, "Digital Twin" <www.gartner.com/en/information-technology/glossary/digital-twin>.

and simulating processes.[129] Moving toward a Metaverse space, the sensors that consistently detect micro-level activities – including gestures, motions, and ambient conditions in virtual reality – can be seen as "physical extensions" of individuals' social identity: the "technological sense of self."[130] All of these emerging technologies, which further integrate and complement physical and virtual spheres, have their own privacy and security risks that must be managed.[131]

6.4.2 Public–Private Convergence: Private Cybersecurity Standards

6.4.2.1 Bottom-Up Approach to Cybersecurity Standardization

Cybersecurity risk management across all sectors, therefore, is more important than ever. Among all of the tools, cybersecurity standards contribute to risk management by establishing "common security requirements and capabilities needed for secure solutions,"[132] at least in reducing the effects of attacks if they occur.[133] Typically, cybersecurity standards, as "set forth in published materials that attempt to protect the cyber environment of a user or organization,"[134] define technical requirements, criteria for managing information and risk evaluation, techniques for handling security failures, and procedures following security breaches.[135] Cybersecurity standards are diverse and varied in scope and function, spanning the specifications of security features in web browsers, the mathematical definition of cryptographic algorithms, and other technical requirements.[136]

In terms of standards governance, there exists a spectrum of cybersecurity standardization models, ranging from more centralized, coercive, top-down governmental involvement to more decentralized, soft, bottom-up private initiatives. China's government-centered

[129] *Ibid.*

[130] Linda Tucci and Davie Needle, "What is the Metaverse? An Explanation and In-Depth Guide" (*TechTarget*, May 8, 2023).

[131] For example, informed consent for digital interactions in the Metaverse could be unprecedentedly challenging.

[132] See generally William Stallings, "Standards for Information Security Management" (2007), 10 Internet Protocol Journal 10.

[133] *Ibid.*

[134] Scholarly Community Encyclopedia, "Cybersecurity Standards" <https://encyclopedia.pub/entry/29282>.

[135] *Ibid.*

[136] *Ibid.*

standardization system represents the most outstanding case of a top-down regulatory approach. In the Chinese ICT market, the government assumes primary responsibility for standardization development, with the policy rationale that state-led standardization creates the most efficient national economy.[137] Conversely, there is a growing trend across the world toward a bottom-up approach to cybersecurity standardization.[138] Empirical studies demonstrate that more and more jurisdictions have been moving toward a bottom-up approach to cybersecurity standardization, which aims to minimize mandatory technical regulation and favors voluntary, private-sector standards to enhance cybersecurity.[139] Under the bottom-up approach, the business sector has actively taken on standardization initiatives, which they contend leads to more cost-effective rules than government regulation.[140] Behind the scenes, the privatization of governance has been driven, at least in part, by governments' lack of requisite technical expertise and the administrative flexibility to respond to rapidly changing regulatory needs.[141] The involvement of public and private sector actors working together has proven to be a more effective model than complete government control.

Emblematic of this movement with regard to the EU is the European Union Agency for Cybersecurity ("ENISA").[142] Mandated by the EU Cybersecurity Act as the hub in coordinating a cybersecurity certification framework throughout Europe, ENISA has actively contributed to cybersecurity standards, and thus, to the proper functioning of the internal market within the EU.[143] By working closely together with EU member states and the private sector, ENISA provides advice and solutions related to cybersecurity, supports policy implementation, and coordinates standardization activities.[144] As ENISA repeatedly stresses in its policy papers, it believes that enhancing the role of PPP should be emphasized in

[137] Dan Breznitz and Michael Murphree, "The Rise of China in Technology Standards: New Norms in Old Institutions" (2016) Research Report Prepared on Behalf of the US–China Economic and Security Review Commission, at 2.

[138] Scott J. Shackelford et al., "Bottoms Up: A Comparison of 'Voluntary' Cybersecurity Frameworks" (2016) 16 U.C. Davis Business Law Journal 217, at 259.

[139] *Ibid.*

[140] Tim Buthe and Walter Mattli, *The New Global Rulers: The Privatization of Regulation in the World Economy* (Princeton University Press 2011), at 5.

[141] *Ibid., at* 5–6, 9–10.

[142] The European Union Agency for Cybersecurity (ENISA) <www.enisa.europa.eu/>.

[143] *Ibid.*

[144] *Ibid.*

standardization processes.[145] Overall, a bottom-up approach to the creation of cybersecurity standards and strong representation from stakeholders are the key elements in ENISA decision-making procedures.[146] It can be said that the ENISA serves as an umbrella, under which a variety of certification schemes are encouraged to mutually recognize each other to mitigate potential fragmentation.[147] For instance, ENISA's Guidelines for Securing the Internet of Things,[148] which aims to provide security guidelines for IoT technologies, was created in conjunction with stakeholders involved in the supply chain of the IoT.

Similarly, the US National Institute for Standards and Technology Cybersecurity Framework (the "NIST Framework") was established to strengthen collaboration between the public and private sectors in their efforts to enhance cybersecurity.[149] In a series of multistakeholder meetings, international representatives across government, business, and civil society worked together to create the NIST Framework.[150] The NIST has been actively engaged with stakeholders through multiple avenues of communication.[151] Such a process demonstrates an active dialogue that relies on a bottom-up approach to cybersecurity regulation – building consensus across sectors and industries through a dynamic PPP. For example, together with stakeholders from government, industry, international bodies, and academia, the IoT Cybersecurity Program was established to develop standards and guidelines to improve the cybersecurity of connected devices.[152]

6.4.2.2 Cybersecurity Standards Chaos

Of course, the idea of governance through public-private networks is not at all new. The academic literature, including research in the field

145 *Ibid.*

146 *Ibid.*

147 See generally Dimitra Markopoulou et al., "The New EU Cybersecurity Framework: The NIS Directive, ENISA's Role and the General Data Protection Regulation" (2019) 35(6) Computer Law & Security Review 2.

148 ENISA, "Guidelines for Securing the Internet of Things" (2020) <www.enisa.europa.eu/publications/guidelines-for-securing-the-internet-of-things>.

149 The National Institute of Standards and Technology (NIST) <www.nist.gov/about-nist>.

150 *Ibid.*

151 NIST, "Cybersecurity Framework" <www.nist.gov/cyberframework>.

152 NIST, "Cybersecurity & Privacy Stakeholder Engagement" <www.nist.gov/cybersecurity/cybersecurity-privacy-stakeholder-engagement>; NIST, "Cybersecurity for IOT Program" <www.nist.gov/itl/applied-cybersecurity/nist-cybersecurity-iot-program>.

of international economic law, has long examined the changing role of the state in market economies and the transformation of public functions.[153] In a world of high complexity, governments are delegating traditionally public functions to the private sector. Therefore, the world is increasingly governed through co-regulation by public and private actors.[154] With respect to cybersecurity, where public and private sectors attempt to adapt to rapid technological changes, it is particularly evident that governments must relax their regulatory power and shift responsibility through privatization.[155]

Nonetheless, bottom-up approaches generally lead to greater fragmentation than top-down approaches, simply because government-centered standardization systems have more influential positions in harmonizing the system. Indeed, cybersecurity standards are proliferating, exceeding 1,000 publications globally and resulting in a complex standards landscape.[156] This "mushrooms after rain" phenomenon surrounding private cybersecurity standards is now problematic in many ways. Although on the one hand it manifests the dynamics of the industry, it might also result in the danger of overlapping and even conflicting standards. From the perspective of international trade, the absence of a defined hierarchy over these private standards makes coordination challenging. The international "standards jungle" of cybersecurity, as a result, may lead to an uncoordinated set of standards and thus work as an impediment to free trade.

The IoT "standards chaos" serves as a strong example here.[157] The industry has been struggling to make sense of the IoT standards, which are currently moving in the opposite direction of the push toward universal standards for baseline security.[158] Dozens of organizations are currently developing various IoT cybersecurity standards and issuing IoT cybersecurity certifications. These disparate schemes, however, are

[153] See, for example, Gregory Shaffer, *Defending Interests – Public-Private Partnerships in WTO Litigation* (Brookings Institution Press 2003), at 12–14.

[154] Shackelford, supra note 138, at 219.

[155] Shin-yi Peng, supra note 124, at 130.

[156] PwC & The UK Department for Business, Innovation and Skills (BIS), BIS/13/1294, "UK Cyber Security Standards" (November 2013) <www.gov.uk/government/uploads/system/uploads/attachment_data/file/261681/bis-13-1294-uk-cyber-security-standards-research-report.pdf>, at 4.

[157] Copper Horse, "Mapping Security & Privacy in the Internet of Things" <https://iotsecuritymapping.uk/by-sector-and-body>.

[158] Brian Buntz, "Amid IoT Standards Chaos, Put Business Matters First" (*IoT World Today*, April 20, 2019).

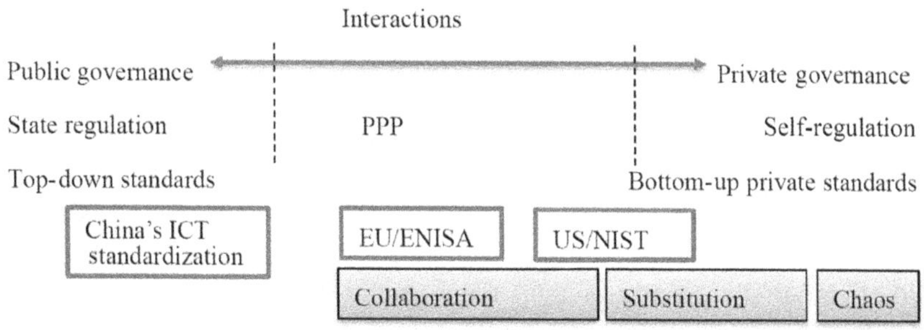

Figure 6.2 Public–private interaction in cybersecurity standardization

"nowhere near in sync" and can also be in conflict,[159] a fact which distorts the IoT value chain. Under such a fragmented landscape, IoT device manufacturers, sensor and chip suppliers, and software companies must manage all of these requirements and certify the security of their IoT products time and time again, with variants present around the world.[160] Evidently, the need to establish a global baseline for IoT cybersecurity is pressing. Turning back to the typologies framed above, public-private interactions in the realm of cybersecurity standards may be conceptualized as "chaos,"[161] as shown in Figure 6.2, in that they display no clear pattern and appear potentially contradictory.[162] From the aspect of international trade, a less fragmented standards regime can reduce barriers to entry into IoT markets. When ICT products are not manufactured with comparable cybersecurity standards, the need for interoperability will require extra gateways to translate one standard to another,[163] which will make it particularly difficult for SMEs to compete in the market.

To conclude, the implications of "standards" are unique in various contexts. Regardless, there is a strong link between technical standards and an efficient international trading system. In a globalized world, standards provide information about goods and services to ensure

[159] Copper Horse, supra note 157.

[160] Connectivity Standards Alliance (CSA), "Now is the Time for a Global Approach to IoT Cybersecurity" (September 12, 2022).

[161] See supra notes 72 and 80.

[162] See Cashore et al., supra note 72, at 1175.

[163] Bruce Sinclair, *IoT Inc.: How Your Company Can Use the Internet of Things to Win the Outcome Economy* (McGraw Hill Education 2017), at 194.

technical compatibility.[164] By sharing a common standard, anonymous manufacturers and services suppliers in markets all over the world can communicate, establish common expectations about one another's products, and evaluate the compatibility of their joint productions.[165] Any innovator in the market can develop new applications with the commercial certainty that an international market for their products will exist.[166] More harmonized cybersecurity standards, therefore, can facilitate "trade flows" from the aspects of both the demand and the supply of digital goods and services.

6.5 Global Architecture for Cross-Border Data Flows

6.5.1 The Reconfiguration of Governance: A Holistic Approach and Hybrid Structure

Taken as a whole, data flow governance is evolving into a debate over the roles of international organizations (IOs), sovereign states, private sectors, civil societies, and other stakeholders. We are facing a crossroads, where (Internet) multistakeholderism meets (trade) multilateralism.[167] This friction is evident. The former features more inclusive and transparent processes, under which public authorities govern alongside private and civic sectors, while the latter is inherently characterized as a series of top-down processes, in which states play central roles (and, in most cases, are the only actors).[168] Should global governance in the cyberspace context follow a multistakeholder approach that is premised on the broad participation of private actors, or move toward a more traditional,

[164] Xiaomeng Lu, "Standards-Related Barriers to Trade in Chinese ICT Market" (2008) Monterey Institute of International Studies, at 7.

[165] *Ibid.*

[166] *Ibid.*; Baisheng An, "Institutional Governance for ICT Standards at the International Level: Within the WTO and Beyond" (2012) World Trade Institute Series Paper.

[167] The term "multistakeholderism" refers to "two or more classes of actors engaged in a common governance enterprise concerning issues they regard as public in nature." In practice, there are various types of multistakeholder governance, produced by variations in the types of actors involved and the nature of authority. See generally William H. Dutton, "Multistakeholder Internet Governance?" (2016) World Bank Background Paper: Digital Dividends, at 2–5; Kal Raustiala, "Governing the Internet" (2017) 110 American Journal of International Law 491; Stefaan G. Verhulst, "The Practice and Craft of Multistakeholder Governance: The Case of Global Internet Policymaking" (2016) Global Partners Digital, at 8–9.

[168] Burri, supra note 26, at 10–11.

multilateral approach through treaty-based international arrangements with greater government oversight?[169]

Considered alone, however, neither approach suffices. On the one hand, the world today tells us that multilateralism has its limits. The analyses above, and throughout this book, reveal and confirm that international economic law alone may not be able to produce significant results to effectively address concerns surrounding datafication. The divergent regulatory goals and approaches of states – in particular, among the US, the EU, and China – render it a "mission impossible" for the WTO JSI on E-commerce to conclude a high-standard, broad agreement with deeper commitments that meaningfully tackle the important issues of cross-border data flows. A governance framework of modesty, as proposed by Shaffer,[170] with limited coverage and obligations that accommodate the divergent regulatory schemes of WTO members, might be the result of political reality.[171]

On the other hand, multilateralism, to which states consent, remains the key source of legitimacy in global trade governance. Controversies over cross-border data flows are at the heart of the digital economy and beyond. In this regard, states' digital policies and data regulations are playing, and will continue to play, a key role in shaping the global rules of the game. As demonstrated in the case studies of CBPR and IoT standards, state involvement and coordination remain significant in addressing problems arising from private regulations, such as the CBPR's lack of accountability and IoT cybersecurity standards chaos.[172] In any event, the role of multilateralism is indispensable in holding states accountable when they impose unjustified barriers to digital trade.

[169] See Joost Pauwelyn, "Rule-Based Trade 2.0? The Rise of Informal Rules and International Standards and How They May Outcompete WTO Treaties" (2014) 17 Journal of International Economic Law 739, at 745; Urs Gasser et al., "Multistakeholder as Governance Groups: Observations from Case Studies" (2015) The Berkman Ctr. for Internet & Society Research Publication Series; Petros C. Mavroidis and Robert Wolfe, "Private Standards and the WTO: Reclusive No More" (2017) 16 World Trade Review 1, at 2–3.

[170] Gregory Shaffer, "Trade Law in a Data-Driven Economy: The Need for Modesty and Resilience" in Shin-yi Peng et al. (eds) *Artificial Intelligence and International Economic Law: Disruption, Regulation, and Reconfiguration* (Cambridge University Press 2021), at 29, 42–52.

[171] At the same time, the fragmentation and uncertainties brought about by the FTAs further challenge international economic legal order. See Section 2.3.4 and Section 5.4.1.

[172] See Sections 6.3.2.3 and 6.4.2.2.

Accordingly, a holistic approach to, and the hybrid structure of, global governance, where the two approaches somehow merge and operate together, may be capable of striking a balance between decentralized, multifaceted initiatives and centralized decision-making.[173] Such a "blended governance regime," as advocated by Gasser,[174] can more proactively coordinate the various elements and actors of both multi-stakeholderism and multilateralism.[175] In the spheres of privacy and cybersecurity regulations, industry-driven soft standards and state-centered international rules can be employed as complements in a strategic and dynamic manner, and the two regimes can be linked and build upon each other. The potential role of each is explored below.

6.5.2 *The Role of (Internet) Multistakeholderism*

We have witnessed the difficulties and complexities associated with concluding digital trade rules through formal international treaties. In this context, the soft law nature of private initiatives can fill the gap left by international trade agreements, regardless of whether it is due to the "thin" obligations of, or the "vague" exceptions to, the trade rules. This book argues that the greater the legal uncertainty surrounding international law, the more critical the soft law norms that should be developed. Pauwelyn observed that the phenomenon of multistakeholderism incorporates not only informal actors and processes, but also soft law output.[176] The "products" of a multistakeholder process are often in the form of nonbinding soft law norms, that is, guidance, best practices, and codes of conduct. These soft private norms may, through various means and under different degrees, emerge and evolve into public regimes.[177] The softness of these informal regulations, although of a voluntary nature, can be linked to state-imposed standards or requirements in terms of both administrative and judicial organs.

[173] See Ayelet Berman et al., "Rethinking Stakeholder Participation in Global Governance" in Joost Pauwelyn et al. (eds), *Rethinking Participation in Global Governance: Voice and Influence after Stakeholder Reforms in Global Finance and Health* (Oxford University Press 2022), at 10–13.

[174] Urs Gasser, "Futuring Digital Privacy: Reimaging the Law/Tech Interplay" in Mira Burri (ed), *Big Data and Global Trade Law* (Cambridge University Press 2021), at 195, 211.

[175] *Ibid.*

[176] Pauwelyn, supra note 169, at 742.

[177] Enrico Partiti et al., "Evolutionary Dynamics of Transnational Private Regulation" (2023) Transnational Legal Theory 1, at 7.

From the aspect of administration, cybersecurity standards are increasingly referred to by relevant regulators, to the degree that compliance with such standards becomes a core requirement in the "duty of care." For example, the US FTC has brought actions against companies whose cybersecurity practices it deemed had failed to take appropriate action in terms of "cybersecurity due diligence."[178] In these cases,[179] the FTC consistently relies on industry experts to prove whether the cybersecurity practices at issue are fully compatible with the NIST Framework.[180] In a broader context, by heavily referring to the NIST Framework established under multistakeholderism, the FTC signals to companies that the "soft, voluntary" nature of the NIST Framework has been recognized by the FTC as the "reasonableness standard for cybersecurity."

Likewise, from the aspects of judicial proceedings and litigation, private standards under multistakeholderism often give meaning to concepts in law, specifically when evaluating the duty of care in negligence cases.[181] Such judicial recognition can extend a binding effect to otherwise "voluntary" private standards.[182] In other words, even though the court does not (and cannot) apply private standards as such, private standards nevertheless serve as guidelines when it comes to the determination of the required standard of care. Compliance with these standards may not be a sufficient defense, but it does have evidentiary value when establishing cybersecurity due diligence requirements.[183] Specifically, the industry-led soft norms provide a baseline for judges in the evaluation of "reasonable care." Considering this, manufacturers may be able to partially mitigate the legal risk by demonstrating conformity to industry standards. Consequently, concerns about legal liability gradually become incentives for companies to comply with the soft law norms, which are

[178] Under its general statutory authority, Section 5(a) of the Federal Trade Commission Act addresses "unfair or deceptive acts or practices in or affecting commerce." Bruce Heiman et al., "The FTC Has Already Set Cybersecurity Standards" (*Law360,* March 5, 2015).

[179] See, for example, *Federal Trade Commission v. Wyndham Worldwide Corp*., 10 F. Supp. 3d 602 (2014).

[180] Vladimir J. Semendyai, "Due Process and the FTC's Fair and Reasonable Approach to Data Protection" (2016) 84 George Washington Law Review 51, at 66.

[181] Buthe and Wattli, supra note 140, at 205.

[182] *Ibid.*

[183] *Ibid.*; Katja Creutz, "Law versus Codes of Conduct: Between Convergence and Conflict" in Jan Klabbers and Touko Piiparinen (eds), *Normative Pluralism and International Law: Exploring Global Governance* (Cambridge University Press 2013), at 190–191.

not legally mandated, but which define best practices.[184] In this regard, soft private law instruments should not be seen merely as self-imposed corporate obligations. Rather, they can be a source of law in court proceedings.

It should be noted, however, that the increasing influence of soft private norms introduces new risks to big tech's dominant position in private norm-settings. Much like the well-organized industry lobbies in the multilateral treaty-making process, the multistakeholder process may become another effective vehicle for private actors with the greatest resources to press their cases. Large companies and well-funded industry groups are more likely to actively participate in multistakeholder processes. The description of multistakeholderism indicating that "everyone can have an equal seat at the table" may be true in theory but not necessarily in practice.[185] This is in addition to the insights of Raustiala, who posited that "U.S. interests in the Internet have in fact been well served by multistakeholder governance … in which the key actors are disproportionately U.S.-based."[186]

Nevertheless, the multistakeholder process, or even "polycentric" governance, which is generally defined as multiple governing authorities with less hierarchical structure and a high degree of autonomy toward a variety of non-state actors,[187] marked a shift away from the top-down governance architecture toward a bottom-up approach that largely relies on voluntary commitments.[188] This trend toward greater polycentricity is primarily attributable to the need to respond to rapid technological changes. For the digital sectors, governments must govern alongside the private sector in a proactive manner in order to adequately drive cross-industry cooperation. As the ICT industry advocated, "polycentric partnerships" should represent the constituency of global governance in

[184] Shackelford, supra note 138, at 225–226, 256.

[185] Aleecia M. McDonald, "Stakeholders and High Stakes Divergent Standards for Do Not Track" in Evan Selinger et al. (eds) *The Cambridge Handbook of Consumer Privacy* (Cambridge University Press 2018), at 262.

[186] In Raustiala's view, "multistakeholder governance over the Internet has triumphed in large part because it reflects hegemonic power, not in spite of it." Kal Raustiala, supra note 167, at 502.

[187] See generally Rüdiger Wurzel et al., "Pioneers, Leaders and Followers in Multilevel and Polycentric Climate Governance" in Rüdiger Wurzel et al. (eds), *Pioneers, Leaders and Followers in Multilevel and Polycentric Climate Governance* (Routledge 2020), at 2–3.

[188] *Ibid.*

the digital sphere.[189] Individual states, although they continue to be functional components, do not play an exclusively dominant role when governing cyberspace. The reality is that cybersecurity certifications are becoming attractive mechanisms to promote a trustworthy digital ecosystem. In Japan, for example, the NIST Framework and the International Organization for Standardization (ISO) 27001 are complementary tools in governing cybersecurity,[190] with more and more companies turning to the NIST best practices as their cybersecurity standards.[191] The fact that the NIST Framework is globally applied indicates its potential to become a recognized baseline standard under international trade agreements and thus serve as an interoperability mechanism that facilitates cross-border data flows between divergent regulatory systems.

6.5.3 The Role of (Trade) Multilateralism

The ongoing shift to multistakeholderism raises pivotal questions concerning international norms development, namely: What is the appropriate role of states-based multilateral norm-setting in Internet governance? How can the WTO's governing function be sustained in the age of datafication? Can international trade agreements provide venues for digital trade dispute settlements regarding soft private standards created through multistakeholder mechanisms, especially the government-backed "voluntary" standards and certifications? More concretely, how can states be held accountable for unjustified barriers to digital trade when multilateralism and multistakeholderism combined shape the regulatory landscape of the digital economy?

To be sure, multilateral governance remains alive as the primary actor in world politics. The WTO has played and is expected to continue to play a useful role in international economic legal order. First, it is more empirically reasonable and economically justifiable to rely on multilateral approaches to safeguard the balance between the free flow of data and other legitimate public policies. On that premise, the role of the WTO in tackling excessive privacy standards or arbitrary cybersecurity risk

[189] The Internet Governance Forum (IGF), for example, brings various stakeholder groups together "as equals" to discuss Internet policy issues.

[190] Inside Cybersecurity "Japanese Industry Leader on Cyber: NIST Framework Increasingly Embraced Overseas" (July 25, 2017).

[191] NIST, "Cybersecurity Framework Success Story: Japan's Cross-Sector Forum" (2020).

assessment procedures would not be easily replaced. Ideally, a "blended governance regime" might occur when WTO trade tribunals exercise the power of review in the case of "unnecessary trade barriers." Certain industry-driven best practices or codes of conduct may be used as baselines in determining whether "less trade-restrictive measures" exist. As illustrated in the previous chapters, the necessity test – especially when operating in the context of "general exceptions"[192] – functions as the key mechanism in distinguishing between protectionist and non-protectionist trade-restrictive measures. In this context, soft private norms can be considered alternatives to state regulations under the necessity test. A trade tribunal can decide, for example, if certain privacy certifications are "less trade-restrictive measures" when compared with "hardish" state privacy laws. Toward that goal, a trade tribunal must consider if alternative, less trade-restrictive measures proposed by the complaining party are reasonably available and can achieve the desired policy goal of the responding party. Here, a complaining party might argue that an anonymization/de-identification certification granted by a trusted certification body or other credible industry self-regulating association is a less trade-restrictive alternative to data-restrictive measures. A complaining party might also propose self-certification programs as a feasible, less trade-restrictive alternative.[193] The responding party, on the other hand, may argue that private governance cannot achieve the equivalent level of protection that state regulation achieves.

Along this line of arguments, private cybersecurity standards appear to have the potential to compete with state regulations and thus constitute "less trade-restrictive alternative measures" in a trade dispute. Considering the global popularity of some cybersecurity certifications, it is not unimaginable that a trade tribunal might find certain information security testing and certifications representative of WTO-consistent measures which are reasonably available to the responding party and less trade restrictive than the state measures in dispute, and

[192] See Section 1.4.3 for more discussions. Note that some of the more recently concluded FTAs specifically record in the digital trade chapter that the general exceptions shall be interpreted "in a manner that takes into account the evolutionary nature of digital technology." See, for example, the EU–NZ FTA, Article 12.4 (Cross-border data flows).

[193] TADP, supra note 33. Like its predecessors, the Privacy Shield and Safe Harbor provisions, the new TADP Framework requires companies to self-certify their adherence to the Principles through the US Department of Commerce. See European Commission, "Trans-Atlantic Data Privacy Framework" (March 25, 2022) <https://ec.europa.eu/commission/presscorner/detail/en/FS_22_2100>.

which could also achieve an equal or higher level of contribution to the objective of protecting cybersecurity. In this way, soft private law norms visibly compete with state regulations – fighting for legitimacy under the multilateral regime.[194] Through multilateralism, the challenged protectionist measures of the responding party might eventually be substituted by "private norms" that are less trade restrictive.[195] In the long run, voluntary private schemes can serve as practical instruments for governments to "assure" compliance with trade rules.

Moreover, multilateral organizations such as the WTO can engage in the coordination of privacy and cybersecurity "international standards." Certain private schemes are highly influential and thus may constitute a "relevant international standard" within the meaning of WTO law. In terms of WTO litigation, technical standards are "rebuttably presumed" not to be more trade restrictive than necessary when they are in accordance with relevant "international standards" within the meaning of TBT Articles 2.4 and 2.5[196] or GATS Article VI:4/5.[197] In practice, when assessing whether a responding state's privacy or cybersecurity regulations constitute unnecessary barriers to trade, a trade tribunal should consider "international standards" established by "relevant international organizations."[198] Taking TBT Article 2.4 as an example, in *U.S. – Tuna II (Mexico)*, the Appellate Body confirmed that by virtue of Article 2.4, if a standard is found to constitute a "relevant international standard," WTO members are required to use it, or its relevant parts, as a basis for their technical regulations.[199]

It should be noted, however, that while the heart of the TBT Agreement is the adoption of international standards for the sake of trade liberalization, the TBT Agreement does not define the term

194 Partiti et al., supra note 177, at 7.

195 *Ibid.*

196 According to Article 2.4 of the TBT Agreement, technical regulations that use international standards are presumed, subject to rebuttal, to be consistent with WTO obligations; on the other hand, the use of a standard that differs from the pertinent international standard may be challenged as an unnecessary trade barrier.

197 See Aik Hoe Lim, "Trade Rules for Industry 4.0" in Shin-yi Peng et al. (eds), *Artificial Intelligence and International Economic Law: Disruption, Regulation, and Reconfiguration* (Cambridge University Press 2021), at 112.

198 TBT Agreement, Article 2.4; GATS, Article VI:4/5.

199 Appellate Body Report, *United States – Measures Concerning the Importation, Marketing and Sale of Tuna and Tuna Products (US – Tuna II)*, WT/DS381/AB/R, May 16, 2012, para. 348.

"international standards" per se. The Appellate Body, in *U.S. – Tuna II*, stated that in order to constitute an "international standard," a standard must be adopted by an "international standardizing body" for the purposes of the TBT Agreement.[200] A "standardizing body" does not need to have standardization as its principal function, or even as one of its principal functions, as long as WTO members "have reason to expect that the international body in question is engaged in standardization activities."[201] In other words, such a "body" simply has to be "active in standardization," and WTO members are aware of the body's standardization activities.[202] One tricky issue here, under TBT Article 2.4 and GATS Article VI:4/5, is the requirement that the membership of the standardizing body must be open to "the relevant bodies of at least all Members of the WTO"[203] – which may be at odds with the characteristics of the multistakeholder process. It is worthy of special note that such a requirement has been reinforced in the recently developed WTO rules, including the "Six Principles"[204] created by the TBT Committee and the DR JSI. With respect to the former, international standards that are developed in line with the "Six Principles" are more likely to be considered "relevant international standards" within the meaning of the TBT Agreement.[205] However, the "Six Principles" explicitly indicate that "[m]embership of an international standardizing body should be open on a non-discriminatory basis to relevant bodies of at least all WTO Members." Similar wording can be found in the DR JSI.[206] If we follow the reasoning of the Appellate Body in *U.S. – Tuna II*, a body is "open" if membership to the body is not restricted; and it is not "open" if membership is *a priori* limited to the relevant bodies of only some WTO members.[207] On this point, it would be interesting to see whether the dispute settlement mechanism of the WTO provides sufficient incentives

[200] *Ibid.*, paras. 355–359.

[201] *Ibid.*, para. 362.

[202] *Ibid.*, paras. 360, 362.

[203] GATS, footnote 2: "The term "relevant international organizations" refers to international bodies whose membership is open to the relevant bodies of at least all Members of the WTO."

[204] WTO, "Principles for the Development of International Standards, Guides and Recommendations" <www.wto.org/english/tratop_e/tbt_e/principles_standards_tbt_e.htm>.

[205] Lim, supra note 197, at 112.

[206] WTO, "Declaration on the Conclusion of Negotiations on Services Domestic Regulation" WT/L/1129 (2 December 2021), at footnote 15.

[207] Appellate Body Report, *U.S. – Tuna II*, para. 364.

for multistakeholder bodies to be fully open to broader public actors, including state membership and ICT sectoral regulators.

In addition to international trade litigation, a more ambitious path is to incorporate multistakeholder standards into international economic law through trade negotiations. In light of this, leading scholars in the field have different candidates in mind. Chander and Schwartz advocate that the Global Privacy Assembly[208] should be able to develop substantive international standards including a set of global privacy norms, just as the Codex Alimentarius Commission set the international standards for food safety.[209] Kulesza and Weber, however, are of the view that among the existing venues, the Internet Corporation for Assigned Names and Numbers (ICANN) seems best equipped to fuel further discussion on relevant standards and offer possibilities for a more harmonized international framework.[210]

6.6 Conclusion

Admittedly, international economic law alone is not adequate in light of concerns surrounding privacy and cybersecurity governance. The global governance architecture of cross-border data flows therefore calls for the "variable geometry" model, which integrates different components of approaches and instruments. Multistakeholderism and multilateralism – at least when it comes to data flow governance – do not have to be two parallel paths. A "right" balance between the free flow of data and other legitimate objectives might never be found, but a more properly balanced approach may be possible if each role and its momentum in the public and private sectors can be reconfigured and restored.

208 Global Privacy Assembly (GPA) <https://globalprivacyassembly.org/>.

209 Anupam Chander and Paul Schwartz, "Privacy and/or Trade" (2023) 90(1) University of Chicago Law Review 49.

210 Joanna Kulesza and Rolf H. Weber, "Protecting the Internet with International Law" (2021) 40 Computer Law & Security Review 1, at 4.

Conclusion

> Technology has built the house in which we all live. The house is continually being extended and remodeled. More and more of human life takes place within its walls, so that today there is hardly any human activity that does not occur within this house. All are affected by the design of the house, by the division of its space, by the location of its doors and walls. Compared to people in earlier times, we rarely have a chance to live outside this house. And the house is still changing; it is still being built as well as being demolished.[1]
>
> —Ursula Franklin

As the house metaphor by Ursula Franklin aptly exemplifies, we are undergoing a wave of datafication practices. If such practices simply continue to evolve without being examined and repaired along the existing path of development, the same issues will continue to accumulate and will more than likely be compounded. Before concluding with an aggregate assessment, the findings from the preceding chapters of this book are summarized below, presenting a complete picture.

Data Network as Enabler

Broadband infrastructure is the prerequisite that enables people to meaningfully participate in the data-driven economy, as well as to put to good use the "beauty" of datafication. Developing countries and LDCs need FDI to build their digital infrastructures. However, the economic benefit of the GATS Mode 3 market access commitments in the telecommunications sector has never been realized in many states. In this context, from *Mexico – Telecom* to *Brazil – Taxation*, the mere fact that the responding parties must have attempted to stretch the scope of the "universal services" or "public morals" to justify their digital inclusion policies within the WTO indicates that the interplay between

[1] Ursula Franklin, *The Real World of Technology* (Anansi Press 1999), at 11.

international economic law and digital inequality invites further reflection. The pressing task for trade negotiators is to find the common ground necessary to balance digital trade liberalization and development needs, rather than creating another "Digital 'Haves' Trade Agreement." One policy direction discussed in Chapter 1 is to impose obligations on big tech companies to contribute their fair share to universal service funds needed for infrastructure upgrades. Such a reform, of course, should be implemented in a transparent, nondiscriminatory, and competitively neutral manner, as required by the Telecom Reference Paper.

Data Network as Critical Infrastructure

Empowering individuals to benefit from innovations and participate in the data economy relies not only on the "availability," but also on the "resilience" of broadband infrastructure. Along the path of datafication, however, the probability of cyberattacks against critical infrastructure increases as well. The weaponization of 5G networks has brought about further challenges to international economic legal order. Major geopolitical players have adopted comprehensive security measures at home and have also strengthened cooperation with geopolitical allies to protect and enhance the resilience of ICT ecosystems. In this regard, the more recent iterations of international trade agreements are equipped with "modernized" security exceptions to ensure that the exceptions to international trade rules are aligned with the policy needs of the data-driven economy. Innovative exception clauses have been incorporated into FTAs to reconcile conflicts between (digital) trade and (cyber) security, which, overall, grant a dramatically expansive scope and excessively unfettered discretion to states when it comes to "national security." Questions as to what constitutes "critical infrastructure" and how it should be designated, however, require due process mechanisms to constrain discretionary abuse. Chapter 2 contends that a consensus concerning the scope of "critical infrastructure" would be politically and economically valuable to filter out overgeneralizations of national security claims.

Data-Driven Platform as Service

Turning to the level of digital applications, today's platformization of services was an "unforeseen" phenomenon when the WTO was established. However, through the pro-liberalization WTO jurisprudence developed in past decades, the GATS market access commitments have played more than a marginal role in the story of the emergence of datafication, leaving the door open for big tech companies. Without question, platforms' associated datafication practices influence human society, in terms of their beauty as well as their peril. The perilous side therefore calls into question whether international trade commitments negotiated in the pre-digital age should be sustained in this datafied world. In the FTA context, Chapter 3 argues that listing nonconforming measures under the Cross-Border Trade in Services Chapter represents the most critical step in reserving a state's "digital sovereignty." Such inscriptions ensure that a state does not risk committing to future services and associated delivery means that did not exist at the time of treaty negotiations. Nonetheless, market access obligations do not prevent states from adopting domestic regulations in pursuit of legitimate national policies. Digital trade liberalization must be accompanied by the introduction of data regulations to address the potential risks and harms.

Data as Speech and Expression

Nonetheless, media platformization has caused problems that a state cannot easily regulate. The media content regulations considered in Chapter 4 are prime examples demonstrating the need to alter the power distribution in the Internet ecosystem. In terms of speech platforms, the "rules-based" platform governance model led by the EU, such as the DSA, now represents a strong power in balancing the US' CDA-based social media self-regulation. The years to come will be critical to the global governance of digital platforms. Key indicators include whether more and more countries will adopt DSA-like regulations along the EU regulatory path. In terms of streaming services, the content quotas for video streaming platforms may constitute performance requirements for investment in services. This measure may also violate the obligations that apply to the nondiscriminatory treatment of digital products. Looking ahead, cultural diversity concerns regarding avatars in the VR space will be even more complex and will propel the "trade v. culture" clash to another level. In any event, media platformization brings about issues surrounding jurisdiction. No matter how carefully crafted, media content regulation must face enforceable reality. International trade rules that ban local presence would enable platform companies to supply services without establishing a local presence, which could constrain a state's ability to enforce platform regulations.

Data as Capital and Algorithmic Input

The role of international economic law in the politics of datafication is rendered even more complex when data becomes capital and is the algorithmic input of digital platforms. Our behavioral data has increasingly become a commodity. Datafication-enabled advertising and other datafication practices, in the absence of proper constraints, will deepen the perils of datafication. A set of cross-border competition disciplines proposed in Chapter 5 may well be an effective instrument to address problems associated with platform monopolies and data capitalism. In this way, there would be less need for *ex-post* competition law enforcement in developing countries and LDCs, where relatively limited resources can be allocated to combat digital cartels and data monopolization. In this context, algorithmic transparency can serve as a starting point for global platform governance. The case study in Chapter 5 investigates the key dimensions of platform transparency requirements in a comparative context and argues that the question of "disclosure to whom" dictates "what to disclose." It also demonstrates that the fragmentation of platform regulation is growing. The proliferation of platform regulations and algorithmic disciplines may place SMEs in an even more difficult situation vis-à-vis big tech companies that have the resources necessary to manage different legal requirements in different countries. The international agenda to foster regulatory coherence, however, depends on the political will of the governments involved. Despite the inherent complexity of the political economy surrounding digital capitalism, Chapter 5 concludes that there are reasons to be optimistic about better governance through international trade agreements.

Data Flows as Digital Trade

Finally, it is worth repeating that digitally enabled goods and services fuel today's economy. In this regard, the question of how to balance free data flows and national policy objectives, especially data privacy and security, is key to advancing the benefits of the digital economy. After establishing that new digital technologies have further integrated physical and digital activities, and thus, more and more of our social interactions are being sensed and datafied, Chapter 6 argues that innovative regulatory approaches are needed to respond to the impact of big data analytics on existing privacy and cybersecurity regimes. As for privacy protections, this book points out that there is an evident gap between private actors' potential governing functions and their current roles in data governance. On the contrary, as demonstrated by IoT cybersecurity certifications, the cybersecurity "standards jungle" may constitute a barrier to data flows. At the crossroads, where multistakeholderism meets multilateralism, the roles of the public and private sectors should be reconfigured for a datafied world. Looking to the future, rapid technological developments and market changes call for further public–private convergence in data governance, allowing both public authorities and private actors to jointly reshape the norms of cross-border data flows. Under such an umbrella, the appropriate role of multilateral, state-based norm-setting in Internet governance includes the oversight of the balance between the free flow of data and other legitimate public policies, as well as engagement in the coordination of international standards.

The Beauty, the Perils, and the Trade-Offs of Datafication

At the level of digital physical infrastructure, substantial digital divides exist, and developed countries' ambitious digital plans are exacerbating the current gap. If left unaddressed, this digital inequality will broaden the divide between under-connected and hyper-digitized regions. At the level of digital application, much like the persistent unequal distributions in the broadband networks, digital capitalism is expanding the inequality between those who provide the data and those who exert control over the use of such data. Taken as a whole, however, the beauty and the perils of datafication vary in different contexts. The more an individual accesses the Internet, the more data digital platforms appropriate and extract for profit. In this regard, the gap at the infrastructure level has resulted in an irony: The broadband "have-nots" tend to be the least represented in big tech's data sources. In other words, those who produce little or no digital data are free from digital platforms' profiling activities and other datafication practices. Of course, they are also consistently excluded from the process of datafication that drives social welfare – insufficiently captured and analyzed by AI health algorithms – and thus are less likely to benefit from the beauty of datafication. Indeed, depending upon the context, digitalization, platformization, and datafication yield the promises and the risks, the beauty and the perils, and the benefits and inequalities associated with big data applications. Necessary policies and regulations must be in place for data's full, beautiful potential to be realized, and, more importantly, for those risky perils to be mitigated.

The Reach and the Limits of International Economic Law

This book has investigated how international economic law can reduce the perils of datafication instead of enhancing them. The discussions throughout the six chapters reveal that international trade agreements should be and can be reformed to better contribute to this journey of regime transformation by safeguarding states' policy space in terms of digital inclusion, national security, digital sovereignty, free speech, cultural expression, platform competition, algorithmic transparency, privacy, and cybersecurity. At the same time, international economic law can ensure that governmental interventions do not constitute unnecessary barriers to digital trade, thus promoting the beauty of datafication. Nevertheless, enormous challenges remain. At this moment, it appears that US allies will commit to new norms on digital trade under the IPEF that promote the US preferred ecosystem for Internet governance. Yet, more and more states have already started to bring their digital competition policy in line with the EU's DMA. Additionally, several neighboring states of China have incentives to follow its authoritarian digital policies. These competing models of data governance are impediments to the effective confrontation of the trend of datafication. More work must be done to restore the relevance of international economic law in this datafied world. To conclude, the interplay between international economic law and the trend of datafication is complex and uneasy. Through its findings, this book has confirmed that international economic law is itself a source of this unease. Importantly, international economic law also has the potential to offer meaningful solutions to the alleviation of our collective discomfort.

SELECT BIBLIOGRAPHY

Aaronson, Susan Ariel and Patrick Leblond, "Another Digital Divide: The Rise of Data Realms and Its Implications for the WTO" (2018) 21(2) Journal of International Economic Law 245.

ACCC, "Digital Platforms Inquiry: Final Report" (July 26, 2019).

ACMA (Australian Communications and Media Authority), "Supporting Australian Stories on Our Screen: Options Paper" (March 2020).

Ala'i, Padideh, "From the Periphery to the Center? The Evolving WTO Jurisprudence on Transparency and Good Governance" (2008) 11(4) Journal of International Economic Law 779.

Alemanno, Alberto, "Is There a Role for Cost–Benefit Analysis beyond the Nation-State? Lessons from International Regulatory Co-operation" in Michael A. Livermore and Richard L. Revesz (eds), *The Globalization of Cost–Benefit Analysis in Environmental Policy* (Oxford University Press 2013).

Allen, Henry et al., "Media Pluralism: What Matters for Governance and Regulation?" (2017) 30(2) Journal of Media Economics 47.

Anderson, Robert D. et al., "Competition Policy, Trade and the Global Economy" World Trade Organization Working Paper (2018).

APEC, "Privacy Framework" (2017).

"Study on APEC's Non-binding Principles for Domestic Regulation of the Services Sector" (2021).

Arner, Douglas W. et al., "The Future of Data-Driven Finance and Regtech: Lessons from EU Big Bang II" (2020) 25 Stanford Journal of Law, Business & Finance 245.

Australian Council of Trade Unions (ACTU), "Australia-Singapore Digital Economy Agreement, Submission to the Joint Standing Committee on Treaties" (September 25, 2020).

Australian Fair Trade & Investment Network, "Submission to the Department of Foreign Affairs and Trade on the Plurilateral Negotiations on Trade-Related Aspects of Electronic Commerce" (February 2020).

AVIA (Asia Video Industry Association), "OTT TV Policies in Asia" (2018).

Baccarne, Bastiaan et al., "The Television Struggle: An Assessment of Over-the-Top Television Evolutions in a Cable Dominant Market" (2013) 92(4) Communications & Strategies 43.

Baiker, Laura et al., "Services Domestic Regulation: Locking in Good Regulatory Practices" WTO Working Paper ERSD-2021-14 (September 17, 2021).

Baldwin, Richard, *The Globotics Upheaval: Globalization, Robotics, and the Future of Work* (Oxford University Press 2019).

Bambauer, Jane, "Is Data Speech?" (2014) 66 Stanford Law Review 57.

Barker, Chris, *Television, Globalization and Cultural Identities* (Open University Press 2000).

Batura, Olga, *Universal Service in WTO and EU Law: Liberalization and Social Regulation in Telecommunications* (Springer 2016).

Benjamin, Stuart M., *Telecommunications Law and Policy* (Carolina Academic Press 2012).

Benjamin, Stuart M. and James Speta, *Internet and Telecommunication Regulation* (Carolina Academic Press 2019).

BEREC (The Body of European Regulators for Electronic Communications), "Draft BEREC Report on the Internet Ecosystem" BoR (22) 87 (June 9, 2022).

"Report on Harmonized Definitions for Indicators Regarding Over-the-Top Services" BoR (21) 127 (September 30, 2021).

Berman, Ayelet et al., "Rethinking Stakeholder Participation in Global Governance" in Joost Pauwelyn et al. (eds), *Rethinking Participation in Global Governance: Voice and Influence after Stakeholder Reforms in Global Finance and Health* (Oxford University Press 2022).

Black, Julia and Robert Baldwin, "When Risk-Based Regulation Aims Low: A Strategic Framework" (2012) 6(2) Regulation & Governance 131.

Blake, Janet, *International Cultural Heritage Law* (Oxford University Press 2015).

Bonnett, Thomas, *Telewars in the States: Telecommunications Issues in a New Era of Competition* (Council of Governors' Policy Advisors 1996).

Brenner, Daniel L., "Creating Effective Broadband Network Regulation" (2010) 62 Federal Communications Law Journal 13.

Breznitz, Dan and Michael Murphree, "The Rise of China in Technology Standards: New Norms in Old Institutions" (2016) Research Report Prepared on Behalf of the U.S.-China Economic and Security Review Commission.

Brownsword, Roger and Han Somsen, "Law, Innovation and Technology: Before We Fast Forward – A Forum for Debate" (2009) 1 Law, Innovation and Technology 1.

Burk, Dan L., "Algorithmic Legal Metrics" (2021) 96 Notre Dame Law Review 1147.

Burkhardt, Marcus et al., "Introduction" in Marcus Burkhardt et al. (eds) *Interrogating Datafication: Towards a Praxeology of Data* (Transcript Publishing 2022).

Burri, Mira, "EU External Trade Policy in The Digital Age: Has Culture Been Left Behind?" (2022) Trade Law 4.0 Working Paper Series University of Lucerne.

"Interfacing Privacy and Trade" (2021) 53 Case Western Reserve Journal of International Law 35.

"The Global Digital Divide as Impeded Access to Content" in Mira Burri and Thomas Cottier (eds), *Trade Governance in the Digital Age* (Cambridge University Press 2012).

"Towards a New Treaty on Digital Trade," (2021) 55(1) Journal of World Trade 77.

"Trade Law 4.0: Are We There Yet? (2023) 26(1) Journal of International Economic Law 90.

Buthe, Tim and Walter Mattli, *The New Global Rulers: The Privatization of Regulation in the World Economy* (Princeton University Press 2011).

Buyya, Rajkumar and Amir Dastjerdi (eds), *Internet of Things: Principles and Paradigms* (Elsevier 2016).

Candeub, Adam, "Reading Section 230 as Written" (2021) 1 Journal of Free Speech Law 139.

Carrilloa, Arturo J., "Having Your Cake and Eating It Too? Zero-Rating, Net Neutrality, and International Law" (2016) 19 Stanford Technology Law Review 364.

CASBAA (Cable and Satellite Broadcasting Association of Asia), "A Titled Playing Field: Asia-Pacific Pay TV and OTT" (2012).

Cashore, Benjamin et al., "Private Authority and Public Policy Interactions in Global Context: Governance Spheres for Problem Solving" (2021) 15 Regulation & Governance 1166.

Chaisse, Julien and Mitsuo Matsushita, "China's 'Belt and Road' Initiative: Mapping the World Trade Normative and Strategic Implications" (2018) 52 Journal of World Trade 163.

Chander, Anupam and Paul Schwartz, "Privacy and/or Trade" (2023) 90(1) University of Chicago Law Review 49.

Chander, Anupam and Haochen Sun, "Sovereignty 2.0" (2021) Georgetown Law Faculty Publications and Other Works (2021).

Chander, Anupam, "Section 230 and the International Law of Facebook" (2022) 24 Yale Journal of Law & Technology 393.

Chi Carmody, "When Cultural Identity Was Not at Issue: Thinking About Canada – Certain Measures Concerning Periodicals" (1999) 30 Law & Policy of International Business 231.

Ciuriak, Dan and Robert Fay, "The Digital Economy Partnership Agreement: Should Canada Join?" (2022) 171 Centre for International Governance Innovation Policy Brief.

Ciuriak, Dan, "The Challenge of Updating Institutions for Digital Trade" (2021) Opinion, Centre for International Governance Innovation.

Claussen, Kathleen, "Trade's Security Exceptionalism" (2020) 72 Stanford Law Review 1097.

Cohen, Harlan Grant, "Nations and Markets" (2020) 23(4) Journal of International Economic Law 793.

Cohen, Julie E., *Between Truth and Power: The Legal Constructions of the Informational Capitalism* (Oxford University Press 2019).

"Law for the Platform Economy" (2017) 51 U.C. Davis Law Review 133.

Condron, Sean M., "Getting It Right: Protecting American Critical Infrastructure in Cyberspace" (2007) 20(2) Harvard Journal of Law & Technology 403.

Cory, Nigel and Luke Dascoli, "How Barriers to Cross-Border Data Flows Are Spreading Globally, What They Cost, and How to Address Them" Information Technology & Innovation Foundation (ITIF) (July 19, 2021).

Cossy, Mirelle, "Cross-Border Supply of Services – Pattern of Specific Commitments" (April 28–29, 2005), WTO Symposium on Cross-Border Supply of Services.

Couldry, Nick and Ulises A. Mejias, *The Costs of Connection: How Data Is Colonizing Human Life and Appropriating It for Capitalism* (Stanford University Press 2019).

Creutz, Katja, "Law versus Codes of Conduct: Between Convergence and Conflict" in Jan Klabbers and Touko Piiparinen (eds), *Normative Pluralism and International Law: Exploring Global Governance* (Cambridge University Press 2013).

Cunningham, McKay, "Next Generation Privacy: The Internet of Things, Data Exhaust, and Reforming Regulation by Risk of Harm" (2014) 2(2) Groningen Journal of International Law 115.

Delev, Christian, "A Moral Stretch? US–Tariff Measures and the Public Morals Exception in WTO Law" (2021) World Trade Review 1.

Delimatsis, Panagiotis, "Concluding the WTO Services Negotiations on Domestic Regulation: Hopes and Fears" (2020) 9(4) World Trade Review 643.

International Trade in Services and Domestic Regulations: Necessity, Transparency and Regulatory Diversity (Oxford University Press 2007).

Dickinson, Gregory M., "Rebooting Internet Immunity" (2021) 89 George Washington Law Review 347.

Dorobantu, Cosmina et al., "Source Code Disclosure: A Primer for Trade Negotiators" in Ingo Borchert and Alan Winters (eds), *Addressing Impediments to Digital Trade* (CEPR Press 2021).

Ducci, Francesco, *Natural Monopolies in Digital Platform Markets* (Cambridge University Press 2020).

Dutton, William H., "Multistakeholder Internet Governance?" (2016) World Bank Background Paper.

Edelman, Benjamin and Abbey Stemler, "From the Digital to the Physical: Federal Limitations on Regulating Online Marketplaces" (2019) 56 Harvard Journal on Legislation 142.

Elms, Deborah, "The Comprehensive and Progressive Trans-Pacific Partnership Policy Innovations and Impacts" (2018) Global Economic Dynamics Focus Paper.

EMAG, "Digital Platform's Market Power" (September 30, 2019).

Emmerson, Andrew, "Conceptualizing Security Exceptions: Legal Doctrine or Political Excuse?" (2008) 11 Journal of International Economic Law 135.

ENISA, "Guidelines for Securing the Internet of Things" (2020).

Erie, Matthew S. and Thomas Streinz, "The Beijing Effect: China's Digital Silk Road as Transnational Data Governance" (2021) 54(1) New York University Journal of International Law & Policy 1.

European Commission, "Better Regulation: Guidelines and Toolbox" (November 3, 2021).

"Competition Policy for the Digital Era" (May 20, 2019).

"Cybersecurity of 5G Networks - EU Toolbox of Risk Mitigating Measures" (2020).

"DSA: Very Large Online Platforms and Search Engines" (April 25, 2023).

"Impact Assessment Accompanying the Document Proposal for a Regulation of the European Parliament and of the Council on a Single Market for Digital Services (Digital Services Act) and Amending Directive 2000/31/EC" SWD (2020) 348 final (December 15, 2020).

"Proposal for a Regulation of the European Parliament and of the Council on Horizontal Cybersecurity Requirements for Products with Digital Elements and Amending Regulation" (2022).

"Shaping Europe's Digital Future" (October 17, 2022).

"The Future of the Electronic Communications Sector and its Infrastructure, Consultation Questionnaire" (February 23, 2023).

"Trans-Atlantic Data Privacy Framework" (March 25, 2022).

"Digital Sovereignty for Europe" (July 2020).

"Europe's Digital Decade and Autonomy" (2021).

"Liability of Online Platforms" (2021).

"The Impact of the General Data Protection Regulation (GDPR) on Artificial Intelligence" (2020).

Ezrachi, Ariel and Maurice Stucke, *Virtual Competition – The Promise and Perils of the Algorithm-Driven Economy* (Harvard University Press 2016).

FCC, "Reports to Congress on Future of the Universal Service Fund" (August 15, 2022).

Fisher, Angelina and Thomas Streinz, "Confronting Data Inequality" (2022) 60(3) Columbia Journal of Transnational Law 829.

Flyverbom, Mikkel, *The Digital Prism – Transparency and Managed Visibilities in a Datafied World* (Cambridge University Press 2019).

Franklin, Ursula, *The Real World of Technology* (Anansi Press 1999).

FTC, "Report to Congress on Privacy and Security" (September 13, 2021).

Gao, Henry, "Digital or Trade? The Contrasting Approaches of China and US to Digital Trade" (2018) 21(2) Journal of International Economic Law 297.

"E-commerce Joint Statement Initiative Negotiation and China" in Shin-yi Peng et al. (eds), *Artificial Intelligence and International Economic Law: Disruption, Regulation, and Reconfiguration* (Cambridge University Press, 2021).

"Google's China Problem: A Case Study on Trade, Technology and Human Rights under the GATS" (2011) 6 Asian Journal of WTO & International Health Law & Policy 349.

Gari, Gabriel, "Recent Preferential Trade Agreements' Disciplines for Tackling Regulatory Divergence in Services: How Far beyond GATS?" (2020) 19(1) World Trade Review 1.

Garlick, Jeremy, *The Impact of China's Belt and Roald Initiative* (Routledge 2019).

Gasser, Urs et al., "Multistakeholder as Governance Groups: Observations from Case Studies" (2015) The Berkman Ctr. for Internet & Society Research Publication Series.

"Futuring Digital Privacy: Reimaging the Law/Tech Interplay" in Mira Burri (ed), *Big Data and Global Trade Law* (Cambridge University Press 2021).

Gellert, Raphaël, *The Risk-Based Approach to Data Protection* (Oxford University Press 2020).

Geradin, Damien and Michel Kerf, "Levelling the Playing Field: Is the WTO Adequately Equipped to Prevent Anti-Competitive Practices in Telecommunications?" in Damien Geradin and David Luff (eds), *The WTO and Global Convergence in Telecommunications and Audio-Visual Services* (Cambridge University Press 2004).

Goldman, Eric, "Five Things to Know about Section 230" (2021) Center for International Governance Innovation.

Goodman, Ryan, "Norms and National Security: The WTO as a Catalyst for Inquiry" (2001) 2 Chicago Journal of International Law 101.

Gough, Ian , "Universal Basic Services: A Theoretical and Moral Framework" (2019) 90(3) The Political Quarterly 2.

Government of Canada, "What Does the CPTPP Mean for Canadian Culture?" (2018).

Grubesic, Tony and Elizabeth Mack, *Broadband Telecommunications and Regional Development* (Routledge, 2016).

Gur, Berna Akcali, "Cybersecurity, European Digital Sovereignty and the 5G Rollout Crisis" (2022) 46 Computer Law & Security Review 1.

Hamilton, Daniel S. and Joseph P. Quinlan, "The Transatlantic Economy 2021: Annual Survey of Jobs, Trade and Investment between the United States and Europe" (2021).

Haskel, Jonathan and Stian Westlake, *Capitalism without Capital: The Rise of the Intangible Economy* (Princeton University Press 2018).

Heath, J. Benton, "The New National Security Challenge to the Economic Order" (2020) 129 Yale Law Journal 1020.

Helmersen, Sondre T., "The Evolutionary Treaty Interpretation by the WTO Appellate Body in Georges Abi-Saab et al. (eds), *Evolutionary Interpretation and International Law* (Hart Publishing 2019).

Hintz, Arne et al., *Digital Citizenship in a Datafied Society* (Polity Press 2019).

Hintze, Mike, "In Defense of the Long Privacy Statement" (2017) 76 Maryland Law Review 1044.

Hovenkamp, Herbert, "Antitrust and Platform Monopoly" (2021) 130 Yale Law Journal 1952.

Howse, Robert, "Importing Regulatory Standards and Principles into WTO Dispute Settlement: The Challenge of Interpreting the GATS Arrangements on Telecommunications" in Ioannis Lianos and Okeoghene Odudu (eds), *Regulating Trade in Services in the EU and the WTO: Trust, Distrust and Economic Integration* (Cambridge University Press, 2012).

Iansiti, Marco and Karim R. Lakhani, *Competing in the Age of AI: How Machine Intelligence Changes the Rules of Business* (Harvard Business Review Press 2020).

IHRB (Institute for Human Rights and Business), "Data Brokers and Human Rights: Big Data, Big Business" (November 2016).

International Trade Union Confederation, "E-Commerce, Free Trade Agreements, Digital Chapters and the Impact on Labor" (2019).

ITU, "Digital Inclusion of All" (2019).

"GSR Discussion Paper: Regulation and the Internet of Things" (2015).

"Setting the Scene for 5G: Opportunities & Challenges" (2018).

"The State of Broadband 2020: Tackling Digital Inequalities" (September 2020).

"Universal Service Funds and Digital Inclusion for All" (2013).

ITU-D, "Digital Inclusion" (2023).

Kamara, Irene, "Co-Regulation in EU Personal Data Protection: The Case of Technical Standards and the Privacy by Design Standardization Mandate" (2017) 8(1) European Journal of Law and Technology 1.

Kamara, Irene, "Misaligned Union Laws? A Comparative Analysis of Certification in the Cybersecurity Act and the General Data Protection Regulation" in Dara Hallinan et al. (eds), *Data Protection and Artificial Intelligence* (Hart Publishing 2021).

Kaminski, Margot E., "Binary Governance: Lessons from the GDPR's Approach to Algorithmic Accountability" (2019) 92 Southern California Law Review 1529.

Kanetake, Machiko and André Nollkaemper, "The Application of Informal International Instruments Before Domestic Courts" (2014) 46 George Washington International Law Review 765.

Katz, Vanessa, "Regulating the Sharing Economy" (2015) 30 Berkeley Technology Law Journal 1067.

Kelsey, Jane, "The Illegitimacy of Joint Statement Initiatives and Their Systemic Implications for the WTO" (2022) 25 Journal of International Economic Law 2.

Kennedy, Charles H., *An Introduction to U.S. Telecommunications Law* (Artech House 2001).

Khan, Lina M., "Amazon's Antitrust Paradox" (2017) 126 Yale Law Journal 710.

Kho, Stephen and Yujin K. McNamara, "Focus on China: The Expansive Use of National Security Measures to Address Economic Competitiveness Concerns" (2022) 17 University of Pennsylvania Asian Law Review 368.

Knight, Lizzie and Tania Voon, "The Evolution of National Security at the Interface Between Domestic and International Investment Law and Policy: The Role of China" (2020) 21 Journal of World Investment and Trade 104.

Krajewski, Markus, *National Regulation and Trade Liberalization in Services* (Kluwer Law International 2003).

Krisch, Nico, "Jurisdiction Unbound: (Extra)territorial Regulation as Global Governance" (2022) 33(2) European Journal of International Law 481.

Krishnamurthy, Vivek et al., "CDA 230 Goes North American? Examining the Impacts of the USMCA's Intermediary Liability Provisions in Canada and the United States" (2020).

Kulesza, Joanna and Rolf H. Weber, "Protecting the Internet with International Law" (2021) 40 Computer Law & Security Review 1.

Lachaud, Eric, "What GDPR Tells about Certification" (2020) 38 Computer Law and Security Review 1.

Lang, Andrew, "GATS" in Daniel Bethlehem et al. (eds), *Oxford Handbook of International Trade Law* (Oxford University Press 2009).

Lim, Aik Hoe, "Trade Rules for Industry 4.0" in Shin-yi Peng et al. (eds), *Artificial Intelligence and International Economic Law: Disruption, Regulation, and Reconfiguration* (Cambridge University Press 2021).

Linderfalk, Ulf, *On the Interpretation of Treaties* (Springer 2007).

Lodge, Martin and Kai Wegrich, *Managing Regulation: Regulatory Analysis Politics and Policy* (Palgrave Macmillan 2012).

Luff, David, "Telecommunications and Audiovisual Services: Considerations for a Convergence Policy at the World Trade Organization Level" (2004) 38(6) Journal of World Trade 1059.

Markopoulou, Dimitra et al., "The New EU Cybersecurity Framework: The NIS Directive, ENISA's Role and the General Data Protection Regulation" (2019) 35(6) Computer Law & Security Review 2.

Matsushita, Mitsuo et al., "Competition Policy and Trade" in Mitsuo Matsushita et al. (eds.) *The World Trade Organization: Law, Practice, and Policy* (Oxford University Press 2015).

"Trade and Competition Policy" in Daniel Bethlehem et al. (eds.), *The Oxford Handbook of International Trade Law* (Oxford University Press 2009).

Mattoo, Aaditya and Pierre Sauve, "Regionalism in Services Trade" in Aaditya Mattoo et al. (eds), *A Handbook of International Trade in Services* (Oxford University Press 2008).

Mavroidis, Petros C. and Robert Wolfe, "Private Standards and the WTO: Reclusive No More" (2017) 16 World Trade Review 1.

Mavroidis, Petros C., *Trade in Goods* (Oxford University Press 2012).

Mayer-Schonberger, Viktor and Kenneth Cukier, *Big Data: A Revolution That Will Transform How We Live, Work, and Think* (Harper Business 2013).

McDonald, Aleecia M., "Stakeholders and High Stakes Divergent Standards for Do Not Track" in Evan Selinger et al. (eds) *The Cambridge Handbook of Consumer Privacy* (Cambridge University Press 2018).

McNealy, Jasmine E., "Sonic Privacy" (2022) 24 Yale Journal of Law and Technology 365.

Meltzer, Joshua P., "The Internet, Cross-Border Data Flows and International Trade" (2015) 2(1) Asia & Pacific Policy Studies 90.

Meuwese, Anne, "Constitutional Aspects of Regulatory Coherence in TTIP: An EU Perspective" (2015) 78 Law & Contemporary Problems 153.

Mishra, Neha, "International Trade Law Meets Data Ethics: A Brave New World" (2020) 53(2) New York University Journal of International Law and Politics 305.

"The Trade – (Cyber)security Dilemma and its Impact on Global Cybersecurity Governance" (2020) 54(4) Journal of World Trade 567.

Misra, Sudip et al., *Introduction to Industrial Internet of Things and Industry 4.0* (Routledge 2020).

Mitchell, Andrew and Neha Mishra, "Digital Trade Integration in Preferential Trade Agreements" (2020) 191 Asia-Pacific Research and Training Network on Trade Working Paper Series 34–36.

"Regulating Cross-Border Data Flows in a Data-Driven World: How WTO Law Can Contribute" (2019) 22(3) Journal of International Economic Law 389.

Mitchell, Andrew D., *Legal Principles in WTO Disputes* (Cambridge University Press 2008).

"Brief of Evidence of Andrew David Mitchell in the Matter of the Trans-Pacific Partnership Agreement Inquiry before the Waitangi Tribunal" (2020).

Moazed, Alex and Nicholas L. Johnson, *Modern Monopolies: What It Takes to Dominate the Twenty-First Century Economy* (St. Martin's Press 2016).

Moyn, Samuel, *Not Enough: Human Rights in an Unequal World* (Harvard University Press 2018).

Mundie, Craig, "Privacy Pragmatism: Focus on Data Use, Not Data Collection" (2014) 93(2) Foreign Affairs 28.

NIST, "Cybersecurity for IOT Program" (2023).

"Cybersecurity Framework" (2022).

OECD, "Algorithms and Collusion: Competition Policy in the Digital Age" (2017).

"Big Data: Bringing Competition Policy to the Digital Era" DAF/COMP (2016).

"Fostering Cross-Border Data Flows with Trust" OECD Digital Economy Papers No. 343 (December 2022).

"Regional Competition Agreements: Benefits and Challenges" (November 29, 2018).

"Regulatory Impact Analysis: A Tool for Policy Coherence" (2009).

"Regulatory Impact Assessment, OECD Best Practice Principles for Regulatory Policy" (2020).

"Reviews of Risk Management Policies Good Governance for Critical Infrastructure Resilience" (2019).

Partiti, Enrico et al., "Evolutionary Dynamics of Transnational Private Regulation" (2023) Transnational Legal Theory 1.

Pauwelyn, Joost, "*Rien ne va plus*? Distinguishing Domestic Regulation from Market Access in GATT and GATS" (2005) 4 World Trade Review 131.

"Rule-Based Trade 2.0? The Rise of Informal Rules and International Standards and How They May Outcompete WTO Treaties" (2014) 17 Journal of International Economic Law 739.

Peng, Shin-yi and Han-Wei Liu, "The Legality of Data Residency Requirements: How Can the Trans-Pacific Partnership Help?" (2017) 51:2 Journal of World Trade 183.

Peng, Shin-yi, "Autonomous Vehicle Standards under the Technical Barriers to Trade Agreement" in Shin-yi Peng et al. (eds), *Artificial Intelligence and International Economic Law: Disruption, Regulation, and Reconfiguration* (Cambridge University Press 2021).

"Cybersecurity and Trade Governance" in Julien Chaisse & Cristián Rodríguez-Chiffelle (eds), *The Elgar Companion to the WTO* (Edward Elgar 2023).

"Cybersecurity Threats and the WTO National Security Exceptions" (2015) 18 (2) Journal of International Economic Law 449.

"Digital Trade" in Daniel Bethlehem et al. (eds), *The Oxford Handbook of International Trade Law* (Oxford University Press 2022).

"GATS and the Over-the-Top Services: A Legal Outlook" (2016) 50(1) Journal of World Trade 21.

"Lessons from the TPP Regulatory Coherence Chapter: The Laws Governing Unsolicited Commercial Electronic Messages as a Case Study" in Shin-yi Peng et al. (eds), *Governing Science and Technology under the International Economic Order: Regulatory Divergence and Convergence in the Age of Mega-regionals* (Edward Elgar 2018).

"Levelling the Playing Field between Sharing Platforms and Industry Incumbents: Good Regulatory Practices?" in Anupam Chander and Haochen Sun (eds), *Data Sovereignty: From the Digital Silk Road to the Return of the State* (Oxford University Press 2023).

"Private Cybersecurity Standards? Cyberspace Governance, Multistakeholderism, and the (Ir)relevance of the TBT Regime" (2018) 51 (2) Cornell International Law Journal 445.

"Public–Private Interactions in Privacy Governance" (Concept Paper) (2022) 11(6) MDPI-Laws Special Issue: International Law as a Driver of Internet Governance 80.

"Regulating New Services through Litigation? Electronic Commerce as a Case Study on the Evaluation of 'Judicial Activism' in the WTO" (2014) 48(6) Journal of World Trade 1189.

"Renegotiate the WTO Commitments? Technological Change and Treaty Interpretation" (2012) 45(2) Cornell International Law Journal 403.

"The Rule of Law in Times of Technological Uncertainty: Is International Economic Law Ready for Emerging Supervisory Trends?" (2019) 22(1) Journal of International Economic Law 1.

"The Uneasy Interplay between Digital Inequality and International Economic Law" (2022) 33(1) European Journal of International Law 205.

"Trade in Telecommunications Services: Doha and Beyond" (2007) 41(2) Journal of World Trade.

"Universal Telecommunications Service in China: Trade Liberalization, Subsidy, and Technology in the Making of Information Equality in the Broadband Era" (2003) 4 Asian-Pacific Law & Policy Journal 21.

Petersmann, Ernst-Ulrich, "Competition-oriented Reforms of the WTO World Trade System-Proposals and Policy Options" in Roger Zach et al. (eds.), *Towards WTO Competition Rules* (Kluwer Law International 1999).

Petit, Nicolas, *Big Tech & the Digital Economy: The Moligopoly Scenario* (Oxford University Press 2020).

Piffaut, Henri, "Algorithms: The Impact on Competition" (2022) 23(1) Business Law International 5.

Polanco, Rodrigo Lazo and Sebastián Gómez Fiedler, "A Requiem for The Trans-Pacific Partnership: Something New, Something Old and Something Borrowed?" (2018) 18(2) Melbourne Journal of International Law 298.

Polanco, Rodrigo, "The Trans-Pacific Partnership Agreement and Regulatory Coherence" in Tania Voon (ed), *Trade Liberalization and International Cooperation: A Legal Analysis of the Trans-Pacific Partnership Agreement* (Edward Elgar 2013).

Raustiala, Kal, "Governing the Internet" (2017) 110 American Journal of International Law 491.

Reidenberg, Joel R. et al., "Trustworthy Privacy Indicators: Grades, Labels, Certifications, and Dashboards" (2019) 96 Washington University Law Review 1409.

Rothchild, John A., "Against Notice and Choice: The Manifest Failure of the Proceduralist Paradigm to Protect Privacy Online or Anywhere Else" (2018) 66 Cleveland State Law Review 559.

Rounseville, Isaac, "Drawing A Line: Legislative Proposals to Clarify the CDA, Reinforce Consumer Rights, and Establish a Uniform Policy for Online Marketplaces" (2020) 60(4) Jurimetrics 263.

Rubinstein, Ira S., "The Future of Self-Regulation Is Co-Regulation" in Evan Selinger et al. (eds) *The Cambridge Handbook of Consumer Privacy* (Cambridge University Press 2018).

Rustad, Michael L. and Thomas H. Koenig, "Creating a Public Health Disinformation Exception to CDA Section 230" (2021) 71 Syracuse Law Review 1255.

Sauvé, Pierre, *Trade Rules Behind Borders: Essays on Services, Investment and the New Trade Agenda* (Cameron May 2003).

Schill, Stephan and Robyn Briese, "If the State Considers: The Self-Judging Clauses in International Dispute Settlement," in Armin von Bogdandy et al. (eds), *13 Max Planck Yearbook of United Nationals Law* (Martinus Nijhoff Publishers 2009).

Segura, María Soledad and Silvio Waisbord, "Between Data Capitalism and Data Citizenship," (2019) 20(4) Television & New Media 412.

Selbst, Andrew D and Julia Powles, "Meaningful Information and the Right to Explanation" (2017) 7(4) International Data Privacy Law 233.

Semendyai, Vladimir J., "Due Process and the FTC's Fair and Reasonable Approach to Data Protection" (2016) 84 George Washington Law Review 51.

Shackelford, Scott J. et al., "Bottoms Up: A Comparison of "Voluntary" Cybersecurity Frameworks" (2016) 16 U.C. Davis Business Law Journal 217.

Shaffer, Gregory and Henry Gao, "A New Chinese Economic Order?" (2020) 23(3) Journal of International Economic Law 607.

Shaffer, Gregory, "Governing the Interface of U.S. – China Trade Relations" (2022) 115(4) American Journal of International Law 650.

"Reconceiving Trade Agreements for Social Inclusion" in Manfred Elsig et al. (eds), *The Shifting Landscape of Global Trade Governance* (Cambridge University Press 2019).

"Trade Law in a Data-Driven Economy: The Need for Modesty and Resilience" in Shin-yi Peng at al. (eds) *Artificial Intelligence and International Economic Law: Disruption, Regulation, and Reconfiguration* (Cambridge University Press 2021).

Shapiro, Stuart, "The Triumph of Regulatory Politics: Benefit–Cost Analysis and Political Salience" (2012) 6 Regulation & Governance 189.

Sidak, Gregory and Daniel Spulber, "Deregulation and Managed Competition in Network Industries" (1998) 15 Yale Journal on Regulation 117.

Skinner, Chris, *Digital Human: The Fourth Revolution of Humanity Includes Everyone* (UNKNO 2018).

Słok-Wódkowska, Magdalena and Joanna Mazur, "Secrecy by Default: How Regional Trade Agreements Reshape Protection of Source Code" (2022) 25 (1) Journal of International Economic Law 91.

Solomun, Sonja et al., "Platform Responsibility and Regulation in Canada: Considerations on Transparency, Legislative Clarity, and Design" (2021) 34 Harvard Journal of Law & Technology 1.

Solove, Daniel J., "Privacy Self-Management and The Consent Dilemma" (2013) 126 Harvard Law Review 1879.

Southerton, Clare, "Datafication" in Laurie A. Schintler and Connie L. McNeely (eds), *Encyclopedia of Big Data* (Springer International 2022).

Streinz, Thomas, "International Economic Law's Regulation of Data as a Resource for the Artificial Intelligence Economy" in Shin-yi Peng et al. (eds), *Artificial Intelligence and International Economic Law: Disruption, Regulation, and Reconfiguration* (Cambridge University Press 2021).

Stucke, Maurice and Grunes, Allen, *Big Data and Competition Policy* (Oxford University Press 2016).

Sullivan, Clare, "EU GDPR or APEC CBPR? A Comparative Analysis of the Approach of the EU and APEC to Cross Border Data Transfers and Protection of Personal Data in the IoT Era" (2019) 35(4) Computer Law & Security Review 380.

Suominen, Kati, "Implications of the European Union's Digital Regulations on U.S. and EU Economic and Strategic Interests" Center for Strategic & International Studies (November 2022).

Sylvain, Olivier, "Platform Realism, Informational Inequality, and Section 230 Reform" (2021) 131 Yale Law Journal 475.

The U.S. White House, "Executive Order on Protecting Americans' Sensitive Data from Foreign Adversaries" (June 09, 2021).

"National Security Strategy" (2022).

Trachtman, Joel P., "Platforms and Global Governance: Globalization on Steroids" (2023) 26(1) Journal of International Economic Law 78.

Trautman, Lawrence J., "Is Cyberattack the Next Pearl Harbor?" (2016) 18 North Carolina Journal of Law & Technology 233.

Tuthill, Lee and Martin Roy, "GATS Classification Issues for Information and Communication Technology Services" in Mia Burri and Thomas Cottier (eds), *Trade Governance in the Digital Age* (Cambridge University Press 2012).

Tuthill, Lee, "The GATS and New Rules for Regulators" (1997) 21 Telecommunications Policy 783.

U.S. Department of Health and Human Services, "Guidance Regarding Methods for De-identification of Protected Health Information in Accordance with the Health Insurance Portability and Accountability Act (HIPAA) Privacy Rule" (2010).

UK Parliament, "Digital Trade and Data" First Report (June 23, 2021).

UK Department for Digital, Culture, Media & Sport, "Consultation Outcome-Audience Protection Standards on Video-on-Demand Services" (April 28, 2022).

UNCTAD, "Digital Economy Report" (2019).

"Technology and Innovation Report" (2021).

"The COVID-19 Crisis: Accentuating the Need to Bridge the Digital Divides" (2020).

United Nations, "World Investment Report 2016" (2016).

"World Investment Report 2022" (2022).

United States President's Council of Advisors on Science and Technology (PCAST), "Big Data and Privacy: A Technological Perspective" (2014).

USTR, "National Trade Estimate Report on Foreign Trade Barriers" (2023).

"Report to Congress on China's WTO Compliance" (2021).

van Aaken, Anne, "Introduction to the Symposium on Digital Trade" (2023) 117 AJIL Unbound 94.

Van Damme, Isabelle, *Treaty Interpretation by the WTO Appellate Body* (Oxford University Press, 2009).

Viljoen, Salomé, "A Relational Theory of Data Governance" (2021) 131 Yale Law Journal 573.

"An Argument for Positive Political Theories of Data Governance" (2022) 6 Georgetown Law Technology Review 464.

Voon, Tania, *Cultural Products and the World Trade Organization* (Cambridge University Press 2007).

Waldman, Ari E., *Privacy as Trust: Information Privacy for an Information Age* (Cambridge University Press 2018).

Wang, Heng, "The Belt and Road Initiative Agreements: Characteristics, Rationale, and Challenges" (2021) 20 World Trade Review 282.

Weber, Rolf H. and Mira Burri, *Classification of Services in the Digital Economy* (Springer 2012).

Weber, Rolf H. and Evelyne Studer, "Cybersecurity in the Internet of Things: Legal Aspects" (2016) 32 Computer Law & Security Review 715.

"Global Law in the Face of Datafication and Artificial Intelligence" in Shin-yi Peng et al. (eds), *Artificial Intelligence and International Economic Law: Disruption, Regulation, and Reconfiguration* (Cambridge University Press 2021).

West, Sarah Myers, "Data Capitalism: Redefining the Logics of Surveillance and Privacy" (2019) 58(1) Business & Society 20.

Wilson, Nigel, "Australia's National Broadband Network: A Cybersecure Critical Infrastructure?" (2014) 30 Computer Law & Security 699.

World Trade Forum, "How Industrial Data Can Help Unleash Productivity, Innovation and Sustainability" (May 13, 2022).

WTO Secretariat, *Guide to the GATS: An Overview of Issues for Further Liberalization of Trade in Services* (Kluwer Law International 2001).

"Background Note by the Secretariat, Advertising Services" S/C/W/47 (July 9, 1998).

"Declaration on The Conclusion of Negotiations on Services Domestic Regulation" WT/L/1129 (December 2, 2021).

"E-Commerce, Trade and the Covid-19 Pandemic Information Note" (2020).

"Guidelines for the Scheduling of Specific Commitments Under the General Agreement on Trade in Services" Council for Trade in Services, S/L/92 (March 28, 2001).

"Joint Initiative on Services Domestic Regulation Reference Paper on Services Domestic Regulation" INF/SDR/2 (November 26, 2021).

"Joint Statement on Electronic Commerce" WT/L/1056 (January 25, 2019).

"Joint Statement on the Negotiations on Audiovisual Service" TN/S/W/49 (June 30, 2005).

"Minutes of the Meeting of the Council for Trade in Goods" G/C/M/139 (June 16, 2021).

"Multilateral Trade Negotiations the Uruguay Round Group of Negotiations on Services" MTN.GNS/23 (July 11, 1989).

Communication by the United States, "Work Programme on Electronic Commerce" S/C/W/359 (December 17, 2014).

Communication from Argentina, Colombia and Costa Rica, "WTO Negotiations on Trade-Related Aspects of E-Commerce" INF/ECOM/1 (March 25, 2019).

Communication from Australia and Canada, "Understanding on the Scope of Coverage of CPC 84 – Computer and Related Services" TN/S/W/60, S/CSC/W/51 (January 26, 2007).

Communication from China, "Joint Statement on Electronic Commerce" INF/ECOM/19 (April 24, 2019).

Communication from India and South Africa, "The E-Commerce Moratorium: Scope and Impact" WT/GC/W798 (March 10, 2020).

Communication from Switzerland, "GATS 2000; Audio-visual Services, Council for Trade in Services" S/CSS/W/74 (May 4, 2001).

Communication from the African Group, "Report of Panel Discussion on Digital Industrial Policy and Development" JOB/GC/133 (July 21, 2017).

Communication from the European Commission, "China's Transitional Review Mechanism" G/TBT/W/326 (October 29, 2009).

Communication from the European Commission, "Elements for Complementary Approaches in Services" TN/S/W/55 (October 27, 2005).

Communication from the European Commission, "Classification in the Telecom Sector under the WTO-GATS Framework" TN/S/W/27, S/CSC/W/44 (February 10, 2005).

Communication from the European Commission, "An Enabling Environment to Facilitate Online Transactions" TN/S/W/64 (May 23, 2017).

Communication from the United States, "Work Programme on Electronic Commerce: Ensuring that Trade Rules Support Innovative Advances in Computer Applications and Platforms" S/C/W/339 (September 20, 2011).

Electronic Commerce Negotiations – Consolidated Negotiating Text, INF/ECOM/62/Rev.1 (December 2020).

Non-Paper for the Discussions on Electronic Commerce, "Work Programme on Electronic Commerce" JOB/GC/100 (July 25, 2016).

Non-Paper from Brazil, "Exploratory Work on Electronic Commerce" INF/ECOM/3 (March 25, 2019).

Wu, Mark, "Digital Trade-Related Provisions in Regional Trade Agreements: Existing Models and Lessons for the Multilateral Trade System" (November 2017) RTA Exchange, ICTSD and IDB.

Wu, Tim & Christopher S. Yoo, "Keeping the Internet Neutral? Tim Wu and Christopher Yoo Debate" (2007) 59 Federal Communications Law Journal 575.

Wu, Tim, "Network Neutrality, Broadband Discrimination" (2002) 2 Journal of Telecomm. & High Technology Law 141.

"The World Trade Law of Censorship and Internet Filtering" 7(1) Chicago Journal of International Law (2006) 263.

Wurzel, Rüdiger et al., "Pioneers, Leaders and Followers in Multilevel and Polycentric Climate Governance" in Rüdiger Wurzel et al. (eds), *Pioneers, Leaders and Followers in Multilevel and Polycentric Climate Governance* (Routledge 2020).

Yoo, Christopher S., "Beyond Network Neutrality" (2005) 19 Harvard Journal of Law & Technology 1.

"Wireless Network Neutrality: Technological Challenges and Policy Implications" (2016) 31 Berkeley Technology Law Journal 1409.

Zuboff, Shoshana, *The Age of Surveillance Capitalism: The Fight for a Human Future at the New Frontier of Power* (Public Affairs 2019).

INDEX

Printed in the USA
CPSIA information can be obtained
at www.ICGtesting.com
CBHW071201270324
5885CB00020B/143